The European dictatorships
Hitler, Stalin, Mussolini

Allan Todd

CAMBRIDGE
UNIVERSITY PRESS

CAMBRIDGE
UNIVERSITY PRESS

University Printing House, Cambridge CB2 8BS, United Kingdom

Cambridge University Press is part of the University of Cambridge.

It furthers the University's mission by disseminating knowledge in the pursuit of education, learning and research at the highest international levels of excellence.

www.cambridge.org
Information on this title: www.cambridge.org/9780521776059

First published 2002
11th printing 2014

Printed in the United Kingdom by Printondemand-worldwide, Peterborough

A catalogue record for this publication is available from the British Library

ISBN 978-0-521-77605-9 Paperback

Text design by Newton Harris Design Partnership

Map illustration by Kathy Baxendale

ACKNOWLEDGEMENTS
Cover, Peter Newark's Pictures; 3, 18, 46, 88, 89, 96, David King Collection; 104, 110, 154, Topham Picturepoint; 128, Peter Newark's Military Pictures; 175, 207 Ullstein Bild; 213, Hulton/Archive

Picture research by Sandie Huskinson-Rolfe of PHOTOSEEKERS.

Contents

Contents

Dictatorships:
ideologies and totalitarianism

Any comparative history of the three interwar dictatorships must involve looking at three main questions. First, to what extent were the ideologies and regimes associated with Lenin and Stalin similar and thus both part of communism? Second, to what extent were the movements of Mussolini and Hitler the same and how far were their fascist states similar? Finally, there is the much more controversial question of the degree of similarity between the communist and fascist ideologies, movements and states, with the related issue of whether the Soviet, Fascist and Nazi states were authoritarian or totalitarian dictatorships.

The first two of these issues will be discussed below. As regards the final question, there are two main viewpoints. Many historians believe that communism and fascism are two politically extreme but fundamentally opposed movements, with drastically different origins and aims, even though their methods of rule were very similar during the 1920s and 1930s. This view sees communism as a revolutionary left-wing movement and fascism as an essentially reactionary right-wing one (despite some 'radical' aspects in its methods and style of rule). The fundamental difference between them is said to lie in the fact that communism is dedicated to destroying capitalism, while fascism is seen as capitalism's most ruthless defender.

Not all historians share the view that these two political ideologies are diametrically opposed. R. Pipes in *Russia under the Bolshevik regime, 1917–24*, for example, sees them as having many 'affinities' and as competing 'for the same constituencies'. In particular, he sees Lenin and Bolshevism as having far more influence on Mussolini and Hitler than on the general socialist movement. Although Pipes attacks liberal and left-wing historians for being unable to examine this issue dispassionately, it is useful to bear in mind that Pipes himself is not quite an entirely neutral authority (in 1981–82, he was director of Soviet and east European affairs under President Reagan).

These questions will be addressed again in the final chapter (see p. 210), after the dictatorships of the Soviet Union, Italy and Germany have been examined.

Ideological terms

The history of the political dictatorships that emerged in Russia, Italy and Germany after the First World War is often seen as extremely complicated. This is partly the result of the large number of different political terms used to describe the ideologies and forms of rule in these dictatorships. An added complication is that different historians use the same terms in slightly different ways.

At first glance, the ideology of these dictatorships appears to be more straightforward than their history as, in many ways, they can be seen to be based on one of two fundamentally opposing political ideologies: communism or fascism. Using the political terminology of the early stages of the French Revolution (when the most radical political groups sat on the left side of the national convention, while the most conservative sat on the right), the communists can be described as being on the far or extreme left, while the fascists are on the extreme right.

Unfortunately, it is not quite as simple as this, as both communism and fascism have more than one strand. Consequently, both historical players and historians have often meant different things when using the same terms. At the same time, some have argued that, instead of seeing the political spectrum as one where the two extremes are separated by being at opposed ends, those ends should be seen as almost forming a circle. Although this relates to practice rather than political theory, this description shows the great similarities, rather than the contrasts, between these two ideologies.

Communism

Marxism

In many ways, communism seems the clearer of the two main conflicting ideologies, as it can trace its political roots to the writings of one man: Karl Marx (1818–83) – or two men, if Marx's close collaborator, Friedrich Engels (1820–95), is included. At the most basic level, Marx's writings were based on the materialist conception of history, which he developed. Using the works of the German philosopher Georg Hegel (1770–1831) and of Charles Darwin (1809–82), Marx explored the idea that human history was largely determined by the class struggles between ruling and oppressed classes, which had conflicting interests. He argued that the ruling class needed to exploit, while the oppressed class wanted to escape from this exploitation.

Marx argued that from the start of human history it is possible to detect five different types of society or modes of production. These are:

- primitive communalism: an early form of communism which existed when humans lived as hunter-gatherers and had no separate or dominating social classes;
- slave society: when society was divided into two classes of slave-owners and slaves, such as the Roman empire;
- feudalism: with land-owning aristocrats and serfs;
- agricultural capitalism: with a wealthy land-owning class and landless labourers;
- industrial capitalism: when the bourgeoisie, the dominant social class, owned the factories, mines and banks, and the work was done by the proletariat, a class of industrial workers who owned no property.

Marx, standing left, with Engels in 1864. Seated are Marx's daughters Jenny, Eleanor and Laura.

All four of the class-divided societies were ones in which the dominant class comprised a small minority of the population and had an extremely unequal distribution of economic and political power.

According to Marx, the move from one type of society to another was brought about by the struggle between the dominant class and the main subordinate class. As soon as a subordinate class overthrew the dominant class, a new class struggle would begin to emerge between this new ruling class and the new subordinate class. Marx also believed that, although at first the new society was more economically efficient than the previous one and so played a historically progressive role, the new class divisions would lead eventually to conflict and decline, even though this process might take hundreds of years.

In his massive study of industrial capitalism in Britain, *Das Kapital* (published between 1867 and 1894), Marx made a case against the Victorian industrialists who believed that the British had created the most advanced society that was humanly possible. Instead, using his theory of class struggle, he argued that the industrial workers would inevitably be thrown into a bitter class struggle against their employers. Marx believed that if the workers were successful in overthrowing capitalism they would construct a socialist society, in which the ruling class would comprise the majority of the population, for the first time in human history. From this proposed sixth form of human society, Marx believed it would be possible to move to a seventh one: communism. This society, which would be based on the economic advances of industrial capitalism, would be one of plenty, not of scarcity, as was the case in primitive communalism. As it would be classless, class conflict and struggle would be absent, allowing the economy to develop more efficiently.

However, Marx did not write much about the political forms to be adopted under socialism (the transitional stage between capitalism and communism) and communism, other than to say that, with the majority of the population in control, it would be a more democratic and less repressive society than those that had existed previously. Although he used the phrase 'dictatorship of the proletariat' to describe the political rule in a socialist workers' state, Marx did not mean a harsh and repressive regime. 'Dictatorship' in this sense meant 'dominance' based on the ownership of the means of production. Thus he described the parliamentary democracy of late nineteenth-century Britain as a 'dictatorship of the bourgeoisie', as he believed ownership of wealth allowed the bourgeoisie to ensure their interests were always protected and advanced. After the Paris Commune in 1871, Marx added to his views on the state and politics after the workers' revolution by saying that measures should be adopted to bring about the eventual 'withering away' of the state. Along with the anarchists, he believed the state was unnecessary and prevented the people from governing themselves.

Marx did not believe that progression through the six stages of society was inevitable – this was to prove important in future developments in Russia. Although class struggle was inevitable, he said that societies could stagnate and remain stuck in an inefficient system if the lower classes were unable to overthrow their ruling class, and that societies could even revert to a less advanced system. He also argued that, in special circumstances, a relatively backward society could 'jump' a stage, but only if that state was then aided by sympathetic advanced societies. He did not believe that a poor agricultural society could move to socialism on its own, as socialism required an advanced industrial base.

Marx parted company with the anarchists on the question of how to bring about the desired revolution. While the anarchists believed all organisation was evil and that the revolution would happen 'spontaneously', Marx argued that a consciously revolutionary political party was necessary to help the oppressed workers use their strength in numbers to end their exploitation. He did not believe that the workers could spontaneously develop a revolutionary conscious-ness and argued that in any society the dominant ideas were always those of the dominant classes as they owned the major means of communication.

Leninism

The fact that Marx did not refer to himself as a 'Marxist', but preferred the term 'communist' (which he had used in the title of the book he and Engels wrote in 1847: *The communist manifesto*), confuses matters somewhat. He preferred this term mainly because it pointed to the ultimate goal: a classless communist society. However, Marx's followers often preferred to call themselves 'Marxists' as well as communists in order to distinguish themselves from other groups which claimed to be communist and also to emphasise that Marxism and its methods formed a distinct philosophy.

One such was the Russian revolutionary Vladimir Ilyich Lenin (1870–1924). Although Lenin developed some of Marx's economic ideas – especially those on capitalism and imperialism in the early twentieth century – his main contribution to Marxist theory was in relation to political organisation. He took Marx's comments about the need to organise a revolutionary party and applied them to the extremely undemocratic political system operating in Tsarist Russia. His main idea was what became known as 'democratic centralism'. Lenin argued that because Tsarist Russia was a police state a revolutionary Marxist party could not operate there in the same way that a mass workers' party would operate in a democratic society. Although he believed that all members of the party should have the right to form factions to argue their points of view (the 'democratic' part of democratic centralism), once a decision had been made by party members, all members should give it their full support, even if they had argued and voted against it and even if the decision had only gained a majority of one (this was the 'centralism' aspect). Lenin also argued that the Marxist party in Tsarist Russia needed to be made up of fully committed revolutionaries who would make up a small vanguard party. These views were put forward in his book *What is to be done?* published in 1902.

Lenin did not refer to himself as a 'Leninist'; as far as he was concerned, he was a Marxist or a communist. However, many Marxists believed he had deviated from Marx's teachings. One of the leading Russian Marxists who disagreed with him on the issue of party organisation was Trotsky, who argued that democratic centralism would allow an unscrupulous leader to become a dictator over the party. His view that Lenin was distorting rather than developing Marx's ideas would gain credence after the Bolsheviks came to power in 1917 and were faced with the practical task of governing Russia.

It is often said that another adaptation of Marxism by Lenin is his theory that the stages of human society as identified by Marx could be 'telescoped', so that there would be an extremely short period between the end of feudalism in Russia and the beginning of socialist construction. To an extent, however, this is based on the mistaken belief that Marx had said there would be clear and distinct stages which would always be separated by many years. In fact, both Lenin and Trotsky (who, independently, developed a similar view) based their ideas on the possibility of moving quickly to the socialist phase on Marx's own ideas of permanent revolution. Marx wrote that as soon as one revolutionary stage had been achieved the struggle for the next could begin almost immediately. According to Lenin, 'orthodox' Marxists like the Mensheviks were not taking all of Marx's writings into consideration and were placing undue emphasis on some of his earlier comments.

However, both Lenin and Trotsky believed that Russia could not succeed in carrying through any 'uninterrupted revolution' without outside economic and technical assistance. When their earlier hopes of successful workers' revolutions in other European states failed to materialise, Lenin proved to be an extremely pragmatic – some would argue opportunistic – ruler, who was quite prepared to adopt policies which seemed to conflict with communist goals and even with those of the socialist stage of development. This is seen most clearly in relation to the New Economic Policy (see pp. 33–34) and in Lenin's ban on factions and other parties. Lenin argued that these were just adaptations to the prevailing circumstances and that as soon as conditions allowed there would be a return to 'socialist norms'.

Marxism-Leninism

This term was invented by Stalin and was not used until after Lenin's death. It was used to show that Lenin was almost as important in the development of Marxism as Marx himself and it soon came to be used in Stalin's Soviet Union to describe 'orthodox Marxism'. Increasingly it came to mean what Stalin himself had to say about political and economic issues. Essentially, Marxism-Leninism was the official ideology of the Soviet state and all communist parties loyal to Stalin and his successors. Many Marxists and even members of the Communist Party itself believed that Stalin's ideas and practices (such as 'socialism in one country' and the purges) were almost total distortions of what Marx and Lenin had said and done.

Stalinism

This term is used by both historians and those politically opposed to Joseph Stalin (1879–1953) to describe the views and practices associated with him and his supporters. Historians and political scientists use it to describe a set of beliefs and a type of rule which are essentially deeply undemocratic and even dictatorial. While it was first used to describe Stalin's actions in the Soviet Union, it has since been used to describe the general style of rule adopted by his successors in the Soviet Union and by those communists who ran the countries of eastern Europe from 1945 until the collapse of the communist regimes in 1989–90.

According to G. Gill, Stalinism has six components:

- a highly centralised economy, in which all important areas are state-owned;
- a social structure which at first allows mobility from working-class occupations into scientific, technical, administrative and intellectual professions but leads to the emergence of a privileged elite who attempt to keep access to such occupations within their families;
- tight political controls over cultural and artistic life;
- a personal dictatorship based on coercion, through the use of secret police and repression;
- total politicisation of all aspects of life, which weakens the political control of state and party because the dictator is seen as the embodiment of the country;
- an ossified conservative ideology which pays lip-service to earlier revolutionary ideals but which, in practice, replaces them.

Historians have also described Stalinism as an ideological adaptation of Marxism which resulted from the particular conditions that existed in the Soviet Union in the late 1920s and early 1930s. D. Lane points out that Stalinism contains many values related to Russia's Tsarist and peasant past, such as Tsarist-style autocracy and the belief in the need for an all-powerful leader, an official orthodox ideology (with communism replacing religion) and the belief in a 'national community', which was transformed into a nationalist belief that the Russian people could achieve 'socialism in one country' without outside help.

Stalinist ideology can thus be seen to have contributed to the rapid industrialisation of the USSR by stimulating national confidence and pride. Another important element of Stalinism is the 'cult of personality', in which the leader is elevated to a position where he is believed to be capable of achieving anything and is always right.

Marxist opponents of Stalin and post-Stalin rulers used the term in some of the ways it is used by historians. However, they were determined to show that Stalinism was not an adaptation of Marxism but a qualitative and fundamental aberration from both Lenin and Marx and from revolutionary communism in general. They stress, in particular, the way in which Stalin and his supporters rejected the goal of socialist democracy in favour of a one-party state and how Stalinism, in theory and in practice, placed the national interests of the Soviet Union above the struggle to achieve world revolution. From the time of the power struggle in the Soviet Union, Stalinism (and the accompanying term 'Stalinist') has been a term of abuse used by those who opposed Stalin's rise and his policies, in much the same way that Stalin and his supporters accused all communists who opposed them of being 'Trotskyists'. Trotskyists came to see themselves as the true defenders of the legacy of Marx, Engels and Lenin, and so the only truly revolutionary Marxists (all others having turned Marxism into a reactionary and even counter-revolutionary ideology which rejected the Marxist commitment to internationalism).

Fascism

Historians have found it even more difficult to agree on a definition of fascism than to agree on a definition of communism. S. Payne's clear definition of fascism as 'a form of revolutionary ultra-nationalism for national rebirth that is based on a primarily vitalist philosophy, is structured on extreme elitism, mass mobilisation and the *Führerprinzip* [leadership principle], positively values violence as an end as well as a means and tends to normalise war and/or the military virtues' says nothing about it being committed to the violent destruction of all independent working-class organisations, especially trade unions and socialist and communist parties. Also absent from this definition is any mention of anti-Semitism or racism in general.

'Fascism' is certainly one of the most controversial and misused terms in the history of the modern world. It is, for example, often loosely used as a term of abuse to describe any political regime, movement or individual seen as being right-wing or authoritarian. In addition, fascism, unlike Marxism and communism, has no coherent, unified ideology or *Weltanschauung* (world view) which is accepted as being specific to it. Even groups calling themselves fascist often fail to agree on any of its essential aspects.

Fascism: the 'third way'

There is a viewpoint whereby fascism is seen as simply a series of unconnected and uncoordinated reactions to the impact of the First World War and the Russian Revolution, that its nature varied from country to country and that it is impossible, therefore, to generalise about it. Here fascism is seen as a series of specific responses to the specific situations that existed in many European countries in the interwar period, rather than as a thought-out ideology. In general terms, therefore, fascism can be seen as an opportunistic form of extreme nationalism which, in political terms, lies somewhere between communism and capitalism; in other words, a political 'third force'.

However, as R. Griffin points out, some historians see fascism as a specific type of ideology, as distinct as liberalism or anarchism, which puts itself forward as an alternative 'third way' to liberal and Marxist modernisation. R. Thurlow has contributed to this debate by pointing out how Italian Fascism can be seen as a synthesis of influences from both the extreme left and right of Italian politics, while Nazism was essentially a far-right ideology that incorporated some left-wing organisational practices, such as mass meetings and rallies. The Israeli historian Z. Sternhell, in particular, has portrayed fascism as a serious 'third way' between capitalism and socialism. He argues that fascism has strong left-wing roots and so he rejects Nazism as a form of fascism. However, R. Eatwell and others point out that most people came to fascism from the right rather than the left.

Eatwell has also argued that it is possible to see fascism as a rejection of both capitalist individualism and socialist internationalism. From this perspective, the argument is that fascism is an attempt to combine the capitalist elements of private property and dynamism with socialist concerns for community and welfare, to bring about a national rebirth.

Nonetheless, even if its ideology was inconsistent – if not non-existent – fascism has had almost as great an effect on the modern world as communism.

Fascism and ideology

Unlike Marxism and communism, fascism does not appear to have existed before the end of the First World War. In Italy Benito Mussolini (1883–1945) and other ultra-nationalists took the term *fascio* (meaning 'band', 'union' or 'group'), which had been used previously by various Italian left-wing and anarcho-syndicalist groups, for their own political organisation. Once he was established as dictator, Mussolini attempted to link his party's name to the *fasces* (bundle of sticks) which had signified the authority of the Ancient Roman lictor (an official who controlled the debates in the Senate).

Before 1919, the political groups that influenced the Italian Fascist Party and the German Nazi Party were small and insignificant. With the benefit of hindsight, however, it is possible to trace the intellectual origins of fascism to the nineteenth century. This basic but rudimentary form of fascism is sometimes referred to as 'proto-fascism'. In general terms, proto-fascism can be seen as a 'new right' reaction against the late eighteenth-century liberal ideas of the Enlightenment and early nineteenth-century positivism. Both these philosophies emphasised the importance of reason and progress over nature and emotion. In addition to a general reaction against other aspects of the nineteenth century, such as the growth of liberal capitalism, which tended to hit smaller businesses and artisans, and the emergence of class struggle, there were two main philosophical and intellectual influences on what was to become fascism.

First was the French philosopher Georges Sorel (1847–1922), who, appalled by the moderation of most socialists, argued that workers should form revolutionary unions known as *syndicats* in order to bring about a revolution through direct militant action, such as the general strike. After the revolution, there would be no state, just workers' control of the factories they worked in, with 'spontaneous' anarchist co-operation between them. Though not a Marxist, Sorel was clearly on the left. Nonetheless, some fascists (in Italy especially) transformed his ideas into the concept of the 'corporate state' (see pp. 117–19).

However, it was Sorel's ideas on political myths which influenced most fascists. Sorel argued that most people were impelled into action by emotion not reason and that, therefore, a revolutionary movement needed to find or invent some powerful myth or big idea (whether true or not was unimportant) that would motivate people to take violent action. This idea was later commented on by Gustave le Bon (1841–1931) in relation to crowd behaviour and by Sigmund Freud (1856–1939) in relation to personality, and was picked up by future fascists, who replaced Sorel's myth of the general strike with the importance of the nation and the need to restore it to its former (mythical) greatness.

Nationalism was an important strand of fascism. In this, fascism was taking to extremes, rather than rejecting, one of the aspects of the Enlightenment. By the nineteenth century, a belief had emerged that there were distinct and separate groups of people who shared the same history, language and culture ('cultural nations') who should all be grouped together in the same nation. Extreme nationalists developed the argument that the nation was supreme and that the individual should be made subservient to the nation and its interests. This ultranationalism was often accompanied by the belief that the nation was in decline, resulting in demands for its dramatic rebirth.

By stressing the nation over the individual in this way, proto-fascism also paved the way for the fascist belief that class struggle should be prevented for the good of the nation. Thus hostility to left-wing political groups was an early feature of fascist movements. According to S. M. Lipset this partly explains why fascism can be seen as an 'extremism of the centre' which originated from and found its main support among the lower middle classes, who felt squeezed between the power of big capitalist firms and the threat of socialism and, especially, communism.

Also influential on early fascism was the strand of thought known as social Darwinism, which was partially based on the evolutionary theories of Charles Darwin. One of Darwin's followers, Herbert Spencer (1820–1903), developed a very simplified version – with racial overtones – of his theories and then applied them to the development of human societies. According to Spencer and the social Darwinists, people and nations were like animals, in that it was natural for them to struggle and fight in order to determine the survival of the fittest. This violence would ensure that weaker groups and nations, which did not deserve to survive, would be eliminated in order to keep the strong healthy.

Friedrich Nietzsche (1844–1900) later contributed his idea of a superman, and his writings frequently referred to the importance of emotion, struggle and war. Yet his views were complex and he was, in fact, against mindless obedience to authority and in favour of individualism. Nonetheless, early fascists used and misused his ideas to justify their actions.

Fascism was also influenced by what has been called 'vitalism', which is the belief that emotion and action are superior to reason. In fact, when Mussolini was asked what fascism was his reply was, 'It is action.' One important result of this was a strong emphasis on the positive benefits of action and violent combat. It is for this reason that fascist parties tend to develop a paramilitary movement along-side their parliamentary section. The vitalists propounded the positive virtues of violent action, especially at times of danger to the nation when, the fascists believed, democratic and liberal political structures were too ineffectual and weak to take the necessary actions. Fascists were also anti-democratic because parliamentary democracy was seen as a way in which large industrialists and the far left could exert influence that was harmful to the small man and to the nation.

In many ways, these political and ideological developments in the latter part of the nineteenth century have led some historians to call this period the 'incubatory period of fascism'. It is important to stress that most of the writers mentioned in connection with the emergence of fascist ideology were not intentional influences.

Generic fascism

Another problem surrounding attempts to define fascism is ascertaining whether there is a general fascist movement to which the different fascist parties belong, in the way that socialist and communist parties belong to clearly defined movements. Connected to this is the issue of comparing the fascist states of Italy and Nazi Germany and assessing to what extent they were similar. Generally speaking, those who argue that there is a general fascist category to which all fascist parties conform, to a greater or lesser extent, tend to see right-wing and left-wing dictatorships as being fundamentally different.

It is certainly true that in the 1920s and 1930s Italian Fascism acted as a model for many fascist parties elsewhere in Europe. Examples include Sir Oswald Mosley's British Union of Fascists and the Nazi Party of Hitler, who in his early days was an admirer of Mussolini. In 1934, in imitation of the socialists, communists and anarchists, all of which had their own international organisations, Mussolini set up the Fascist International and gave funds to several emerging fascist parties.

Marxist historians are generally agreed in seeing both fascism and Nazism as essentially similar, in that they were both fanatically anti-communist and anti-socialist, and were also defenders of capitalism, especially of the interests of the large industrialists involved in armaments and associated firms. Many of these people were often important financial supporters of the fascist parties in their rise to power. The Marxist historians also point to their common aggressive and militaristic nationalism, which inevitably led to wars of conquest.

Other historians have gone back to the intellectual origins of fascism in order to determine its core beliefs and characteristics. R. Griffin sees the call for national rebirth at the centre of fascism and describes it as an ideology and movement based on 'populist ultranationalism'. Despite certain national variations, Griffin argues that Italian Fascism and German Nazism shared the desire to destroy the existing political structures and create a new order instead. Essentially, Griffin believes that the features fascist movements have in common are more significant than any differences between them or omissions they might have from a definitive list of characteristics. S. Payne and R. Eatwell have developed interpretations similar to that of Griffin in some respects, pointing out the negative and reactionary aspects of fascist ideology.

Fascism and Nazism

One problem with attempts to portray all fascist parties as broadly similar is the issue of racism and, more specifically, anti-Semitism. While anti-Semitism was not a core belief of Italian Fascism, it was one of the main elements of German Nazism. In general terms, racism towards non-whites was common and widespread in Europe in the nineteenth century and was used to justify imperial expansion in Africa and Asia. The belief that whites were superior and that other races were inferior was supported by various pseudo-scientific writers such as Arthur de Gobineau (1816–82) and Houston S. Chamberlain (1855–1927). De Gobineau argued that there was a hierarchy of races and that those with lighter skins were higher up the evolutionary scale, and that this inequality led to natural antagonism between the races. Chamberlain argued that in order to safeguard 'culture', which could only be produced by the superior Europeans, it was essential to ensure racial purity. Chamberlain saw European history as a struggle between the Germanic peoples (Aryans) of northern Europe, who had inherited the culture of Ancient Greece and Rome, and the Jews, who Chamberlain described as the enemies of culture and mankind. These arguments were connected to the idea of eugenics (a social movement which advocated methods of improving the population through selective breeding), which became popular in some quarters during the 1920s.

In Germany and Austria, in particular, traditional religious hostility to Jewish people was increasingly replaced in the nineteenth century by this pseudo-scientific approach to race and racial purity. These ideas were extremely influential on Adolf Hitler (1889–1945) and the emerging Nazi Party and its supporters in Germany. Hitler actually met H. S. Chamberlain in 1923 and praised him in his book *Mein Kampf*. In the early stages of Italian Fascism, however, anti-Semitism was not an issue and even after Hitler put pressure on Mussolini to introduce racial laws against the Jews there was never the fanatical hatred of Jews in Italy which marked so many of the Nazi Party's leaders, members and supporters.

It is this difference, among others, which has led many to argue that fascist parties were too disparate for there to be a model to which all fascist parties conformed. Others have countered this argument by pointing out that, apart from anti-Semitism, the two main European fascist parties (and the states they constructed) shared many similar beliefs and practices. Consequently, if the racist element developed by German fascism is excluded from the core of fascist beliefs, then it is still possible to talk of the existence of a general fascism.

Dictatorships: authoritarian or totalitarian?

As well as having to understand the meanings of the various political ideologies which came to prominence and power in the interwar period, it is also necessary to be familiar with several terms used by political scientists as these terms are frequently used to compare and contrast the three regimes and ideologies.

A 'dictatorship' is the general term used to describe a political regime in which democracy, liberal individual rights and genuine parliamentary rule are absent. However, historians and political scientists have tended to divide dictatorships into two categories: authoritarian and totalitarian. Authoritarian dictatorships, according to K. D. Bracher, do not come to power as the result of a mass revolution, but come about as the result of an existing conservative regime imposing increasingly undemocratic measures intended to neutralise and immobilise mass political and industrial organisations. They can also arise following a military coup. Whatever their origin, authoritarian regimes are firmly committed to maintaining or restoring traditional structures and values. Totalitarian dictatorships, on the other hand, come to power as the result of a mass movement or revolution and are, at least in theory, committed to a radical ideology and programme of political, economic and social change.

Of particular relevance to any comparative study of the dictatorships of Stalin, Mussolini and Hitler is an understanding of the debate surrounding the application of the 'totalitarian' label to one or more of the regimes in question. In general, those historians who argue that fascist and communist dictatorships are basically similar tend to believe that all three regimes were totalitarian dictatorships and had many features in common.

The concept of totalitarianism (or total political power) was first developed by Giovanni Amendola in 1923. He was a political opponent of Mussolini's Fascist Party and came to the conclusion that the Fascist regime was qualitatively different from other dictatorships. In fact, Mussolini took over Amendola's term in 1925, claiming that fascism was based on a 'fierce totalitarian will' and that all aspects of the state – its politics as well as its cultural and spiritual life – were now fully politicised. He stated that everything should be 'fascistised' in order to create a situation which could be described as 'Everything within the State. Nothing outside the State. Nothing against the State.' Giovanni Gentile, the main theoretician of Italian Fascism, also used the term on many occasions.

Since then, several historians have attempted to define 'totalitarianism' by identifying certain characteristics that are not usually features of authoritarian dictatorships. As well as Bracher, these have included H. Arendt (*The origins of totalitarianism*, 1951) and C. Friedrich and Z. Brzezinski (*Totalitarian dictatorship and autocracy*, 1956). According to W. Laqueur in *Fascism. A reader's guide*, the term 'totalitarian' was developed to cover the basic 'common features of communist and fascist states'. In 1973, L. Schapiro's *Totalitarianism* updated totalitarian theories. Overall, there are five main aspects which are said to be central to any totalitarian regime. These are as follows:

- a distinctive, 'utopian', all-embracing ideology which both dominates and attempts to restructure all aspects of society;
- a political system headed by an all-powerful leader, around whom a deliberate cult of personality is created, and in which party, parliament and the state are under the control of the leader;
- the deliberate use of censorship and propaganda aimed at controlling all aspects of culture and at indoctrinating (and at times mobilising) all sections of society, especially the young;
- a systematic use of coercion and terror to ensure total compliance on the part of the people, with all decisions made by the leader and the regime;
- the establishment of absolute state control and co-ordination of the economy, which is subordinated to the political objectives of the political regime.

Although these points should ease the task of deciding if the three regimes we will be discussing were authoritarian or totalitarian, the question is further complicated by the fact that, as pointed out by R. Pipes and others, since the end of the Second World War and the start of the Cold War, the use of these terms has been clouded by attempts to score points in the 'great contest' between East and West, which did not end until 1991. While some politicians and historians have tried to establish that both the Soviet Union and Nazi Germany were similar totalitarian regimes, others have denied any similarities between the two dictatorships or the two ideologies of communism and fascism.

From Leninism to Stalinism, 1918–28

Russia was one of the many countries adversely affected by the First World War and the resultant peace treaties. Even before the war began in 1914, Russia had been experiencing several difficult problems, which were exacerbated by the war. However, unlike Italy and Germany, which did not undergo major transformations until the war had ended, Russia experienced two revolutions in 1917. In some respects, though, the situations in Russia, Italy and Germany during and immediately following the war were quite similar: all three countries experienced economic dislocation, dissatisfaction about the war and the peace treaties, and growing support for more extreme political parties, and all three had relatively ineffective political systems.

The impact of the First World War, 1914–17

Although many sections of Russian society had serious social and economic grievances, Russia had not seemed – even to Lenin – to be on the verge of revolution in 1914. It was Russia's participation in the First World War that helped push Tsarist Russia from a state of crisis to a revolution. The main factors leading to revolution were economic, social and political.

Economic and social factors

Russia's economy, already relatively backward compared with those of its western European neighbours, was devastated by three years of total war. It had disastrous repercussions on all sections of society, but especially on the peasants and the industrial workers.

The countryside

The backward agricultural system was highly dependent on both manpower and horses and as these were drafted to the front lines agriculture was deprived of both. After just two years of war over 15 million men and over 60 per cent of horses had been removed from farming and the agricultural sector began to crumble. The war also destroyed the financial stability that had existed before 1914 and resulted in high inflation rates that far outstripped the peasants' incomes. As trading became unprofitable for them, peasants began to reduce their sales of grain and, instead, began to hoard it or use it to make vodka.

The towns

The peasants' reluctance to sell their grain increased the pressure on food supplies that had been created by the size of the army which, by 1917, numbered over 36 million. Daily bread rations dropped from 2.7 pounds in January 1916 to 1.8 pounds per person in March 1917.

Furthermore, the war disrupted the transport system to such an extent that, by 1916, the railway network was on the point of collapse. This meant that it was increasingly difficult to transport what limited food there was even to major urban centres such as Moscow and Petrograd. Growing inflation led to many firms going bankrupt, resulting in an increase in unemployment, while those still in work saw their real wages drop by as much as 30 per cent in 1917 alone. As social unrest in the form of strikes and food riots increased, fearful factory owners shut down their firms and fled, thus adding to the problems of unemployment and hunger in most major cities.

Political factors

The political situation in Russia was dictated by the inherent weaknesses of the Tsarist state and the role of revolutionary parties and leaders.

The Tsarist state and the March Revolution of 1917

By 1917, Russia's long-term and short-term social and economic problems gave revolutionaries a far bigger audience than they had ever had before. The political and administrative machinery of Tsarist Russia was fragile, leaving the regime vulnerable to any serious crisis. The war and the defeats suffered by the Russian troops put massive and ultimately fatal strains on the undemocratic Tsarist state. When Nicholas II assumed personal command of the army and left for the front in 1915, the influence of Gregori Rasputin and the scandals that surrounded him alienated many among the political elites who had previously supported the Tsarist system and had rallied to Nicholas at the start of the war. By the time Rasputin was murdered in December 1916, many influential people had withdrawn their support from the Tsar, especially after he refused to dismiss incompetent ministers and create a cabinet with wider national backing. By 1917, many were too weary or too angry to attempt to save him.

At the same time, a series of demonstrations and strikes in Petrograd spread and developed into a general strike. More ominously for the Tsar, the troops of the Petrograd garrison became unreliable and many units began to fraternise with the demonstrators. As it became clear that the police and Cossacks were unable to disperse the crowds, the authorities became paralysed and many of the Tsar's ministers fled from the capital. The combination of the resultant political vacuum at the top and disaffection at the bottom transformed the protests into what became known as the March Revolution. The highest-ranking generals persuaded the Tsar to abdicate, but failed to establish a constitutional monarchy when his uncle, Grand Duke Michael, refused to accept the crown. Tsardom thus collapsed from within, and Russia was declared a republic.

Dual power

From March to November 1917, an uneasy political truce existed between the two bodies that emerged in Petrograd following the collapse of Tsarism. One was the provisional government set up by a self-appointed committee of the *duma* (parliament), which itself had only been elected on the very narrow franchise allowed by the Tsar. This provisional government had no electoral mandate and thus had no political legitimacy; instead its power rested on the tacit consent of the army high command and therefore it failed to solve the crisis of legitimacy left by the collapse of Tsarism. The other was the Petrograd Soviet, which was a workers' strike committee (with delegates regularly elected and able to be instantly recalled) and was first set up during the 1905 Revolution. It was revived on the same day that the provisional government was formed. Initially, the idea was that these two bodies would work together, with the populist Soviet co-operating with the elites in the provisional government. From the beginning there were problems with having two conflicting authorities: for example, the Soviet's Order Number 1 instructed workers and soldiers to obey the provisional government, but only if the Soviet agreed with its decisions. This effectively undermined the provisional government's control of the armed forces.

Despite the Soviet's opposition to the war, the provisional government decided to continue Russia's involvement in the war, but as the army disintegrated the political gulf between these two bodies widened and the authority of the provisional government began to crumble.

Revolutionary parties

Despite these economic, social and administrative problems, it was the crucial involvement of political groups (particularly, though not exclusively, the Bolsheviks) that pushed Russia beyond collapse towards the emergence of a revolutionary state. When Lenin returned from exile in April 1917, he constantly pushed the Bolsheviks to take a more revolutionary position. Before his return and his 'April theses' (Lenin's ideas about Bolshevik policy), the Bolsheviks (including Stalin) had given limited support to the provisional government, even though it was continuing to fight in the war. At the same time, class conflict was deepening as militant factory workers and rank-and-file soldiers became increasingly radicalised. One result of this was that the Mensheviks and Social Revolutionaries (the mainly peasant party of more moderate socialists who had initially dominated the Petrograd Soviet) began to lose their seats to the Bolsheviks and the even more militant anarcho-syndicalists. These political groups were not prepared to support an unelected government which refused to end Russia's involvement in the hated First World War.

The failure of a military offensive in July led to increased discontent with the provisional government. As the disorder and violence spread to Petrograd, the Bolsheviks led the demands for the Soviet to seize power. The government moved further to the right, becoming increasingly discredited and isolated in the growing political vacuum. The government took strong action against the Bolsheviks and Lenin fled to Finland. Out of step with the public, the provisional government experienced one political crisis after another and frequent ministerial changes. Soon the compromise between the elites and the popular movements evaporated and the middle ground in politics all but disappeared. In September the Bolsheviks won substantial electoral victories in both town and city councils and especially in the soviets; in both the Petrograd and Moscow soviets they won a majority of the seats. (The franchise had been extended to all adults over 21 – including women – in 1917.)

These electoral victories encouraged Lenin in October to urge the Bolshevik Central Committee to overthrow the provisional government. Though some leading Bolsheviks (such as Zinoviev and Kamenev) were opposed to this (and actually leaked the decision to opposition newspapers), the majority supported Lenin and, under the day-to-day organisation of Trotsky, the Bolsheviks began their preparations. By then, Russia had become an extraordinary political arena, with wide public debate and participation. In both urban and rural areas, soviets were established. They held unofficial, non-government elections in which workers, peasants and soldiers voted for delegates to the national All-Russian Congress of Soviets. The soviets not only raised political demands, but often became *de facto* administrative bodies.

Elections were frequent and the All-Russian Congress of Soviets was the only nationally elected body which could – and increasingly did – claim to speak for the people as a whole. As the provisional government failed to deal with food supplies, transport, law and order, and army organisation, the soviets moved to fill the political and administrative vacuum. All this exacerbated the impotence of the provisional government.

In rural areas, the government refused to deal with the land question until after the war. This built up pressure for an immediate practical solution, resulting in rural soviets and individual peasants beginning their own land expropriations. In urban areas, lock-outs, closures and absent employers (many had fled the country) led to workers seizing factories and establishing their own factory committees. By the autumn of 1917, the government was almost totally isolated and existed in name only. The November Revolution, which resulted in the fall of the provisional government, was, therefore, more a case of the Bolsheviks stepping into the political vacuum rather than embarking on a serious overthrow.

Why the Bolsheviks succeeded in establishing power, 1917–18

Actions by other parties

Immediately after the November Revolution in Russia, the Bolsheviks announced to the second All-Russian Congress of Soviets (in which the Bolsheviks were the largest party) that the provisional government had fallen and that the All-Russian Congress was now the government. However, many of the parties in the soviets opposed replacing the government and refused to accept this. Deputies of the Mensheviks' right-wing faction immediately walked out in protest at the Bolsheviks' announcement. The other left-wing parties demanded that a coalition government be set up, but insisted that Lenin and Trotsky should be excluded and that the Bolsheviks' Red Guards should be disarmed. The Bolsheviks refused to be involved in such a coalition, so these parties also joined the boycott. Thus an entirely Bolshevik government (known as the Council of

This painting shows Lenin addressing a group of Red Guards during the November Revolution of 1917.

People's Commissars or Sovnarkom) was voted into power, with Lenin acting as chairman. This new government faced several major problems, including how to stay in power and extend its control over the country as a whole, how to bring a rapid end to the war and remove the German armies that were occupying large parts of European Russia (the area west of Moscow) and how to bring about economic stability and recovery. Once civil war began in January 1918 (see pp. 22–23), the Bolshevik government found itself having to cope with all these (and other) problems in the context of a bloody internal struggle for survival and power, which ensured there would be no peaceful transition to a new economic and political system.

Despite Lenin's misgivings, some Bolsheviks wanted to widen the government by forming a coalition with the other left-wing parties. After a special conference, the majority of Bolsheviks voted to continue discussions with the Social Revolutionaries (SRs) and Mensheviks, provided that the Bolsheviks continued to hold the majority of seats. A coalition was formed in December with the Left Social Revolutionaries. (Following a split, the SRs had divided into two separate parties: the Right SRs and the Left SRs.) Later that same month, elections for a new constituent assembly were also held, before news had reached the vast rural areas of Russia that the SRs had split.

Later Bukharin and other Bolsheviks came to believe that the rise of Stalin was linked to several of the decisions taken in the first few weeks after November 1917, especially those that identified the party too closely with the soviets and the revolution itself. While Lenin and Trotsky were committed to upholding soviet constitutionalism, the actions of Stalin and his supporters would prove that the more moderate Bolsheviks had been right to be concerned about the implications of not having a wider basis for the government.

Early actions

The first decisions taken by the new regime allowed the Bolsheviks to consolidate their position and led some of their opponents to turn to military resistance. Lenin and the Bolsheviks had always believed that, although Russia's specific circumstances might lead it to revolution first, workers' revolutions in the more developed countries of Europe, such as Germany and France, were imminent. They also believed that, while it might be possible to begin the construction of socialism in Russia, this could only be carried further with the economic and technical assistance of the more advanced economies of Europe. None of the leaders in 1917 ever believed that it would be possible to construct socialism in Russia in isolation or even to remain in power for very long. Consequently, they did not work out any specific plans for legislation. Instead, they concentrated on working for revolution and, at first, believed that their main role was to carry out a few propaganda actions which would speed up the European revolutions. This reflected their belief that eventually they would be overthrown by a victorious counter-revolution.

As a result, many of the Bolsheviks' early legislative acts were hasty and often confused or even contradictory; they gave little thought to dealing with practical problems. They rushed through legislation that fulfilled the promises they had made: the first decrees issued by the congress on the day after the revolution dealt with peace and land.

Apart from the Bolsheviks' genuine desire to end the destructive 'imperialist' war, it was also politically imperative to do so, as the effects of the war had already brought down the Tsar and then the provisional government. Their decree on peace was rushed but speedily accepted; it called on the government to conclude an 'immediate' and 'just and democratic' peace, with no annexations or indemnities. While it might have been possible to achieve one or other of the two objectives, to achieve both proved impossible. The main problem was that the Bolsheviks tried to get all the countries involved in the war to negotiate a general peace, without success. Thus in December 1917 they had begun separate talks with the Germans, which led to a ceasefire. However, the Bolsheviks and Left SRs had only agreed on separate talks, not on whether a separate peace should be concluded without the participation of the Allies. These talks were also held in public in order to aid the advent of a European-wide revolution, which seemed to be fast approaching. The Bolsheviks also tried to insist that there should be no transfer of German troops to the Western Front as they did not want to help Germany defeat the Allies. They further demanded that they should be allowed to conduct revolutionary propaganda among German and Austro-Hungarian troops.

The Bolsheviks wanted to see the establishment of larger and more efficient co-operatives, and collective ownership of the land was still their main aim. Nevertheless, the decree on land formally approved all land seizures that had taken place before November 1917 and sanctioned whatever decisions the peasants might choose to make about the land. This was really just a pragmatic acceptance of the effects of earlier Bolshevik agitation and independent action by the peasants, and of the long-standing demands of the SRs. In the event, the Peasants' Soviet voted for the break-up of all surviving estates, with the land to be divided among the peasants. In all, about 25 million privately owned smallholdings were created. This decree was quickly approved by the Soviet's delegates.

The other main promise made by the Bolsheviks was to provide food and jobs for the industrial workers. This also proved difficult as many workers had simply taken over their places of work and established their own factory committees in the months leading up to November 1917. In many cases, these were dominated by anarcho-syndicalists who were strongly opposed to the Bolsheviks' ultimate aim of creating a centrally planned economy. The factory committees wanted total control, which clashed with the Bolshevik decree on workers' control (which defined 'control' as giving the workers a say in the decision-making process, along with managers, experts and government representatives). Lenin argued that the workers needed to learn how to manage factories more efficiently before they could be given full management powers. The main problem for the Bolsheviks was that, although their members had strong positions in the various trade unions, they did not have a majority in the All-Russian Central Council of Trade Unions, the national executive body. Most unions wanted to preserve their independence from the state and believed they should have a major say in determining economic policy; they also tended to be run by political groups to the left of the Bolsheviks.

Initially, Lenin and the majority of Bolsheviks were more interested in establishing central state control while leaving ownership mainly in private hands, as they did not believe the fragile Russian economy was ready for any quick moves to socialism via a programme of nationalisation. Although key aspects of the economy would be taken over by the state, the immediate plan was to introduce a form of 'state capitalism'.

Growing political isolation

Once these early decisions had been made, the Congress (by now consisting only of the Bolsheviks and their supporters) elected the permanent All-Russian Central Executive Committee (CEC) to act when it was not sitting. The Bolsheviks and the Left SRs held 90 out of the 110 seats; the remainder were left vacant for other left-wing parties, should they decide to participate. Though the formal institutional shape of the new revolutionary government had now been created, the new government still had to establish effective power over the country as a whole. The Bolsheviks' growing political isolation eventually led them to take measures against other political parties.

As soon as the Bolsheviks assumed power, they had faced a strike by the bureaucrats working in government departments and the banks. To break this, the government had set up the All-Russian Extraordinary Commission for Combating Counter-Revolution, Sabotage and Speculation (Cheka) in December 1917. As the first signs of counter-revolutionary preparations emerged later in December, Cheka's scope was expanded from dealing with the anti-revolutionary bureaucrats to dealing with the counter-revolutionaries who were beginning armed resistance. The leader of the former government, Kerensky, was establishing himself about 20 miles from Petrograd, while several generals had begun to form what soon became just one of several White Guard armies.

The constituent assembly

One of the last acts of the former government had been to permit elections for a new constituent assembly. These elections eventually took place in December but, as Lenin argued, before news of the revolution and the split in the SRs had spread to all parts of Russia. Although the Bolsheviks had called on Kerensky to hold such elections, they had done so mainly to embarrass the provisional government because what they really wanted was for all power to be transferred to the soviets. 'All power to the soviets' had been their main call from April 1917 right up to the November Revolution. Some Bolsheviks had believed Lenin was wrong to call for all power to be given to the soviets at a time when the SRs and the Mensheviks had majority control of some of the soviets, especially as the SRs supported the provisional government. In the local areas, even under the Tsar, it was difficult for central government or institutions to maintain control.

Lenin stated in *State and revolution* in August 1917 that the revolution would be followed by the dictatorship of the proletariat, with an organised state that would disappear once the economy had progressed to communism. In practice, however, the Bolsheviks at first lost effective power to the thousands of soviets set up in the winter of 1917–18. Nonetheless, even before the civil war began, the Bolsheviks used a variety of tactics – including forced amalgamations, exploiting procedural rules and harassment – to assert greater central control over the soviets. However, even if a soviet had a Bolshevik majority, this did not automatically mean it supported all party or government decisions, as party members followed the party practice of debate and dissension for some time after 1917.

Despite this, the Bolsheviks seem to have believed that the majority of the people supported them. This was based on the fact that the second All-Russian Congress of Soviets represented about 20 million electors, the majority of whom had been voting for the Bolsheviks – or at least the policies only they advocated – since September. Although only about 30,000 people had been directly involved in the events of November 1917, ten times as many had helped the Bolsheviks to victory simply by not opposing them. However, the results of the elections to the constituent assembly were not what the Bolsheviks had wanted. Almost 42 million people voted: the clear winners were the SRs, with 48 per cent of the vote (over 20 million), while the Bolsheviks received 24 per cent (almost 10 million votes). Lenin was encouraged when the Left SRs won a majority of the seats on the new executive committee at the Second Congress of the Peasants' Soviet, which met in December.

When the Kadets and the Right SRs attempted an anti-Bolshevik rising in early December 1917, they were outlawed, their leaders arrested and newspapers banned. The newly elected constituent assembly deputies of these parties were also excluded from its first meeting on 18 January 1918. Despite these actions, the Right SRs had a majority of seats in the constituent assembly and they refused to ratify the Soviet's decrees on peace and land or to accept the transfer of all power to the soviets. As the Kadets and some Right SRs were already involved in military action against the new government, the Bolsheviks and their Left SR coalition partners agreed to disband the assembly the following day. Although they sought to justify this action on the grounds that the elections in November had given undue weight to the minority of wealthier peasants and that it had been too soon for the decrees on peace and land to have an effect on the results, it was clear that the two political systems (the direct democracy of the soviets and the indirect democracy of parliament) and their attendant institutions were incompatible.

Civil war and foreign intervention, 1918–21

After the Bolshevik Revolution of November 1917, a civil war between Reds (communists and their supporters) and Whites (anti-communists) broke out. It was further complicated by the intervention of 14 foreign armies in support of the Whites.

Early stages

By the end of December 1917, armies led by White generals had already begun military actions against the new Bolshevik-Left SR government. At the same time, a Cossack rebellion had broken out. The White generals were united only by their hatred of the revolution: some were in favour of restoring the Tsar, while others were more concerned with establishing their own power. They were certainly not in favour of restoring the provisional government and it soon became clear that they also wanted to take back the land that had been seized by the peasants before and after November 1917. In addition to these developing White armies, the Right SRs began a series of armed risings in central Russia and formed an anti-Bolshevik government at Samara, south-east of Kazan.

Although the Bolsheviks presented this as a class war, it had other aspects to it: apart from the inevitable local factors to be expected in such a massive and poorly connected country, there was the important issue of the different nationalities which had made up the Tsarist empire. Many had wanted independence from the empire and now saw their chance, especially as the Bolshevik government had promised the right of self-determination. Particularly strong were the independence movements in the Ukraine and Georgia. Nationalist partisan forces (known as Greens) were formed in these regions and often fought the Reds as well as the Whites.

The civil war was complicated and was made more bitter by the intervention of foreign armies on the side of the Whites from April 1918. Even before November 1917, Allied representatives in Russia had pressed the various provisional governments to ban the Bolsheviks and arrest their leaders. Later, they had moved almost immediately to try to bring down the Bolshevik government. These activities intensified when Trotsky, as commissar of foreign affairs, began publishing secret treaties between the Allies and the Tsar which promised him extra lands in the Balkans, even though the Allies claimed to be fighting for freedom, democracy and the rights of small nations.

The Treaty of Brest-Litovsk

Lenin had always been concerned that the Central Powers and the Allies might join forces to crush the Russian Revolution before similar revolutions were sparked off elsewhere. For this reason he had argued that a separate peace with Germany was necessary, especially as discipline in the Russian army was continuing to break down as hundreds of thousands of war-weary troops deserted from the front. This issue ended the coalition with the Left SRs, and came near to splitting the Bolshevik Party.

On 21 January 1918, the Bolshevik Central Committee debated the question of peace in the presence of the Bolshevik delegates to the Third All-Russian Congress of Soviets. It soon became clear that there was a three-way split. Lenin, supported by Zinoviev and Stalin, now commissar for nationalities (neither of whom believed, as Lenin did, that a European revolution was likely), was in favour of accepting the very harsh terms that had recently been presented by the Germans, arguing that if Germany was defeated by the Allies all the Russian territory demanded by Germany would be reclaimed, and pointing out that Russia no longer had an effective army because of desertion and anti-war sentiment. The left of the party, led at this stage by Bukharin, wanted to reject Germany's terms and instead fight a revolutionary war to help spark off other revolutions in Europe. In between these two positions were those who, like Trotsky, wanted 'neither war nor peace'. They argued that if the talks were prolonged, there would be more opportunity for revolution to occur in Germany and the Austro-Hungarian empire, thus bringing about the disintegration of their armies; in fact, this did happen less than a year later. When it came to a vote, the biggest group was Bukharin's war faction, with 32 votes; next came Trotsky's group with 16 votes, while Lenin and his supporters received only 15 votes. Of special significance for the government was the fact that the Left SRs supported Bukharin's position on fighting a revolutionary people's war.

At first, a compromise was reached in which Trotsky would delay accepting Germany's terms, but would sign a peace treaty if the Germans renewed their offensive. The Germans, annoyed at the delays, attacked on 17 February and, because of the state of the Russian army's morale, received no serious resistance.

After much hesitation, Trotsky finally decided not to oppose Lenin on the question of an agreed peace, however bad the terms. The Bolshevik majority in the government accepted this, even though both the Bolshevik Central Committee and the Left SRs were still opposed to peace on such terms. In the end, Trotsky (and three of the war faction) abstained, allowing Lenin to win by seven votes to four.

The leading members of the war faction, including Bukharin, then resigned from all their party and government posts, despite Lenin's urgent pleas for them to remain. At the same time, Trotsky also resigned as commissar for foreign affairs because he could not bring himself to sign a treaty which imposed such harsh terms. The Treaty of Brest-Litovsk was thus signed on 3 March, but not before it had been condemned as a German diktat imposed on a weaker nation. A subsequent emergency congress of the party on 19 March, which finally agreed to recommend ratification of the treaty to a forthcoming meeting of the Congress of Soviets, saw criticisms of Trotsky which led him to comment that perhaps the party would have to admit that 'we have come before our time'.

The treaty was extremely punitive. Among other measures, about 30 per cent of European Russia, including the Ukraine, Russia's most important grain-producing area, containing over 60 million people (along with 30 per cent of its factories and 75 per cent of Russia's iron and coal mines), was lost to Germany and its allies. Lenin acknowledged that these terms were harsh, but reminded his comrades that the Russian Communist Party (as the Bolsheviks were officially renamed in March 1918) was internationalist, not nationalist, and that its most important task was to gain time and a 'breathing space' for the international revolution to develop, even if that meant damage to Russia and perhaps even the overthrow of the Communists themselves. Later, in August 1918, following the collapse of the German armies on the western front, the Germans withdrew almost all of their troops from Russian soil, thus effectively tearing up the Treaty of Brest-Litovsk.

The Red Army

The growing threat of counter-revolution led the Bolshevik-Left SR coalition to establish their own volunteer Red Army. Although a decree was issued in January 1918 to form a Workers' and Peasants' Red Army, no organisation was created to set this in motion. It was not until April that regional offices were opened to recruit people. This first step was taken by Trotsky who, on his resignation as commissar of foreign affairs in March, had been appointed commissar of war and president of the Supreme War Council. The only troops the Communists could rely on were a division of Latvian riflemen, the Red Guards and several bands of partisans, which meant that at the start of the civil war they were greatly outnumbered. At first the Communists found it hard to recruit a new central army as most of them were anti-militarist. In addition, since the March revolution soldiers' committees had become accustomed to electing their own officers and by this time most Russians had had enough of war. Nevertheless, by the end of 1920, Trotsky had created and equipped an army almost 5 million strong (although only about 500,000 were combat troops, the rest being involved in transport, labour and administrative duties).

Trotsky began by creating a nucleus of an army, using the military skills of ex-Tsarist officers to begin with because of the lack of expertise and experience of ordinary workers. The plan, however, was to establish a proletarian core which would be both trustworthy and capable of taking command. This use of 'specialists' was generally disliked, both in the army and in all other aspects of administration and the state. Trotsky's plans were presented on 22 April 1918. They were attacked by the Mensheviks (who had returned to the soviets), the Left SRs and the left-wing of the communists. The centre also opposed them as they resented the lack of opportunities available for loyal Red Guard and partisan commanders. In 1918 such people held only about 25 per cent of all commanding and administrative posts (by the end of the civil war, Trotsky had created a new officer corps from NCOs and ordinary workers which provided almost 70 per cent of all commanding officers). In an attempt to limit the risk of betrayal, Trotsky ordered that a register of officers' families be kept and threatened they would be taken as hostages if officers deserted their commands. He also appointed political commissars to accompany all officers and insisted that all orders be signed by both parties. Initially, Trotsky was able to build up the forces of the Red Army as the White Guards were still in the process of forming armies, while foreign armies were still establishing themselves in various coastal areas. This meant that the Communists, who controlled the central areas, were able to consolidate their position.

The civil war finally took a serious turn in May, when the Czech Legion (a group of about 40,000 Austro-Hungarian POWs who had formed an army to fight against the Central Powers) wrongly feared that the Communists were about to hand them over to the Germans. They revolted, took over a large part of Asian Russia (including the Trans-Siberian Railway) and then joined up with a group of White Guards. Faced with this crisis, Trotsky tried an experiment with conscription in Petrograd and Moscow which yielded about 10,000 soldiers. He also began to centralise the Red Army under a single command, which involved disbanding the Red Guards and the partisan detachments. Many of the latter were strongly influenced by anarchism and, on principle, opposed centralisation and the creation of regular divisions and regiments, often under the command of ex-Tsarist officers. Trotsky also faced opposition to his plan from Communist-led units, especially from Voroshilov and the 10th Army Group, with which Stalin was closely associated.

In August, the continued military successes of the Whites led to the compulsory call-up of commissioned and non-commissioned officers, while Trotsky moved to a special train which became almost his second home for the duration of the civil war. From it, he attempted to improve the morale of the Red Army troops.

The collapse of the coalition

Though the Fourth Congress of Soviets had ratified the Treaty of Brest-Litovsk, the Left SRs had immediately withdrawn from Sovnarkom. Their members remained in administrative posts in most government departments (including the Cheka) and the executive bodies of the soviets. However, in July 1918, following the Fifth Congress of Soviets, the Left SRs decided to make a complete break from the Communists. Left SR leaders accused Lenin and Trotsky of having betrayed the revolution and threatened them with 'the revolver and the bomb'. This led the Communist government (which had moved from Petrograd to the relatively greater safety of Moscow) to ask the Congress for emergency powers to severely discipline those responsible for armed attacks.

On 19 July, following the assassination of the German ambassador by two Left SR high-ranking officials of the Cheka and with the Czech Legion advancing, the Left SRs began an insurrection. Cheka chiefs were taken prisoner by the insurgents and the Post and Telegraph building was occupied. The Left SRs then announced that Lenin's government had been overthrown. Within three days, however, the insurrection had been suppressed and its leaders arrested, even though the most reliable troops had earlier been sent east to fight the Czech Legion. Although some Left SRs who had senior positions within the Cheka were executed, the majority were granted amnesty a few months later. This insurrection, and the continued advance of the Czech Legion, led to the execution of the Tsar and his family, who had been under arrest since November 1917. The Communists were concerned that they would fall into the hands of the Whites and act as a rallying point for the opposition.

Foreign intervention

It was also from August 1918 that foreign intervention on the side of the Whites became more serious. After the revolution and the Treaty of Brest-Litovsk, the Allies' immediate concern had been whether the new government would keep Russia in the war and so prevent Germany from transferring its troops from the eastern to the western front. For this reason they had at first offered the Communists the same financial and military help they had given the provisional government. After serious fighting on the eastern front began to die away in December 1917, Allied forces landed in Russia. Just before the Treaty of Brest-Litovsk was signed, this was stepped up, ostensibly to prevent weapons supplied by the Allies to the Tsar from falling into the hands of the Germans, but in reality the Allies were there to help the Whites against the Communists. The Allies then began supplying arms to those Whites in favour of continuing the fight against Germany.

The foreign countries were also aggrieved that the Communists had repudiated the foreign debts run up by the Tsar and then the provisional government, especially when they later went on to freeze all foreign assets in Russia and to nationalise firms, including those in which there had been significant foreign investments.

However, as the civil war continued, foreign involvement soon turned into a crusade on the part of 14 nations that were opposed to the very existence of a communist regime. This involvement became much more determined after the end of the First World War and when revolution erupted in Germany and

Hungary. These foreign powers included France, Britain, the USA and Japan, as well as the various nations that had wanted independence from Tsarist Russia, such as Poland, Czechoslovakia, Finland, Lithuania and Romania. However, these foreign forces were almost as disunited as the Whites themselves, and the war-weary troops ordered into Russia after 1918 did not wish to fight another serious war. As a result, some French and British regiments became mutinous, while in Britain many workers took industrial action and began to threaten a general strike if Allied intervention against the new workers' state was not ended. Only in the Baltic were significant results produced; here British forces joined up with national troops to ensure that Estonia, Latvia and Lithuania were able to secure their independence from Russia's new rulers.

In October 1918, after the SRs had assassinated Uritsky (an important Communist) and wounded Lenin, the government proclaimed a Red Terror to rid the country of counter-revolutionaries. The terror was intended to force the traditional administrators to serve the workers' state as an alternative to execution. By then, the military structures of the Red Army had been reorganised, with the Revolutionary War Council of the Republic replacing the Supreme War Council. This put Trotsky, as the president of this new body, in charge of the revolutionary war councils of the 14 armies that now made up the Red Army. Conflict between Trotsky and Stalin (now the chief political commissar for the southern front) continued.

By now the Communists were facing three major threats on different fronts (with a total circumference of over 5,000 miles) from the Whites and their foreign allies. The Reds survived these three dangers because the Whites were separated from each other by vast distances and because their personal rivalries and ambitions meant that they refused to co-ordinate their offensives. As the Reds controlled the centre and had a single command, they were able to switch their troops (numbering 500,000 by March 1919) from front to front as required. To meet this crisis, the trade unions had called up 50 per cent of their members to defend the republic; by the end of April, the Red Army had 1.5 million troops.

Clashes over military strategy between Trotsky and Stalin continued, however, and resulted in the removal of Vatzetis as commander-in-chief and his replacement by Stalin's man. Many of Trotsky's supporters were also removed from their positions on the Revolutionary War Council. When Trotsky offered to resign all his posts, Lenin persuaded the Politburo (see p. 38) to reject his resignation and give him a blank endorsement for any future orders. In October, however, Stalin supported Trotsky's plans for the defence of Petrograd and Moscow against Lenin, who argued that Petrograd should be abandoned. Stalin went so far as to adopt the very points Trotsky had been making since August 1919. By December 1919, it was clear that the Reds were going to win, even though the fighting was not yet over. The civil war finally came to an end in September 1920.

The Russo-Polish War, 1920–21

By the end of 1919, Soviet Russia expected to reach agreement with Poland, which, armed and encouraged by France, was still active on the side of the

Whites. As a result, sections of the Red Army were removed from active service and were being formed into labour armies to help in much-needed reconstruction. The government was further encouraged in January 1920 when the Allies lifted the blockade they had imposed against Soviet Russia.

Then in March 1920 Pilsudski, the Polish dictator, launched an invasion of Soviet Russia. Despite Soviet offers of a favourable territorial settlement, the invasion continued and the peace reforms approved by the Congress of Soviets were suspended. In June the Red Army expelled Polish forces and Britain offered to mediate. Despite their promises to grant independence to Poland (which had been part of the Tsar's empire), Lenin and the majority of the government decided to pursue the Polish army across the border in order to assist the soviets that had been set up in some parts of Poland. Trotsky had reservations about this attempt to export revolution, which was mainly the result of desperation at Soviet Russia's isolation in Europe. As he feared, most Poles saw the Red Army as invaders, not liberators, and by August the Red Army had been defeated and forced to retreat.

This setback encouraged one final attack by surviving White Guard forces in the Crimea, which was soon defeated. In October 1920, a ceasefire was agreed between Soviet Russia and Poland, although the Treaty of Riga was not signed until March 1921.

More fighting occurred within Soviet Russia in February 1921 when Ordjonikidze, the chief commissar in Georgia and a friend of Stalin's, falsely claimed that a strong Communist insurrection had broken out that had great popular support. (Georgia, along with Armenia and Azerbaijan, had declared its independence in May 1918; since then, it had been governed by the Mensheviks and had allowed German and, later, British troops to occupy its territory and had ruthlessly suppressed the Georgian Communists.) After two weeks of bitter fighting, the Red Army defeated the Mensheviks and, against earlier declarations for self-determination, Lenin's government annexed Georgia. Although Lenin urged conciliation with the defeated Mensheviks, evidence later showed that Stalin and Ordjonikidze ignored his injunctions. The Georgian question was later to play a part in the power struggle that developed just before Lenin's death.

Reasons for the victory of the Reds

The Reds were successful in the civil war because they were able to gain control over the central part of Russia. The greater industrial capacity this gave them meant they were better able to supply their troops. In addition, the Reds' troops were fervently committed to the cause of revolution, both national and international. Crucially the Reds had also won the acceptance of the peasant population, who were keen to hold on to their newly acquired land. Finally, the Whites were unable to make any political capital of the atrocities committed by the Reds as they had committed so many themselves.

The revolutionary state, 1921–24

When the Bolsheviks came to power in November 1917 they were committed to bringing about revolutionary transformations of Russia's economy, political system and society. The tremendous economic and administrative problems facing them, as well as their realisation that Russia, on its own, could not achieve socialism, led them to make several pragmatic departures from orthodox Marxism.

Why did a one-party state emerge?

The eventual emergence of a one-party state, which was a significant departure from Marxist theory, resulted from several crucial economic and political decisions taken early in the history of Soviet Russia.

When Lenin and the Bolsheviks assumed governmental responsibility, most Bolsheviks accepted that they would have to use the existing economic structures until workers' revolutions in Europe had produced socialist governments that would give them financial and technical assistance. In the meantime, Lenin argued that they would have to adopt interim measures that would allow Russia to continue to function and, at the same time, begin to lay the foundations for socialism.

From 1917 to 1924, the Soviet government presided over three distinct economic policies, all of which seemed to have as much to do with pragmatic adaptation as with Marxist theory.

State capitalism, 1917–18

Although many Bolsheviks wanted to implement revolutionary socialist policies, Lenin was more concerned with preventing total economic collapse. The serious food shortage and rampant inflation were compounded by the loss of the grain-rich Ukraine, following the harsh Treaty of Brest-Litovsk. The new government's ability to transform the economy was also restricted by the fact that, in the early days, their authority was limited to Petrograd, Moscow and a few other major towns. It was these factors – and the realisation that they would have to appease the peasants who produced the food – that lay behind the Bolsheviks' acceptance of the peasants' desire to split up the large estates into many small private holdings. The Decree on Land of November 1917 formally sanctioned a revolutionary change in land ownership, in which the elite landlord class (the monarchy, the nobility and the church) was totally deprived of its property. The part of the decree that dealt with the abolition of private ownership of land was ignored. By the end of 1919, only about 65 per cent of land was state-owned or held by collective farms.

Similarly, the Bolsheviks were forced to accept the prevailing reality regarding Soviet Russia's industry. As we have seen, many of the workers' committees set up by workers in factories had anarcho-syndicalist majorities and were opposed to any central control. As a result, the Decree on Workers' Control, which attempted to establish central control over the workers' committees in order to improve productivity, was largely inoperative. Though the decree legislated for the official nationalisation of all factories, they continued to be taken over by unofficial independent workers' committees, in what was described as 'proletarian nationalisation from below'.

Despite this situation, the Communist government set up the Supreme Council of the National Economy (Vesenkha) in December 1918. Its task was to draw up plans for national economic development and co-ordination. The decree did not nationalise all capitalist enterprises, as Sovnarkom believed their owners' co-operation was necessary to speed up industrialisation and urbanisation, both of which were essential before socialism could be constructed. It was also hoped that this would reasssure foreign investors. Instead, Vesenkha was to work with owners, factory committees, the soviets and the various government commissariats. Banks and railways, though, were nationalised in an attempt to bring some order to the currency and transport systems.

This co-operation between the state and private owners was known as 'state capitalism'. Many on the left of the party, however, were deeply uneasy about this approach to industry.

War communism, 1918–21

At the start of the civil war in June 1918, the Communist government introduced emergency economic policies which replaced state capitalism and later became known as war communism. It was a desperate attempt to ensure the survival of the revolutionary regime until the spread of revolution to other parts of Europe.

War communism involved the nationalisation of industry, increased central government control, the requisitioning of food from the peasants and the formation of the Cheka to combat counter-revolution. The Decree on Nationalisation was issued in June 1918 and finally ended private ownership of all major factories and mines. All industrial enterprises were now owned by the state.

War communism thus achieved one of the central revolutionary aims of the Bolsheviks. In many respects, though, it was not a thought-out policy, but one that was reluctantly undertaken by Lenin and his government. The introduction of war communism did not result in an automatic improvement in industrial productivity, which, in the context of the civil war, was even more essential if the Red Army was to remain supplied.

By 1921, coal production was 10 per cent and iron was 3 per cent of 1913 levels, the railways were virtually destroyed and the populations of major cities such as Moscow and Petrograd were down by 50 per cent and 33 per cent respectively. In addition, by 1921 some 2 million people had emigrated, many of them the educated and the technical experts the new state so badly needed. In fact, Soviet Russia was less urbanised in 1921 than it had been in 1897. It was thus clear to some leading communists that war communism was showing signs of general collapse.

Industrial and agricultural problems

The government had several problems to overcome: many industries were short of raw materials, the transport system was at best unreliable, and the shortage of Bolshevik specialists and skilled managers left many factories dependent on the managers appointed by the previous capitalist owners. There was also a shortage of experienced factory workers. Many had been recruited by the Red Army, first as volunteers and then as conscripts, while others had recently migrated to the rural areas in search of food. In addition, many of the factory committees resented central control, although this was partly solved by the fact that, since November 1917, the Bolsheviks had gained increasing control over these committees.

All these problems were made worse by the fact that, at first, Sovnarkom simply printed bank notes as they were needed. This led to hyperinflation and the collapse of the rouble. The outcome was that money was abolished and a system of barter replaced a money economy. This pleased some Communists on the left of the party (such as Bukharin and Preobrazhensky), as the disappearance of money was one of the ultimate aims of a communist society. However, it did nothing to increase productivity.

Thus, although war communism led to increased state control of industry and kept the Red Army supplied, it was a complete failure as regards the economy as a whole. By 1921, the combined effects of war, civil war and revolutionary upheaval led to a fall in all the important economic indicators. Between 1913 and 1921, gross industrial output dropped by over 60 per cent. The working day was increased to 10 or 11 hours because so many workers had left the towns (almost 1.5 million out of 2.6 million over the period 1917–20) and labour discipline was enforced by harsh penalties against absenteeism.

The most important reason for the shift from state capitalism to war communism, however, was the serious food shortage which threatened to leave the Red Army and industrial workers without sufficient food. Lenin and his government were determined to increase food production by establishing central control over agriculture. They also believed the richer peasants (*kulaks*) were deliberately hoarding grain in order to keep prices high. This was partly the case as the government, to whom the peasants had sold most of their grain since 1917, could no longer afford the prices demanded. Sovnarkom decided to deal with this 'counter-revolutionary' resistance by using more forceful methods of repression.

In June 1918, a new People's Commission of Supply (Narkomprod) was set up. Its task was to organise committees of poor peasants (kombedy) to collect the grain that was needed and arrange its transport to the towns. Although over 120,000 such committees were established, most peasants were more interested in helping themselves than central government. When this scheme failed, the government decided to send in armed Cheka units and workers' detachments to requisition the supplies needed from the richer peasants. The often violent collections did not, however, result in increased yields, as the peasants simply produced only what was necessary for their own consumption. At the same time, the Whites were carrying out similar forced requisitions in the areas they controlled.

As with industrial production, the combination of the various disruptions to rural life since 1914 produced such a shortfall in grain supplies that, in 1920 and

1921, grain harvests were less than 50 per cent of what they had been in 1913. In the Volga region, which had been affected by not only the civil war but also droughts, sand blizzards and locusts, the result was a famine. By July 1921, it was feared that 10 million peasants would be affected; by December, the estimate had risen to over 30 million and the Communists appealed to Western charities (such as the American Relief Association) for assistance. In all, it is estimated that as many as 7.5 million Russians starved to death in the period 1918–21, out of a total of 8 million deaths resulting from the civil war.

Political impact and dissent

As early as February 1920 Trotsky had recommended changing war communism, but this was rejected, so he dropped his suggestions and began to use the troops of the Red Army as labour and construction teams. The Ninth Congress of Soviets in December 1920 had seen the Mensheviks and SRs join in the demands to end grain requisitioning. Despite this, Lenin continued to argue right through 1920 that war communism – and the grain requisitions in particular – should carry on. However, by early 1921, its clear failure to increase production, the famine, as well as several anti-Communist risings that had taken place in 1920, persuaded him that a change of policy was vital. When he first outlined his new policy, however, the majority of the government rejected it. It would take a more serious revolt to persuade them to change their minds.

Many of the supporters of the November Revolution were anarcho-syndicalists, who resented central government control of industry. Many, including several Communists, also objected to Trotsky's centralised control of the Red Army and his use of former Tsarist officers. They began to demand a 'third revolution'. In 1920, two left-wing factions emerged within the Communist Party: the Democratic Centralists and the Workers' Opposition. They demanded an end to the bureaucratic controls of war communism. Other divisions also began to appear within the Communist Party: Trotsky argued for a 'producers' democracy' (with trade unions absorbed into the structures of the state, in order to raise productivity), while the left Communists rejected all calls for the militarisation of labour and called for the restoration of full 'proletarian democracy'. Lenin and Zinoviev found themselves somewhere between these two positions. There were clear signs that the Mensheviks and the SRs, which had continued to operate after a fashion during the civil war, were becoming increasingly popular, as were the anarchists and anarcho-syndicalists. Had totally free elections to the soviets been held in 1920, it is likely that the Communists would have lost their majority.

After the civil war and foreign intervention in 1920 and the Russo-Polish War of 1920–21, discontent finally exploded. There were several outbreaks of armed opposition during 1920. One of the most serious took place in the Tambov province, where peasants seized grain convoys that were going to the cities of central Russia; it took 50,000 Red Army troops to regain control.

In March 1921, dissatisfaction with war communism and demands for the restoration of full soviet democracy erupted in the Kronstadt Rising (or Rebellion) of sailors and workers. Though this naval base had previously been a Bolshevik stronghold, there had been new influxes of workers (mainly peasants from the Ukraine) and sailors since 1917, who were mainly anarcho-syndicalist supporters. The mutiny was eventually crushed by Red Army troops, but only after bitter and bloody fighting.

This event finally persuaded most of the Communists that Lenin's earlier call for an end to war communism and the adoption of a new economic policy was correct. This step, though, caused great political controversy and played an important role in the eventual emergence of a one-party state, partly because it led to serious divisions in the Communist Party and partly because it strengthened capitalist elements in the economy at a time when the regime was politically weak.

The New Economic Policy (NEP)

At the Tenth Party Congress, in March 1921 Lenin introduced the New Economic Policy, in order to revive industrial and food production. This time, despite a split vote, a majority of the Communist leaders voted for it.

The NEP not only ended war communism, it also introduced a partial step back towards capitalism, as there was a limited return to market economics in some areas of the economy. In some ways, it was a return to the earlier policy of state capitalism, with a mixed economy that was under the control of the state. Though the major banks and industries and foreign trade remained nationalised, small firms and retail businesses were returned to private control, while peasants were allowed to sell part of their surplus produce for profit. State requisitions were ended immediately and replaced by a much lower tax-in-kind. Many communists were angered and worried by these concessions to small-scale capitalism: the Workers' Opposition called the NEP the 'new exploitation of the proletariat'.

Lenin, however, recognised that one of the major reasons for the peasants' reluctance to produce and sell grain had been the inability of industry to produce the manufactured goods they wanted. It was hoped that, by restricting the powers of Vesenkha over small industries and getting the State Bank to provide credit to small firms, production of goods would increase. In 1922 the introduction of a new re-valued rouble led to the return of a money economy. Also in 1922, Lenin persuaded the party's Eleventh Congress to agree to allow peasants to hire labour and rent land. Soon – as feared by those on the left of the party – wealthy businessmen (Nepmen) and peasants (*kulaks*) emerged, but the economy did begin to improve. For many Communists, the NEP was, at best, a dispiriting retreat to pre-revolutionary ways. Bukharin, however, parted company with the left Communists during the 1921 crisis and soon became an enthusiastic supporter of the NEP and its central idea of establishing and maintaining an alliance (*smychka*) with the peasantry.

By 1924, the economy had made significant improvements. According to A. Nove (who has adjusted the figures to account for possible bias and inaccuracies), grain production was up from 38 million to 51 million tons, while factory output had doubled; the average wage of factory workers had also more than doubled. These real achievements as well as those in 1925–26 led some

Communists to argue that the NEP could now be abandoned and more substantial industrial expansion begun.

Agriculture recovered much more quickly than industry. While unemployment continued to exist in many industrial towns, it was clear that the Nepmen and the *kulaks* were prospering. Good harvests in 1922 and 1923 highlighted the relative failure of industrial production to recover from the damage and disruption suffered in the period 1914–21. As food prices fell, those of the much scarcer industrial goods rose, to create what Trotsky termed the 'scissors crisis' in October 1923. As the peasants found the price of their grain falling and industrial goods either absent or expensive, the fear was that they would begin to cut back on production again and to consume more of their surplus production or feed it to their animals, rather than sell at lower prices. This was seen as such a serious potential problem that the Central Committee set up a special 'scissors committee'. More immediately, however, the economic picture began to improve after October 1923 when industrial production began to make more significant improvements. By 1924, there were signs of a real industrial recovery.

The crisis played an important role in the struggle for power which, in the light of Lenin's serious illness, was beginning to emerge. It also showed that Vesenkha had not been able to draw up, let alone implement, a coherent national plan for economic recovery and continued growth.

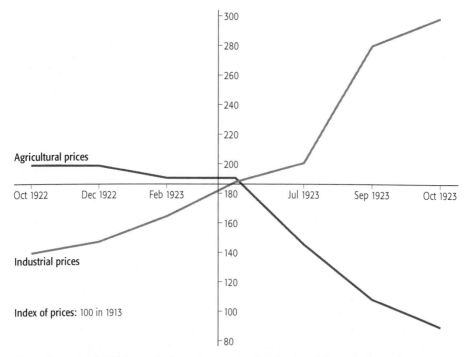

The 'scissors crisis'. This graph shows how agricultural prices fell and industrial prices rose during the NEP in 1923. (Adapted from M. Lynch, *Reaction and revolution: Russia 1881–1924*, 1922.)

Party and state

Lenin and the Bolsheviks believed, in line with Marxist theory, that an ideal society should have no standing army, no police and no bureaucracy. In *State and revolution*, Lenin wrote of the state in a classless communist society 'withering away'. After the revolution, the Bolsheviks tried at first to make the new workers' state as similar to this ideal as possible. They envisaged that their proletarian dictatorship would be superior to the bourgeois dictatorships of capitalist parliamentary democracies. In particular, they wanted the soviets to combine all legislative and executive powers, electors to have the power to revoke and replace deputies at any time and the soviets to be able to dismiss the government at a moment's notice with a vote of no confidence. Immediately after the revolution, Lenin and the Bolsheviks continued to take for granted the idea that the soviets would contain different parties and voice opposition. For example, when the Right SRs and the Mensheviks walked out in protest at the revolution, their seats on the CEC were left vacant in case they decided to return. Although Lenin was against forming a coalition, he did not favour banning any opposition party which accepted the new constitutional framework of the soviet system. In fact, the early days of the new regime did not point to the establishment of a dictatorship.

The Bolshevik Party, however, had come to power during the disruption of war and revolution, and both state and party were transformed during the murderous chaos of the civil war and the foreign intervention that followed. It can be seen, therefore, that the civil war played a major role in the change from a system where the soviets were an important part of the political process to one where one party came to exercise a dictatorship. In addition, during the period 1917–21, the Communist Party had a significant influx of new members who had grown accustomed to central direction and obedience to the higher party organs during the military threats to the regime. It seemed obvious to them that they should do their best to prevent the return of the old order and the exploiting classes. Repressing opposition groups – especially those that resort to violence – is common to all types of regimes at times of war. The assassinations carried out by the SRs opposed to the Communists created a situation in which the Cheka rapidly extended its role from arresting middle-class and aristocratic opponents to moving against ordinary workers and peasants.

Some historians, such as R. Tucker, stress the degree to which the party machine became accustomed to administrative diktats rather than democratic discussion as an acceptable form of government. The party also increasingly resorted to appointment rather than election of officials during the civil war; with the introduction of the NEP in 1921, this was continued and developed into a system known as the *nomenklatura*, whereby the party kept lists of reliable people and their skills and identified over 5,000 party and state posts that could only be filled by central appointment from the approved lists. This did not necessarily mean that Lenin and the Communists originally intended to create an authoritarian regime – the conditions which existed in Russia in 1917–21 would have led any party which wanted to stay in power to develop authoritarian methods. Under the pressures of war and its disruptions, Sovnarkom and the soviet system – and the party itself – were increasingly by-passed by the smaller party bodies such as the Politburo and the Orgburo which, being smaller, could take rapid decisions. For instance, in the period 1917–18 alone, only 68 out of 480 decrees were presented to the Soviets' CEC for approval. Under the chairmanship of Sverdlov, the powers of the full CEC were increasingly transferred to the higher bodies of the Soviet, and especially to its presidium, on which the Bolsheviks had a majority. This tendency was speeded up by the start of the civil war and the expulsion of the Mensheviks and most of the SRs from the soviets' executive bodies for 'counter-revolutionary acts'.

It was a surprise to everyone, including the Communists, when the new workers' state emerged victorious from the civil war. When it became clear, by 1921, that the Communists were isolated both internally and externally, they were faced with a dilemma: should they remain in power or resign because of the unfavourable circumstances in which they found themselves and, if they decided on the former, how were they to rule? As R. Service noted, the Communist Party believed that the overlap of function and personnel in the party–state structures was the only element capable of holding the 'soviet compound' together in the extreme circumstances of 1921; if they fell apart, the soviet state would soon dissolve and the old order would return.

The 1921 ban

The NEP and its plans for the limited revival of capitalism, the shock of the Kronstadt Rising (which had been supported by all the opposition parties and had thus shown the growing isolation of the Bolsheviks) and the ultimate failure of revolutions in the rest of Europe led Lenin to introduce a ban on organised factions within the Communist Party and a ban on opposition parties in the soviets at the Tenth Congress in March 1921. Until then, even during the civil war, strong disagreements within the Communist Party had been a usual part of the party's democratic centralism. Parties such as the Mensheviks and Social Revolutionaries had continued to operate within the soviets, although they had experienced temporary restrictions and even bans, and the use of tactics and force to reduce their representation, depending on the seriousness of the military situation at the time. The ban on the Mensheviks had been lifted as early as December 1918 and that on the Right SRs in February 1919. Opposition parties were allowed to function if they did not call for armed resistance to the Bolsheviks. Even when other parties were restricted, this was never on the basis of a principle of a one-party state.

Lenin's ban on factions was based on the view that the isolation of the Soviet state and the partial return to capitalism of the NEP required the party to be extra disciplined in order to prevent possible fragmentation and the victory of counter-revolutionary forces. The idea was to hold power in the name of the working class until the economic reforms had rebuilt the working class. Evidence would suggest that Lenin and Trotsky and most other Communists hoped that, once the civil war was over, the opposition parties would play a full and active part in the soviets. As a first step, the powers of the Cheka had been reduced and the death penalty abolished in January 1920.

Several Communists strongly opposed the 1921 ban and Lenin later stated that it was a temporary measure, intended to deal with an acute political and economic crisis. At this point, most Communists held the fate of the revolution to be paramount, so they were prepared to accept their party's political monopoly. As the Soviet state's international isolation continued, some began to argue that this emergency measure might have to be continued. It was, however, never intended to be a ban on inner-party opposition and dissent in general. Nonetheless, the views of the Workers' Opposition and the Democratic Centralists were judged to be syndicalist, anarchist 'deviations' which were incompatible with party membership. Several of the more prominent leaders were given posts far away from Moscow and the other major towns. This set a dangerous precedent for the years to come, even though Lenin's methods were not as extreme as those later adopted by Stalin.

Substitutionism

Nonetheless, the ban was a further step in the process of 'substitutionism' (whereby the party was substituted for the people, then the party organisation for the party, then a single leader for the party organisation) that would end in the dictatorship of Stalin. Part of the problem in the early 1920s was that the Communists had never envisaged obtaining or holding power without the support of the majority of the working industrial class. Yet by 1921, the government's power rested on a soviet system from which the workers were largely absent, because of losses during the civil war, workers taking up administrative posts or the fact that economic collapse and subsequent unemployment meant many workers had migrated to rural areas and so played a smaller part in the political process. All of these factors combined to create a significant political vacuum.

In addition, the party itself was not the same as the one that had led the November Revolution. The party grew rapidly, but this growth was unplanned. In early 1917, Bolshevik membership had stood at about 25,000; this had almost quadrupled in the period 1917–19 – an additional 250,000 members had joined in 1919 alone. Such increases continued so that by 1922 the Communists had about 750,000 members. After 1919, when it became clear that the Reds were going to win the civil war, many who joined the party were committed careerists rather than committed Communists. Then after the 1921 ban on other parties, those who might have joined the Mensheviks or the SRs turned to the only legal party. Membership among the peasants increased, which also contributed to the reduction in working-class membership. Thus many of the early members came to see themselves as being an authentic, if minority, 'old guard' with a responsibility to purge the party of what, according to Zinoviev, were 'unconscious Mensheviks or unconscious SRs'.

Ironically, among the first to call for such a purge was the Workers' Opposition at the Tenth Party Congress in 1921. This was approved and, later that year, public meetings were held to assess genuine political commitment. The only punishment was loss of party membership and anyone could speak for or against the person under investigation. Significantly, the police and courts were not involved and mere criticism of party policy or leadership was not grounds for expulsion. In all, about 200,000 members were expelled from the party, most of whom were careerists, former members of anti-Bolshevik parties who had joined after the civil war, corrupt communist officials or the politically unsure who had little idea of Marxist principles.

This purge, however, set a dangerous precedent. In later years, Stalin came to see purges as a way of removing critics and rivals. It also taught many party members to feel that it was wisest not to voice any serious differences.

This reinforced a trend that had become increasingly obvious during the civil war: the old guard was deciding party policy, rather than the party congresses. In January 1919, an Organisational Bureau (Orgburo) was established to implement decisions. The secretariat of the Central Committee was also expanded and separated from the Orgburo and given the power to make decisions provided there were no objections from the Orgburo. Then in March 1919, a Political Bureau (Politburo), under the authority of the party's larger Central Committee, was set up to make decisions about urgent issues. They all contributed to a shift from decisions being made by the whole party to their being made by smaller bodies. The Orgburo began to take over many of the functions of the Central Committee. This happened more and more after April 1922 when Stalin became the general secretary of the Communist Party. (He was the only party member with seats on all four of these bodies.)

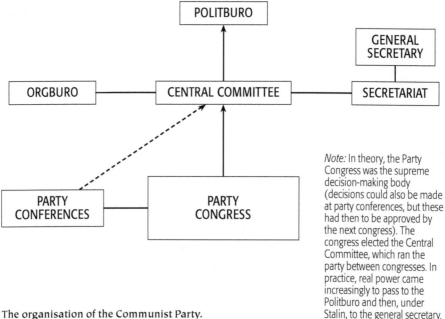

Note: In theory, the Party Congress was the supreme decision-making body (decisions could also be made at party conferences, but these had then to be approved by the next congress). The congress elected the Central Committee, which ran the party between congresses. In practice, real power came increasingly to pass to the Politburo and then, under Stalin, to the general secretary.

The organisation of the Communist Party.

As early as March 1922, Lenin voiced concern that only a 'very thin stratum' of the party determined policy, a tendency that was being reinforced by the decline and dispersal of the politically mature workers. At the Eleventh Party Congress (which turned out to be the last one Lenin was able to attend), Lenin was joined by Zinoviev and Trotsky in expressing concern about the merger of party and state and suggesting that some attempts should be made to separate their functions. Lenin was particularly concerned about the way in which the Politburo, not Sovnarkom, was becoming the chief decision-making body. During 1921–23, with his health failing, he tried to enlist Trotsky's help in getting the party bureaucracy to divest itself of many of its governmental functions. This view was not shared by other Communists such as Stalin, Zinoviev and Kamenev, who believed that the presence of members of the traditional state bureaucracy in most government departments meant the party had to control all levels of the administrative system.

While the larger bodies of the party (like the party congresses and conferences) and the soviets were becoming weaker, the state was expanding its power. In 1918, the Council of Labour and Defence (STO) was set up to organise the supplies of the Red Army; in 1920, this became a separate commissariat which frequently by-passed or overruled local soviets, as did Vesenkha. The local soviets increasingly came to be seen as centres for local administration. At the same time, the Red Army and the police also became involved in the controlling of the regions by the centre.

Initially at least there was the added problem that all government departments were dependent on administrators who had been appointed by the Tsar or the provisional government. Lenin argued that, in view of the general low educational standards of most workers, the workers' state would have to rely on these 'bourgeois specialists' until cultural levels of workers had been raised. This was essential for administrative purposes, but also for specific skills such as accounting and government finance.

The party was concerned about these issues early on: in March 1919, the Eighth Congress attacked the growth of bureaucracy and, the following month, passed a decree that set up the People's Commissariat for State Control under Stalin's leadership; in February 1920, this was renamed the Workers' and Peasants' Inspectorate (Rabkrin). Stalin soon began to use his position to appoint party members who were loyal to him. Lenin, much more concerned with government matters, was not really aware of the full extent of the growth in power of the party machine until 1922: in that year, he referred to the Politburo as an 'oligarchy'. Although Lenin was concerned that the old professional administrators and bureaucrats, rather than the government, were directing the workers' state, and that they were 'swamping' Communist values with pre-revolutionary ones, he believed that they were needed. This was a view shared by many of the leading Communists, but not by most rank-and-file party members, who resented the use of such experts and wanted to see them replaced with loyal Communists. Lenin's failing health kept him away from Sovnarkom meetings, which added further to its loss of influence in relation to the leading organisations of the party.

Historians are divided on whether or not these developments under Lenin led inevitably to the dictatorship established by Stalin after 1924. Those who see a distinct line of continuity, such as L. Schapiro and G. Leggett, point to the fact that the Cheka, which was set up by Lenin, later became the NKVD and then the KGB, upon which Stalin's rule depended. In addition, S. Fitzpatrick believes that the evidence suggests that Lenin himself, if not his party, was not in favour of sharing power with other parties in the soviets and that, although Lenin eventually urged Stalin's removal as general secretary, he did not suggest that the post should be abolished. Some of the documents that have become available since the collapse of the former Soviet Union appear to support such a view.

Others, such as E. H. Carr and E. Mandel, point out that, while Lenin (and Trotsky) were authoritarian and approved the use of terror at times, they never attempted to destroy the party's organs or to justify, as a matter of principle, the practice of one-party rule. Also important in assessing the degree of continuity between Lenin and Stalin is the much greater thoroughness and ruthlessness used by Stalin to get his own way and the extent to which Stalin was not prepared to accept Lenin's position of being 'first among equals'. In many ways, it is possible to argue that it was the military experience of the civil war which pushed the administrative system away from earlier ideals and in the direction of coercion and authoritarianism. According to this view, Stalin should be seen as someone who used and abused the system that arose between 1917 and 1924, and not as the logical heir of Lenin.

Society
The idea of the 'dictatorship of the proletariat' dictated that Russian society would have to be fundamentally overhauled. Before the new government could begin to tackle social issues, however, the civil war broke out. One of its most significant social results was the temporary disintegration and dispersal of the industrial working class that had brought the Bolsheviks to power.

Nonetheless, there were attempts to at least lay down the basis for a future new society. The Communists were strong supporters of the emancipation of women. By the end of the civil war, laws had been passed to make divorce available to all women, abortion was permitted, and equal rights and equal pay for women had been granted. Special women's departments (*zhenotdely*) were set up to organise and educate women and to help them play an independent role in all aspects of life. The rights of children in the family were also promoted, especially by Communist youth groups such as the Young Communists (Komsomol for young adults and the Young Pioneers for those aged 10 to 14).

As regards class mobility, which was central to communist politics, the early years of the revolutionary state were not a huge success. Certainly, by the end of the civil war, tens of thousands of ordinary workers and soldiers had been promoted to important administrative posts in government departments, in industry and in the armed forces. However, many more reliable and trustworthy workers had been lost during the civil war, leaving the traditional bureaucrats and 'bourgeois specialists' to continue to play an important role in administration and industry. Nonetheless, in the period immediately after the Bolshevik Revolution the middle and upper classes experienced fundamental losses in their economic and political power. By 1921, all large-scale firms had been expropriated by the state and the constitution of 1918 had withdrawn the right to vote from all those who employed workers for profit or lived by financial investments. As far as ownership of land, mines, banks and factories was concerned, a total revolution had taken place. While a few former landowners and industrialists had at first joined in the civil war in an attempt to recover their property, most decided to emigrate. Though the NEP restored some elements of a market economy, bankers, big industrialists, stockbrokers and large landowners belonged to the past.

Although an avowedly atheist party, the Bolsheviks had not at first taken direct steps to suppress the Orthodox Church. Then in February 1918, Sovnarkom issued a Decree on the Separation of Church and State, which banned the teaching of religion in schools and the church from owning property. The government and the party issued a considerable amount of atheist literature, which led the patriarch of the Orthodox Church to declare that all who supported these measures were liable to be excommunicated. Other Christian denominations as well as the Muslim religion (which was strong in the Asiatic republics) adopted a less hostile stance to the communist government and were treated quite liberally in the early 1920s. Meanwhile, the state-funded League of the Militant Godless stepped up their propaganda and those who engaged in public worship often lost government posts. The outbreak of famine in 1921 was used by Lenin as an opportunity to confiscate church buildings and valuables, ostensibly to provide funds for food relief. Many 'reactionary' clergy were also shot by the Cheka in an attempt to stamp out the influence of an organisation which was loyal to the Tsar and which continued to have considerable influence over the peasantry.

One of the biggest problems facing any government of Russia was the fact that in 1918 it was still a multinational empire. Under both the Tsar and then the provisional government, there had been much unrest in areas that were demanding their national independence. At first, Lenin argued that all the subject nationalities of the old empire should have the right of secession and he accepted that Poland, Finland and probably the Ukraine would want to exercise that right. He assumed that the rest of the nations would be happy to remain in a multinational soviet federal state that would not reflect the old Russian chauvinism and would instead guarantee the rights of all nationalities. In March 1918 the first soviet constitution established the Russian Soviet Federal Socialist Republics (RSFSR). It soon became clear that, as a result of Stalin's activities as commissar for nationalities, Russia would dominate the federation. Lenin later opposed what he saw as Stalin's 'great Russian chauvinism' and the new constitution for a Union of Soviet Socialist Republics (USSR) that he was shaping and which became law shortly after Lenin's death in 1924.

Propaganda and education

Although Lenin had great personal authority, which usually – but not always – resulted in the party finally accepting his suggestions, the Communist Party did not formally have a leader. There was no leadership or personality cult and Lenin did not want or approve of flattery and blind obedience. However, after his death, a 'cult of Lenin' was created by Stalin, in an attempt to attribute special powers to the leader, to which Stalin then laid claim for himself after his success in the power struggle.

As regards education, Lenin and the Bolsheviks wished to eradicate illiteracy (about 50 per cent of the population was illiterate in 1917). The Bolsheviks' aim was partly the result of their general desire to eliminate ignorance and barbarism from Russian society and partly a reflection of their need to raise the cultural and technical levels of the workers and peasants so that they could play an effective role in supervising the economy and the state. Thus in December 1919, a decree was approved which stated that all illiterates should attend school, even though the circumstances made this impossible for the immediate future. As the civil war drew to a close, Lenin turned his attention once more to education, with the emphasis on educating the masses in technical skills in order to speed up industrial and agricultural progress; political indoctrination appeared to be of secondary importance. The commissariat of enlightenment proved to be extremely innovative in its attempts to spread literacy and numeracy and as a result the literacy rate for men in the period 1897–1927 rose from 40 per cent to over 70 per cent.

The propaganda which existed in the early Communist state was often of a 'modernist' nature, as several avant-garde artists were early supporters of the revolution. Posters and cartoons were especially important in trying to spread the political and cultural ideals of the revolution. Also important were propaganda trains and ships, which carried the message to the far-flung corners of the new state; theatre, too, played a significant 'Agitprop' role in the years before Stalin. However, this did not mean that the Communists wanted the old bourgeois culture to be destroyed at the same time that a new proletarian culture was being created. Unlike Stalin, Lenin and Trotsky appreciated the cultural achievements of western Europe and wished to build on these rather than destroy them. Although Lenin did not always appreciate the newer art forms, there was a large degree of artistic experimentation in the period 1917–24, especially in the art of the Constructivists and in cinema. There were, however, some limitations on the artists' free expression and in 1922 a number of prominent writers and scholars who had overtly attacked the Communist state were deported.

Foreign policy

The main aim of early Soviet foreign policy was to assist the outbreak of the 'international revolution' which they believed was imminent. As commissar of foreign affairs, Trotsky had believed he would have little to do but issue a few declarations and then wait to do business with the new workers' states. His early actions when negotiating peace with the Germans were clearly meant to be an example of revolutionary diplomacy, especially his attempts to incite revolution among the troops of the Central Powers on the eastern front. He also upset traditional diplomats by openly publishing the various secret treaties and agreements made by different states with previous Russian governments.

In March 1919, the Communist Third International (Comintern) was set up to instigate and co-ordinate revolutionary activity in Europe. Communist parties were established in Germany, Italy and France during 1920, with the aim of helping along the expected European revolutions. However, by 1921, with the defeat of revolution in Germany and the overthrow of the Hungarian Soviet Republic, even the most optimistic of the internationalists were forced to accept that the revolutionary tide which had swept much of Europe in the years 1917–19 had passed without resulting in a single ally. It was at this point that Soviet diplomacy began to revert to a more traditional format.

One effect of the Red Army's defeat at the hands of the Poles in 1920 and the failure of any victorious revolution in Europe was to make Lenin realise that it would be necessary to adjust foreign policy and be prepared to reach agreements with individual countries. This did not mean abandoning their Comintern activity, however, which continued to revolve around assisting the outbreak of revolution in the rest of Europe. In some ways, this can be seen as a continuation of earlier Russian anti-Western foreign policy, in as much as the new workers' state felt threatened by the surrounding capitalist states that were clearly more powerful. This feeling of insecurity was increased when, after 1921, they imposed an economic blockade against Soviet Russia. Significantly, this foreign policy was based on the desire to avoid conflict – the Russo-Polish War had confirmed earlier beliefs that expansion was not a legitimate aim. As a result, treaties were signed with the former territories of the Tsarist empire (Finland, the Baltic republics and eventually Poland) during 1920–21 which formally accepted their independence.

One of the reasons that some of the Communists, including Lenin, had supported the introduction of the NEP was their recognition of the fact that by 1921 the prospect of an international revolution was receding. They realised that it would be necessary to compromise, even to the extent of adopting policies that conflicted with aspects of Marxist theory. In March 1921, for example, a trade agreement was signed with Britain, and Soviet commercial delegations were soon established in several other west European states. At the same time, the commissariat of foreign affairs began to act independently of the Comintern. This led to a situation in which Soviet foreign policy started to take on a national rather than international and revolutionary slant. In 1922 Soviet Russia participated in the Genoa conference to settle problems created by the First World War peace treaties. While other states refused to recognise Lenin's government, Germany concluded the Treaty of Rapallo with Soviet Russia to increase trade and to provide Germany with military facilities in return for its technical assistance. Nonetheless, while holding discussions with foreign countries, the Comintern encouraged the communist parties in those countries to conduct revolutionary political campaigns. In his *Left-wing communism: an infantile disorder*, published in 1920, Lenin urged communists to work within established trade unions and to participate in parliamentary elections in order to gain positions and recruits.

Lenin's illness

In May 1922, Lenin had the first of a series of strokes, which increasingly restricted his ability to take an active part in politics. There is evidence that by the end of 1923 he was becoming concerned that Soviet Russia was turning into a workers' state 'distorted' by bureaucracy and he began to develop plans to enlarge the Central Committee and to reduce the powers of the Politburo and the Secretariat. Over the next two years, however, the economy under the NEP began to show signs of improvement, especially as regards agricultural production. By 1924, the Communists were becoming increasingly divided over economic policy: some wished to end the NEP and begin to move towards socialist economic planning and especially industrialisation. However, the success of the NEP led many to believe that it should be a more long-term policy, leading to a gradual transition to socialism via a mixed economy by encouraging private enterprise but also building up the socialist state sector at the same time. However, by 1922, Trotsky and others had come to believe it was necessary to begin to build up heavy industry.

The rise of Stalin, 1924–28

At this time, there were also significant political differences over internal political democracy, the policy towards the nationalities that made up Soviet Russia and what attitude to adopt towards furthering world revolution.

The origins of the power struggle

These economic and political divisions became bound up in personal rivalries between leading Communists who, in view of Lenin's ill-health, began to consider what would happen if Lenin died. The most important Communists after Lenin were the other members of the Politburo: Trotsky, Zinoviev, Kamenev, Bukharin, Rykov, Stalin and Tomsky. Of these, Trotsky seemed the most likely to replace Lenin: he had been the main organiser of the November Revolution, had built up the Red Army that had defeated the Whites and was commissar for war. After him, Zinoviev and Kamenev were strong political leaders of Petrograd and Moscow respectively and had long been associated with Lenin. Their weak spot was that they had been opposed to the November Revolution at first and had leaked early plans to the opposition's press. Bukharin, too, was a well-known and popular revolutionary leader. Stalin was not well known and seemed unlikely to emerge as a major force. However, he had been appointed commissar for nationalities after the revolution and, in April 1922, had been appointed general secretary of the Communist Party. In this latter post he had the power to appoint and dismiss Communist officials.

A week after Stalin's appointment as general secretary, Lenin proposed that Trotsky be appointed one of the deputy chairmen of the Council of People's Commissars. There were two, and later three, other deputies but, given Trotsky's importance, he would have been the most senior and thus effectively second-in-command of the government, after Lenin. Trotsky, however, refused and did so again when Lenin returned to this issue in September and December 1922.

Apart from their political differences, these leading Communists were split by personal jealousies and animosities. Many of the leading Communists resented Trotsky's rapid rise to the top of the party. While they had supported Lenin in 1903 when the Russian Soviet Democratic Labour Party (RSDLP) split into Bolshevik and Menshevik factions, Trotsky had sided with the Mensheviks in 1903–04 and had then formed an independent grouping until he joined the Bolsheviks in August 1917. Trotsky's manner was often arrogant and he made little effort to cultivate political alliances. Zinoviev and Kamenev, weakened by their earlier attitude to the November Revolution, turned to Stalin to stop Trotsky succeeding. As early as December 1922, they began to form an alliance to prevent Trotsky from obtaining majority support.

Lenin's Testament

Lenin's strokes kept him from active involvement in politics, but his awareness of these political and personal tensions (especially after October 1922) caused him growing concern. This came to a head in December 1922 when he learned of a Central Committee proposal to weaken the state monopoly of foreign trade. (The state monopoly of foreign trade was seen as essential in order to prevent foreign capitalist businesses from exploiting and weakening the Soviet economy.) At the same time, he decided to support Trotsky's idea that Gosplan should be allowed a bigger role in the running of the NEP. Though he sent a letter to the Politburo outlining his views on these matters, he was shocked to discover that, at first, the Politburo refused to publish the letter. At last realising what Trotsky had meant by the growing bureaucracy, he proposed that he and Trotsky should form a Joint Bloc for Democracy.

At the end of December, however, Lenin suffered his second stroke. Concerned about what might happen after his death, he dictated his initial thoughts for his last Testament, outlining the strengths and weaknesses of all the leading Communists. Afterwards, Lenin's growing concern over Stalin's power, his draft constitution for the USSR and policies towards the national groups (especially in Georgia) led him to add a Postscript in January 1923, recommending Stalin's removal. From then, until his death the following year, Lenin urged Trotsky on several occasions to launch a campaign against bureaucracy and for the restoration of party and soviet democracy.

The early stages and the campaign against Trotsky, 1923–24

By January 1923, the alliance between Stalin, Zinoviev and Kamenev (known as the triumvirs) had been finalised. Stalin then began an attack on Trotsky over his continued refusal to accept the post of deputy chairman, accusing him of

(Left) This photo shows Lenin and Trotsky, the co-leaders of the 1917 November Revolution, celebrating its second anniversary in Red Square on 7 November 1919. The man to the left of Lenin is Kamenev.
(Below) This photo, published in 1967, shows how Trotsky and Kamenev were later airbrushed out of Soviet history. Why did Stalin want to remove proof of Trotsky's closeness to Lenin?

wanting to take Lenin's place instead. In February Lenin showed signs of recovery and wrote a letter criticising the Workers' and Peasants' Inspectorate; once again the Politburo voted not to publish it. The triumvirs then decided to open up party records to all Central Committee members. Soon a 'whispering campaign' was underway, concerning Trotsky's non-Bolshevik past, his earlier disagreements with Lenin, and his 'ambitions'. Trotsky wrote a letter of protest to the Central Committee, refuting the implications and threatening to reveal all at the forthcoming Twelfth Party Congress in April; Stalin quickly had Lenin's recent letter published in *Pravda*.

By March 1923 Stalin appeared to be in serious trouble. His rudeness to Lenin's wife, Krupskaya, had caused Lenin to send him a harsh letter. Kamenev was aware of this and of Lenin's intention to politically crush Stalin. Lenin sent Trotsky his notes about affairs in Georgia criticising Stalin's activities and asked him to explode this 'bombshell' at the congress – he stressed that there should be no compromise with Stalin.

Trotsky, however, then fell ill; when Kamenev (his brother-in-law) visited him, promising changes would be made, Trotsky said that if Stalin announced a new nationalities policy he would not oppose him. Receiving such promises, and believing Lenin would recover, Trotsky handed Lenin's notes over to the Politburo. Lenin then suffered a third stroke, which left him paralysed and speechless for most of the time until his death in January 1924.

The Twelfth Congress in April 1923 opened with the customary greetings from party cells. All mentioned Lenin and Trotsky, several mentioned Zinoviev and Kamenev as well, while hardly any referred to Stalin. As far as the party's rank-and-file were concerned, it was clear who Lenin's successor was going to be. However, with Lenin absent, and now that they had Lenin's notes and Trotsky's promise not to explode Lenin's 'bombshell', the triumvirs felt confident. They urged party unity in view of Lenin's serious illness. The Workers' Opposition wanted the triumvirs to be removed (as they were seen to be restricting party democracy) and the 1921 ban on factions to be ended. Their motion was defeated. The triumvirs persuaded congress to vote for the motion that any criticism of the leading party group would be equivalent to Menshevism.

The Georgian Communists – having had a letter from Lenin before his stroke – were furious when Trotsky said nothing; their demand that the Politburo publish Lenin's notes was refused. Trotsky only spoke on economic issues, but his call for a new socialist planning offensive in the NEP led to concern among many delegates that there might be a return to war communism. The congress then re-elected Stalin as general secretary and elected a new, enlarged Central Committee. Of its 40 members, only 3 were strong supporters of Trotsky. A new control commission was also set up to deal with party membership.

Stalin then set about replacing Trotsky's supporters with those of the triumvirs, especially those loyal to him. By the end of 1923, Stalin already had enough control of the party machine at local level to ensure that most of his nominees were elected as delegates to future congresses.

In July and August 1923 a wave of unofficial strikes broke out in Moscow and Petrograd. The triumvirs immediately blamed the Workers' Opposition and called for the expulsion of all party members who broke the 1921 ban on factions. The GPU (which Cheka became in February 1922; later it was renamed OGPU) discovered the existence of two other left communist factions, the Workers' Group and the Workers' Truth. Although Trotsky did not support these groups, he did oppose the disciplinary measures demanded by the triumvirs. On 8 October Trotsky wrote a letter to the Central Committee, blaming the strikes on the lack of economic planning. A week later, 46 leading Communists issued a statement (known as the Statement of the 46) making similar points to those made by Trotsky; they also attacked Stalin's abuse of power, demanded an end to the 1921 ban and called for an emergency party conference.

Although Trotsky was not involved with this statement, several of his supporters were among the 46, as were members of the Workers' Opposition and the Democratic Centralists. The extent of the opposition shocked the triumvirs; they refused to publish the statement or to call a conference. Instead, they persuaded the Central Committee to censure Trotsky and the 46 for their actions and to threaten them with expulsion if they circulated the statement.

It was at this point that Trotsky and the 46 joined forces to form what became known as the Left Opposition. The standing of its members led Zinoviev, on 7 November, to promise to restore party democracy and to open the pages of *Pravda* to the critics. Within a short time, many party cells indicated their support for the 46. The triumvirs panicked and dismissed the chief commissar of the Red Army (a supporter of Trotsky), replaced the leadership of Komsomol and demoted other critics. However, the three did promise a 'new course' which would include inner-party democracy and freedom of expression. Trotsky, who was still ill, agreed to give his support to the Politburo's new course. As Stalin began to use his power to stifle criticisms, Trotsky wrote an open letter to party meetings in December 1923, warning that some leaders were not fully committed to the promises of the new course. Despite much support for Trotsky's views, secretaries (who were Stalin's nominees) 'lost' most of the resolutions that favoured Trotsky's position. A pamphlet on the new course, written by Trotsky for the Thirteenth Party Conference, due in January 1924, was not printed until after the conference had ended.

Stalin also used his growing power over the party machine, and the fact that the preparations for the conference were in the hands of his nominees, to ensure that as many supporters as possible of the Left Opposition were removed by the processes of indirect election of delegates to the conference.

Trotsky's illness prevented him from attending the conference. In the event, it condemned the views of Trotsky and the 46 as a 'petty bourgeois deviation from Leninism' and accused him of disloyalty to the Politburo and the old guard. Only three delegates supported Trotsky. The conference also voted that the old guard should maintain their control as the party now had over 400,000 members, not all of whom were true Communists. By this time, Trotsky was already on his way to convalesce at the Black Sea, as advised by his doctors. While on this journey, he received a telegram from Stalin informing him of Lenin's death. When Trotsky spoke of returning, Stalin told him to continue his journey as he would not be able to get back in time for the funeral and that it was now more important than ever that Trotsky recover from his illness. In fact, Stalin had deliberately given him the wrong date; at Lenin's funeral, the triumvirs presented themselves as Lenin's successors and raised doubts about Trotsky's absence. They also decided, in honour of Lenin, to recruit 100,000 new party members who would be known as the 'Lenin levy'. Meanwhile, more and more Oppositionists were demoted or dismissed from posts of responsibility.

The defeat of the left, 1924–26

First stage

Before the Thirteenth Party Congress met in May 1924, Lenin's widow revealed Lenin's Testament to the Central Committee and senior congress delegates. Its clear recommendation for Stalin's dismissal seemed guaranteed to prevent him ever succeeding Lenin as leader. Stalin was saved by Zinoviev and Kamenev. They argued that he had changed his policies and that the party needed to stick together. Trotsky, who had only just returned from his convalescence, said nothing and, despite Krupskaya's protests, the Central Committee decided not to remove Stalin as general secretary and not to publish Lenin's Testament; in fact, its existence was kept a secret in the USSR until 1956. The congress voted to accept the condemnation of Trotsky made by the previous conference.

By this time, hopes of revolution in Germany, Poland and Bulgaria had been dashed and this accelerated the drift of the Russian Communist Party to the right. In June 1924, the Fifth Congress of Comintern confirmed the condemnation of Trotsky and elected Stalin in his place as a full member of its executive. Trotsky was threatened with expulsion if he engaged in any further political controversy. His Left Opposition had been defeated, thus ending what turned out to be the first stage of the power struggle.

Second stage

The next stage in the power struggle lasted from 1924 to 1926 and was relatively quiet. Almost immediately after the end of the Thirteenth Congress, the triumvirs began a campaign against 'Trotskyism' (said to be opposed to 'Leninism') and started to present an 'official', distorted history of the revolution and the civil war. At first, Trotsky remained silent but another dispute was sparked off in November 1924 with the publication of his speeches and writings of 1917. This showed how close his views were to those of Lenin. The triumvirs launched a counter-attack, once again dragging up all Trotsky's disagreements with Lenin, before and after 1917, and attacking his theory of permanent revolution (developed from Marx by Trotsky in 1906 and, by 1917, shared by most of the leading Bolsheviks).

In the autumn of 1924, Stalin first revealed his alternative to Trotsky's idea of permanent revolution: 'socialism in one country'. It stressed the need for peace and stability and argued that, despite its backwardness and isolation, the new Soviet state could construct socialism on its own. It rejected Trotsky's continued call for world revolution and was supported by Bukharin who, during 1924–25, completed his shift to the right in the Communist Party. Stalin for the centre and Bukharin for the right thus argued that, with the failure of revolution in the rest of Europe, it was even more important to maintain the alliance (known as the *smychka*) with the peasantry, who still comprised about 70 per cent of the population. They also accused Trotsky of lack of faith in Russia and its people.

In January 1925, the triumvirs used their control of party and state bodies to deprive Trotsky of his position as commissar for war, which had been an important political base for him. Trotsky was warned that any renewed controversy would result in his expulsion from the Politburo and the Central Committee. Trotsky gave up his position without a fight. In May, he was given a new economic post on Vesenkha. Soon he found himself in opposition again, pointing out the threat posed by US capitalism and arguing for moves towards socialist planning to strengthen the NEP and for Comintern to adopt a more revolutionary line.

Many Communists had come to enjoy the relative peace and prosperity of the NEP and feared Trotsky's proposals and his permanent revolution would threaten both internal and external peace. Stalin and Bukharin seemed to offer a more attractive future.

At first, the main protagonists in the power struggle were not Stalin and Trotsky but Bukharin and Preobrazhensky, but their disputes over the NEP and beginning industrialisation soon developed into a serious controversy which led to a split between the triumvirs, and another realignment in the Communist Party. By 1925, the party was clearly split into a left, centre and right. The left now comprised Zinoviev, Kamenev and Preobrazhensky. As early as January that year they had tried to ease Stalin out of his post as general secretary and by April they had begun to oppose socialism in one country as anti-Leninist. The right – Bukharin, Rykov and Tomsky – supported Stalin and the centre, which included Molotov, Kaganovich and Andreev.

By the summer of 1925, these disagreements between the triumvirs became public when Zinoviev's base in Leningrad, formerly Petrograd (known as the Leningrad Opposition) attacked the growing dominance of Bukharin's rightist views. In September, Zinoviev and Kamenev voiced their concerns about some developments in the party and called for a renewal of the struggle for equality and a revival of Leninist internationalism. In October, Zinoviev and Kamenev were joined by Krupskaya and Sokolnikov, and presented a joint statement calling for a free debate on all these issues. With the support of the right, Stalin was able to defeat this call, and the left were warned not to make any public criticisms of official policy.

Stalin then began to remove Kamenev's supporters from their positions in the Moscow party. He had less success with the Leningrad party, where Zinoviev was still strong. Zinoviev also controlled the area around Leningrad, one of the largest and most populous industrial areas, was president of Comintern, and even had the support of Krupskaya. All this time, Trotsky remained silent, partly because of his illness and partly because of his isolation, even though Zinoviev and Kamenev were now advocating views very similar to those of the Left Opposition of 1923–24 and were taking their stand on the proletarian and internationalist traditions of Marxism and Leninism. In fact, in September Trotsky agreed to deny that Lenin's Testament existed.

At the Fourteenth Party Congress in December 1925, despite a fierce debate between the differing groups, Trotsky remained silent – even when Zinoviev referred to Lenin's Testament and his warnings about Stalin's abuse of power, and when Krupskaya expressed her opposition to the campaign against Trotskyism. The congress (which Stalin had packed with his and Bukharin's supporters) then elected a new Central Committee with a Stalinist-Bukharinist majority. The newly elected Politburo also had a centre-right majority. Kamenev was demoted to a candidate member, while three of Stalin's supporters were moved from candidate to full membership.

Despite this defeat, Zinoviev continued his campaign in Leningrad. When the new Central Committee proposed disciplinary measures, these were opposed by Trotsky. As a result, Stalin began a new campaign against Trotsky and accused Zinoviev of Trotskyism. In early 1926, Zinoviev was forced to hand over the leadership of the Leningrad party to Kirov, one of Stalin's supporters, and his supporters were removed from their positions.

Third stage
So far, Trotsky had not sought a link with Zinoviev and Kamenev. In April 1926, he at last offered them support. In secret talks, they revealed how they had fabricated the anti-Trotskyist campaign, and their fears regarding Stalin's methods and policies. With some support from Krupskaya, Sokolnikov and a few other prominent party members, Trotsky, Zinoviev and Kamenev formed a United (Joint Left) Opposition. This began the next stage in the power struggle. At first little happened because from April to June Trotsky was in Germany for treatment for his illness.

On his return, Stalin launched an attack on Trotsky's views. Trotsky in turn wrote to the Politburo, warning them of the possible rule of an autocrat if the party was not reformed. A decisive contest took place over the next 18 months. The United Opposition formally declared its existence in July 1926. It argued for greater party democracy, more industrial planning, moves towards extensive (but not compulsory) collectivisation of agriculture and, above all, the rejection of socialism in one country. Their campaign faltered in the summer, as Stalin's control of the party enabled him to ban meetings and dismiss Oppositionists. The remnants of the Workers' Opposition joined the United Opposition, giving them just over 6,000 supporters out of a total party membership of about 750,000 (although only about 20,000 members were actively involved in this inner-party conflict).

Stalin then accused the Oppositionists of breaking the 1921 ban on factions and focused his attack on Zinoviev, who was still president of Comintern. The Central Committee voted to remove him from the Politburo, leaving only Trotsky to oppose Stalin in the Politburo. The United Opposition decided that they would appeal directly to the party rank-and-file, but again Stalin's control of the party machine and his appeal to national pride meant they had little success. The radical views of some members who wanted to form a new party, and their growing isolation, led Zinoviev and Kamenev to fear expulsion from the only legal party; soon, they began to move away from Trotsky. In October 1926, in an effort to keep the United Opposition together, Trotsky agreed that they should offer the Politburo a truce, which was accepted by Stalin and his supporters.

However, while plans were being made for the Fifteenth Party Conference, one of Trotsky's supporters published the full text of Lenin's Testament in the *New York Times*. The Politburo angrily ended the truce and a Central Committee meeting condemned the United Opposition as a 'social democratic deviation'. Trotsky then accused Stalin of being 'the grave-digger of the revolution'. Trotsky was expelled from the Politburo and Zinoviev was removed from his position as president of Comintern. The conference confirmed the expulsion of the three leaders from the Politburo, and threatened them with further actions if they re-opened the controversies. Their obvious isolation led Krupskaya (who feared the Communist Party was in danger of splitting) and former leaders of the Workers' Opposition to break away and make their peace with Stalin.

The newspapers continued their attacks on the United Opposition and lesser members lost their jobs. Though Zinoviev and Kamenev decided to keep quiet, Trotsky decided to fight on when, in December 1926, the executive committee of Comintern agreed to expel all Opposition supporters. Dissent flared up again in April 1927 over the leadership's policy towards events in China, following Jiang Jieshi's massacre of Chinese Communists. At the end of May, Trotsky was able to force a debate on this issue at the Comintern's executive. However, because 84 prominent Communists had drafted an appeal that was signed by over 300 others, Stalin again accused them of forming a faction. Consequently, Oppositionists continued to be demoted, sent to isolated parts of the Soviet Union or dismissed from their jobs.

As a result, Stalin asked the Central Committee and the control commission to expel Trotsky and Zinoviev from the Central Committee in June 1927. He did not want them to have the opportunity to speak at the Fifteenth Party Congress, planned for November 1927. Stalin was at first unable to persuade them to take this action and he had to postpone the congress until he finally got his way in October. Attempts by the Opposition to address the crowds at the tenth anniversary celebrations of the November Revolution were foiled by Stalin's supporters and the police. At this point Stalin demanded that Trotsky and Zinoviev be expelled from the party. This was agreed to on 14 November and Kamenev and Rakovsky were expelled from the Central Committee. Hundreds of lesser Oppositionists were also expelled.

When the congress met, in December 1927, the United Opposition issued a statement, signed by 121 of their leading members, asking for the expulsions to be annulled. This was overwhelmingly rejected. By this time, Trotsky was coming round to thinking that a new party might be necessary. This alarmed Zinoviev and Kamenev, who were attracted by signs that Stalin was about to abandon the NEP in favour of a programme of industrialisation and collectivisation of agriculture. As a result, during the congress, Kamenev announced that, in order to stop the expulsions and to prevent the formation of a second party, he and Zinoviev would surrender and would make no more criticisms. By 10 December 1927, therefore, the United Opposition was defeated.

The congress was followed by more expulsions and thousands of capitulations. Stalin insisted that all former Oppositionists should repudiate their earlier views. On 18 December, in front of congress, Zinoviev and Kamenev announced that their ideas had been 'wrong' and 'anti-Leninist'. Despite Bukharin's willingness, Stalin refused to readmit them until they had served at least six months' probation. Immediately after the congress, another 1,500 Oppositionists were expelled and 2,500 signed statements repudiating their views. Trotsky was forcibly deported to Alma Ata in Turkestan, near the Chinese border. It was also decreed that the state publishers would no longer print his works; those already in existence were removed from bookshops and libraries.

The defeat of the right, 1927–28

The final stage of the power struggle began almost immediately. As early as the autumn of 1927, a crisis had been brewing in rural areas. Despite three good harvests, there were bread shortages and high food prices all over the USSR, as peasants refused to sell their produce at the prices fixed by the state. There had been rioting in many places and forced grain collections had been made in some areas. Events such as these, and Stalin's consequent decision to adopt a new 'left' course as regards industry and agriculture (see Chapter 3), began to produce a rift between the Bukharinists (who wanted to make concessions to the peasants) and the Stalinists (who preferred more forceful methods). On 6 January 1928, the Politburo issued secret instructions to party organisations to be severe with those who obstructed grain collections and *Pravda* began to run articles attacking the *kulaks*.

In April, the Central Committee began to use the arguments of the Left Opposition against the *kulaks*, and introduced emergency measures such as taking compulsory loans from the *kulaks* and requisitioning their grain. At the same time, those who were seen as having been too lenient with the *kulaks* (mainly Bukharinists) were removed from positions of power, which strengthened Stalin's position.

At first, Trotsky's supporters were pleased to see some of their policies being adopted and expected that they would be readmitted into the party. Some even thought that they might have been wrong about Stalin and that they should join forces with him against Bukharin and the right in this left course against the forces of re-emerging capitalism. Trotsky himself believed that Stalin and the centre should be encouraged to break with the right. Since early 1927, in fact, Trotsky had seen Bukharin's faction (which included Rykov and Tomsky) as more of a danger to the gains of the November Revolution than Stalin's, as it was bigger and more right-wing.

Stalin, however, was determined to do without Trotsky or Zinoviev, although he did try to win over their respective supporters. By May 1928, it was clear that Stalin was planning a 'second revolution' and Trotsky's supporters began to split into 'conciliators' and 'irreconcilables'. In particular, Preobrazhensky, Radek and Piatakov called for an offer of critical support to be made to Stalin; Trotsky, however, argued that the first move must be made by Stalin, when he really needed their help. In June, Zinoviev and Kamenev (and about 3,000 other Oppositionists) were reinstated in the party.

As the food crisis became worse during July, it seemed that Bukharin's faction was gaining the upper hand when he surprisingly won a Central Committee vote to slow Stalin's left turn. The emergency measures were stopped and a 20 per cent increase in the price of bread was announced. By August Stalin (having secured a majority in the Politburo) had renewed his leftward course and the breach with Bukharin was confirmed. Both factions then turned to the defeated Left Oppositionists for support.

Bukharin used Kamenev as a go-between for an approach to Trotsky, saying he feared Stalin was the 'new Genghis Khan' and that he 'will strangle us'. Bukharin now argued that the main issue was not economic policy but freedom of the party and the state, claiming that Stalin was preparing to create a police state and take total power. For his part, Stalin refused any direct contact with the Left Oppositionists, though he dropped many hints of a possible alliance.

By September 1928, Trotsky had become alarmed at Stalin's increasing use of violence against the peasants and was attracted by the idea of an alliance with Bukharin to restore full inner-party and Soviet democracy. However, the two leaders' respective supporters were extremely reluctant to co-operate with their former enemies. The left objected to an alliance with the right just when Stalin seemed about to implement some of their own economic policies. As a result, Stalin was able to defeat the right without the formal support of the left. Bukharin and the right, now in panic, surrendered, while the left remained divided. There was no need for Stalin to recall the exiled Left Oppositionists as he had managed to defeat both factions by relying solely on his own supporters.

In February 1929 Stalin decided that Trotsky needed to be expelled entirely from the Soviet Union, partly because he feared a left–right alliance in the future and partly as he suspected that some of his own faction still had some sympathy with the Opposition. During the same period, Stalin moved against the right. Bukharin, Rykov and Tomsky were charged with factionalism. In April 1929, Bukharin was removed as editor of *Pravda* and political secretary of Comintern, while Tomsky was dismissed from the Central Council of Trade Unions. The right were warned that further violations of party discipline would result in their expulsion from the Politburo. In November 1929 Bukharin was removed from the Politburo for leading the 'right deviation'. Stalin now appeared to have almost complete control of the Communist Party, though Tomsky still had a seat on the Politburo and Rykov continued as a member of the Central Committee.

Why did Stalin emerge as leader?

Historians are not agreed on the reasons for Stalin's emergence and rise to power, as no one factor seems to offer a satisfactory explanation. In fact, the main historical approaches often overlap in several respects.

Power politics

The proponents of the view that all Stalin wanted was power argue that Stalin's rise was a deliberate manipulation of genuine political and ideological differences among the Bolshevik leaders either, according to R. Conquest, to gain supreme power for himself by crushing all other factions or, according to R. Tucker, to make himself into a revolutionary hero as important and famous as Lenin. His success is seen as depending not only on his political shrewdness and ruthlessness, but also on the weaknesses and mistakes of his rivals. E. H. Carr portrays Zinoviev and Kamenev as, respectively, careerist and weak-willed, while S. Cohen argues that Bukharin's commitment to the NEP blinded him to the dangers posed by Stalin until it was too late. Perhaps more importantly, Lenin did not realise the threat from Stalin until 1922, just two years before his death, and in that time he was too ill to be politically active.

Trotsky made several serious errors and miscalculations, perhaps because he dismissed Stalin as a 'grey blur' and a 'mediocrity'. One of his most serious mistakes was handing over Lenin's notes to the Politburo almost at the very beginning of the struggle. This meant that he was left with no documentary proof of Lenin's growing opposition to Stalin's actions. Trotsky also either refused, or did not have the skill, to organise a faction of his own; I. Deutscher has argued that this is because, without Lenin, Trotsky was virtually isolated at the top of the party from the beginning.

Structuralist explanations

While historians have several different structuralist explanations, which are based on history and society's structure, they have one theme in common: that Stalin was a product of Russian history and the administrative system set up (often in a haphazard way) after 1917. Some historians see Stalin as a ruler in the long Tsarist tradition of absolutist rule of dictatorial and often brutal methods. Lenin and other Bolshevik rulers had, on several occasions, worried about the re-emergence of Asiatic absolutism (a reference to the brutal dictatorships of Genghis Khan and Ivan the Terrible) and Russian chauvinism.

Others point to the impact of emergencies such as the civil war which led to the development of appointment rather than election for party and state positions. As the party grew in size, the secretariat and Orgburo became increasingly important for the administration of Politburo decisions. As the administrative apparatus grew, so did Stalin's power to appoint, at both national and local level. As a result, bureaucracy increased, which enabled Stalin to control party congresses, the Central Committee and the Politburo itself. R. Daniels calls this a 'circular flow of power', by which Stalin appointed local party leaders who, in turn, controlled elections to party organisations.

Connected to this was the fact that the impact of revolution and civil war led to the displacement or death of the militant industrial workers who had been the Bolsheviks' main supporters before 1917. Survivors of the civil war were given administrative posts in the government, army or party. Their replacements in the factories were from peasant traditions which had tended to support the Social Revolutionaries rather than the Bolsheviks. As a result, the elected soviets were seen as less reliable and were increasingly ignored. As the administrative bureaucracy increased, communist leaders were forced to recruit former Tsarist bureaucrats, who had administrative experience but lacked initiative, and had contempt for the people and a supine attitude to authority. This, too, caused the leaders to stress strict central control. The Stalinist bureaucratic state was the logical outcome of these factors.

Sociocultural explanations

These are closely linked to structural explanations and emphasise the impact of Russia's social structure on the politics and development of the Communist Party and the Soviet Union. According to S. Fitzpatrick, for example, during the civil war the Communists attracted Russian patriots who resented the alliance between the Whites and the foreign states. Then, when it looked as if the Reds were winning, a large number of careerists (often former Tsarist bureaucrats) flocked to join the winning side in order to secure jobs. This became worse after 1921, when all opposition parties were banned. In addition, the loss of the politically mature vanguard of the working class in the war (see above) left a vacuum in Communist support that was often filled by other workers (often ex-peasants) who had no real understanding of Marxism or even recent Bolshevik history. All these groups were more easily manipulated by the party leadership, who distrusted them anyway, especially in view of the political risks involved with the NEP.

Ideological explanations

Several historians stress the genuine nature of the political differences between the Communist leaders of the 1920s, especially over the NEP. The left were sticking to orthodox Marxism by stressing the dangers inherent in the NEP. They believed that it would stimulate capitalist tendencies and that this might lead to the restoration of capitalism, unless the state sector was strengthened at the same time. They were particularly concerned, given the sociocultural developments referred to above, as many of the new groups tended to favour capitalist rather than socialist policies.

The right argued that, because the Soviet Union was overwhelmingly agricultural and backward, and industry was in crisis, the NEP and the *smychka* were essential if the economy was to revive. However, the right tended to overlook the conflicts that could arise between the Nepmen and the *kulaks* on the one hand and the workers' state on the other. They also envisaged a long period of a mixed economy.

Stalin's rise can thus be seen as a genuine political response by the centre to steer a middle policy course. At the beginning, the centre believed the NEP was essential for recovery and so opposed the left, who seemed to endanger it. Later, once the peasants began to defend their interests against the workers' state, they came to see that a change was needed and for this reason they began to attack the policies of the right.

It can be said that Stalin's policies were consistent and also in tune with the majority of the party membership, who desired stability most of all. To them, Stalin's policy of continuing the NEP and socialism in one country seemed a safer bet than Trotsky's idea of permanent revolution and it appealed to their national pride. Stalin's dramatic change of course in 1927–28 can be seen as a response to a real rural crisis (albeit one predicted by the left). His switch to rapid collectivisation and industrialisation seemed entirely logical and correct. This was one reason why so many ex-Oppositionists moved to support him in 1928.

An explanation that combines elements of the sociocultural explanation was developed by Trotsky himself. Pointing to the failure of international revolution and the consequent isolation of the new Soviet state, he argued that Russian backwardness and the growing political apathy of the working class were undermining the early Soviet democracy. This allowed conservative and reactionary elements to come to the fore and resulted in what he called 'bureaucratic degeneration'. Trotsky argued that the new social and political elite, with increasing privileges, at first supported the right but that, once the problems of the NEP exploded in 1927–28, shifted their allegiance to Stalin and the centre as this was their best bet for maintaining their positions. Thus Stalin's victory can be seen as the result of unforeseen historical and cultural developments after 1917, rather than the result of his opponents' mistakes.

Document case study
The struggle for power

2.1 Lenin's Testament and Postscript

Since he became General Secretary, Comrade Stalin has concentrated in his hands immeasurable power, and I am not sure that he will always know how to use that power with sufficient caution. On the other hand Comrade Trotsky . . . is distinguished not only by his outstanding qualities (personally he is the most capable man in the present Central Committee) but also by his excess of self-confidence and a readiness to be carried away by the purely administrative side of affairs.

The qualities of these two outstanding leaders of the present Central Committee might lead quite accidentally to a split . . . I shall not try to describe any other members of the Central Committee according to their personal qualities. I will simply remind you that the October episode involving Zinoviev and Kamenev was not, of course, accidental but that it ought not to be used seriously against them, any more than the non-Bolshevism of Trotsky . . .

Testament, 25 December 1922

Stalin is too rude, and this fault, entirely supportable in relations among us communists, becomes insupportable in the office of General Secretary. Therefore, I propose to comrades to find a way of removing Stalin from that position and to appoint another man who in all respects differs from Stalin only in superiority; namely, more patient, more loyal, more polite, less capricious, and more attentive to comrades.

Postscript, 4 January 1923

Source: M. Lynch, *Stalin and Khrushchev. The USSR 1924–64*, London, 1990, pp. 15–16

2.2 Trotsky on Stalin and the Testament

In conclusion, we shall merely recall once again Lenin's 'Testament' . . . In the 'Testament,' Lenin, calmly weighing every word, offered his last counsel to the party, evaluating each one of his collaborators on the basis of his entire experience with them. What has he to say of Stalin? That Stalin is (a) rude, (b) disloyal, (c) inclined to abuse power. Conclusion: remove Stalin from the post of General Secretary.

A few weeks later Lenin also dictated a note to Stalin in which he announced that he was 'breaking off all personal and comradely relations with him.' This was one of the final expressions of Lenin's will. All these facts are recorded in the protocols of the July 1927 Plenum of the Central Committee.

Source: L. Trotsky, *The Stalin school of falsification*, New York, 1972, p. 198

2.3 The campaign against Trotsky, according to one of his supporters in 1937

Beginning in 1923, the Opposition found a leader in Trotsky; the bureaucratic system began to find its incarnation in Stalin . . . an agitational campaign unlimited in its violence was launched against Trotsky; he was everywhere denounced as anti-Leninist, the evil spirit of the party, the enemy of the Bolshevik tradition, the enemy of the peasants. His old disagreements with Lenin, dating from 1904 to 1915, were exploited by professional polemicists under Stalin's orders; under the name of Trotskyism they forged an entire, distorted ideology which was made into the most criminal heresy . . .

The official press, circulated in the millions, smothered his voice, and tirelessly hammered away at its campaign of falsification. We subsequently learned the inside story of these campaigns; we learned that neither error nor passion was behind this deliberate falsification of facts and ideas. We have a number of signed statements, regarding the 'fabrication' of Trotskyism . . . (though it is true that several of their authors were recently shot).

Source: Victor Serge, *From Lenin to Stalin*, New York, 1973, pp. 41–42

2.4 Condemnation of Trotsky's views by the Thirteenth Conference of the Russian Communist Party, January 1924

The opposition, headed by Trotsky, came forth with the slogan of smashing the Party apparatus, and tried to shift the centre of gravity of the struggle against bureaucratism in the governmental apparatus to 'bureaucratism' in the apparatus of the Party . . .

Trotsky came out with vague insinuations about the degeneration of the basic cadres of our Party and thereby tried to undermine the authority of the Central Committee, which between congresses is the only representative of the whole Party . . .

The opposition clearly violated the decision of the Tenth Congress of the Russian Communist Party which prohibited the formation of factions within the Party . . . The All-Union Party Conference comes to the Conclusion that in the person of the present opposition we have before us not only an attempt at the revision of Bolshevism, not only a departure from Leninism, but also a clearly expressed petty-bourgeois deviation . . .

Source: Extract from the conference resolution 'On the results of the controversy and on the petty-bourgeois deviation in the party', in J. Laver, *Russia, 1914–41*, London, 1991, pp. 51–52

2.5 Stalin on the defeat of the United Opposition

How could it happen that the entire Party, as a whole, and following it the working class too, so thoroughly isolated the opposition? After all, the opposition are headed by well-known people with well-known names . . . It happened because the leading groups of the opposition proved to be a group of petty-bourgeois intellectuals divorced from life, divorced from the revolution, divorced from the Party, from the working class . . .

If the opposition want to be in the Party, let them submit to the will of the Party, to its laws, to its instructions, without reservations, without equivocation. If they refuse to do that, let them go wherever they please.

Source: Stalin speaking at the Fifteenth Party Congress on 3 December 1927, in J. Laver, *Joseph Stalin. From revolutionary to despot*, London, 1993, pp. 30–31

2.6 The defeat of the right

The destruction of the United Opposition was compounded by mass desertions of its supporters. After repudiating their 'errors' Kamenev and Zinoviev were readmitted to the party in June 1928 – two of the 3,000 or so Bolsheviks who recanted in the six months following the fifteenth party congress . . .

Castigated for 'rightist errors' [for opposing Stalin's policies on collectivisation] Bukharin arranged a clandestine meeting with Kamenev, beseeching him not to help the General Secretary 'cut our throats' and complaining that Stalin 'manoeuvres so that we appear as splitters' while 'changing his theories depending on whom he wants to get rid of at the moment . . .'

Bukharin's meeting with Kamenev, taken together with a speech delivered on the fifth anniversary of Lenin's death ('Lenin's political testament' – its very title a scarcely veiled attack on the General Secretary), presaged his overthrow . . . On 17 November 1929, 10 days after Stalin's 'The year of the Great Breakthrough' extolled the 'socialist offensive' in town and countryside, Bukharin was ousted from the Politburo for leading the 'right deviation'.

Source: C. Ward, *Stalin's Russia*, London, 1999, pp. 16–18

Document case-study questions

1 From what you have read in this book and elsewhere, explain *briefly* the references in document 2.1 to 'General Secretary' and the 'October episode involving Zinoviev and Kamenev'.

2 What are the strengths and weaknesses of documents 2.2 and 2.3 as historical evidence about Lenin's Testament and the campaign against Trotsky?

3 Comment briefly on the importance of the decision of the Tenth Party Congress referred to in document 2.4 in Stalin's rise to power.

4 How do the explanations in documents 2.5 and 2.6 differ on the reasons for the defeat of the United Oppositions and the right?

5 To what extent do these six documents, and any other evidence known to you, explain Stalin's victory over his political rivals?

Stalin's 'revolution from above', 1928–41

Stalin's 'turn to the left' and the abandonment of the NEP

In the course of securing the defeat of Trotsky, Zinoviev and Kamenev, Stalin presented himself, together with Bukharin and the right, as loyal supporters of Lenin and his New Economic Policy of 1921. Yet in 1928, Stalin completely reversed the NEP and, at least as far as scale and speed were concerned, went way beyond the policies advocated by the left. The NEP, with its combination of state and private enterprise, had always been a matter of concern for those in the party who feared the long-term consequences of tolerating and even encouraging capitalist forces in a society as politically and culturally limited as that of the USSR in the 1920s. Many felt uneasy about being surrounded by hostile capitalist states which, in any future economic crisis, might try again to invade the workers' state; only an industrially strong USSR would have the military capacity to defeat such a threat.

Problems with the NEP, 1926–27

In August 1924 Preobrazhensky published *The fundamental law of socialist accumulation*, in which he argued that the state should obtain food cheaply from the peasants and then sell it at a higher price to consumers. This method of 'primitive socialist accumulation' would create the surplus funds necessary to finance industrialisation. Trotsky had come to similar conclusions by 1923. This marked the start of a serious debate about industrialisation within the party and was an underlying factor throughout the power struggle of the next five years. Initially, Stalin and the right rejected these calls which threatened the NEP and the *smychka* to the extent that in 1925 Bukharin actually encouraged peasants to 'enrich' themselves.

Industry

In the mid-1920s, when Trotsky and the Left Opposition were already arguing for a shift towards industrialisation, Stalin and his supporters defended the maintenance of the NEP as a Leninist policy. Bukharin was also dismissive of Preobrazhensky's ideas, although in 1924 he did oppose the call by Lev Shanin of the State Bank for free market forces to be allowed to operate with no controls. By April 1925, however, he had moved further to the right and closer to Shanin. He dismissed the left's arguments that the NEP was generating class forces (in the developing capitalist class of *kulaks* and Nepmen) and that they were threatening the socialist nature of the Soviet state. He warned against the dangers of creating 'a state of war with the peasantry'.

There is evidence, however, that as early as November 1925 Stalin was contemplating a new revolutionary shift in order to make possible a transition from the NEP to a socialist economy. At this stage, with Zinoviev and Kamenev having formed the United Opposition with Trotsky, he continued to work with Bukharin. At the Fourteenth Party Congress in December 1925 (later called the 'industrialisation congress'), Zinoviev's and Kamenev's criticisms of the NEP were rejected, but the principle of economic modernisation was supported. At the Fifteenth Party Conference in the autumn of 1926 Stalin called for the Soviet Union to catch up with and overtake the West as regards industrialisation, but he still insisted that this had to be achieved by maintaining the worker–peasant alliance.

Meanwhile, Gosplan was busily involved in economic planning and produced its first economic plan in August 1925. Its second plan, in 1926, included an outline five-year plan, with specific plans for each year. At the same time, Vesenkha was also drafting schemes for the development of the Soviet economy. There were, however, divisions in these organisations between non-party specialists who were more conservative about short-term possibilities and the party specialists who believed that rapid industrialisation was possible and that the NEP was hindering this. As existing industry had mostly been restored to pre-1914 levels of production, they began to look forward to a period of 'socialist construction'.

By 1927 the fear of an imminent war – Britain broke off diplomatic relations in 1927, relations with France and Poland were poor and Japan seemed threatening – led many to believe that rapid industrialisation was now necessary to enable the Soviet Union to meet any invasion. Furthermore, by now the United Opposition had been defeated, so Stalin felt able to adopt (albeit in a crude and distorted form) some of the economic policies advocated by Trotsky and Preobrazhensky. To prepare the way for this, a 'Hero of Labour' medal was introduced in the summer of 1927 to encourage increased productivity and labour discipline, while cuts in administrative costs were ordered so that more funds would be available for industrial expansion.

At the Fifteenth Party Congress in December 1927, there was still talk of maintaining the basic elements of the NEP, though Stalin did stress the foreign threats and the need to develop heavy industry. Despite approval of several railway, canal and hydroelectric developments, no general agreements were reached on growth targets. In fact, Vesenkha and Gosplan actually produced rival plans.

The agricultural grain crisis in 1927–28 persuaded Stalin that the NEP should be abandoned in favour of rapid industrialisation. This led to a serious split between Stalin and Bukharin at a Central Committee meeting in July 1928. As the conflict with the right developed during 1928, Stalin and his supporters accused their opponents of lacking faith in the Soviet people and of betraying the socialist ideals of Lenin and the Bolsheviks. By the end of 1928, with the right virtually defeated, Stalin pushed for higher production targets from Vesenkha and Gosplan, and non-party specialists were purged. By April 1929, two draft five-

Stalin's 'revolution from above', 1928–41

Steel (million tonnes)

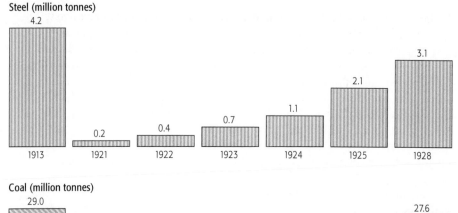

Coal (million tonnes)

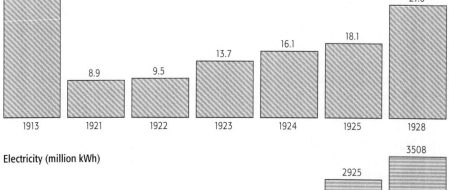

Electricity (million kWh)

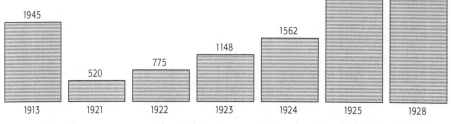

Details of production in some industrial categories in the period 1913–28, showing the achievements of the New Economic Policy. (Adapted from R.W. Davies, 'The New Economic Policy', *New Perspectives*, 3, 3, March 1998.)

year plans – the 'basic variant' and the 'optimum variant' – developed by Vesenkha and Gosplan together were presented to the Sixteenth Party Conference. Under Stalin's leadership the Politburo recommended the 'optimum' plan, which forecast the doubling of Soviet industry by 1932; this was a much bigger increase than the left had called for or even believed possible.

Agriculture

From 1924 to 1926, the NEP had led to a gradual increase in agricultural production. In 1926, despite a good harvest, state collections were only 50 per cent of what had been expected. This was mainly because, as peasants prospered, they consumed more of their produce and had little incentive to sell their surplus as there were insufficient consumer goods to buy. As a consequence, only about 13 per cent of the grain harvest found its way into the towns. Fearing another 'scissors crisis' like that of 1923 (see p. 34), emergency measures were taken against *kulak* 'speculators' and Nepmen in some areas, including seizing grain and increasing taxes on *kulaks* to force them to sell more grain. At the same time there was still unemployment, even though heavy industrial production figures had virtually returned to pre-war levels. This led many in the party to think the state sector needed to be developed.

Although the government reduced prices of grain in 1927, deliveries declined still further. This was due, in part, to poor weather, but many Communists believed it was because the *kulaks* were deliberately withholding grain; in fact, because of a war scare over a possible Polish attack, hoarding did take place. State purchases of grain in 1927 were considerably less than what was required. This not only threatened hunger in the expanding towns, but also undermined the possibility of stepping up industrialisation.

Thus, by the time of the Fifteenth Party Congress in December 1927 (later known as the 'collectivisation congress'), many Communists were beginning to believe that the NEP was blocking both agricultural and industrial development. Stalin argued that the problems could be overcome by strengthening co-operative farms, increasing mechanisation and supporting the voluntary collectivisation of farms (*kolkhozes*). Land, buildings and equipment would become the property of the *kolkhoz* and would result in bigger farms and higher yields. At this stage, there was no mention of forced collectivisation or of destroying the *kulaks* as a class.

In 1928, the problem of insufficient grain purchases continued. Stalin instructed local officials in Siberia to increase state grain procurements. Their response was to seize more grain and to close markets and arrest those who resisted, charging them as *kulaks* under Article 107 of the criminal code (passed in 1927 to deal with speculation). After the 1928 harvest, these actions (which became known as the Ural-Siberian method) began to result in serious unrest in rural areas and subsequent bread shortages, as grain was hidden to avoid requisitioning or to await higher prices.

At a Central Committee meeting in July 1928, Bukharin was able to get through an increase in the price of grain and an end to the forcible measures by arguing that the *smychka* must be maintained. Stalin was determined that industrial development would not be disrupted by any diversion of money to the *kulaks* and after the meeting he ordered that emergency actions should continue. This provoked Bukharin into publishing in September a defence of the NEP, which was also an implicit criticism of Stalin's actions.

The crisis in agriculture continued. By the end of 1928, the combination of a fall in grain sales to the state and a crop failure in the central and south-eastern regions of the USSR led to dramatic increases in free-market prices, a further slump in grain deliveries to the state and the introduction of rationing during the winter of 1928–29. During 1929, the forcible Ural-Siberian method of grain collection was carried out in most of the Soviet Union and the NEP and the *smychka* were destroyed in all but name.

Collectivisation and the five-year plans

Communists, including Marx, always argued that industrialisation and urbanisation were dependent on the modernisation of agriculture so that food production could be increased, at the same time releasing large numbers of peasants and landless agricultural workers for work in the factories. For this reason, Stalin and his supporters felt that it was essential to carry through a two-pronged economic programme. It is clear that Stalin believed that fundamentally changing the economic policy was a way of continuing Lenin's revolutionary work and that successfully concluding a 'second revolution' would establish his position as one of the great revolutionary Marxist leaders. It can be seen that there was a large degree of class warfare in Stalin's determination to end private ownership, especially as regards collectivisation.

Collectivisation of agriculture

By the end of 1929, with the fear of war and an extremely ambitious five-year plan in place, Stalin was determined that the crisis in agriculture would be resolved before the spring sowing for the 1930 harvest. As a first emergency measure, a massive grain procurement campaign was launched, with extremely high quotas. Officials, who were determined to avoid punishment for failure, as had happened in 1928, used their power to arrest, deport and confiscate the property of any peasant who failed to hand over their quota. In all, some 16 million tonnes of grain were collected – in some areas, over 30 per cent of the entire crop was taken.

Campaign against the *kulaks*

The grain procurement campaign of 1929–30 was a short-term emergency measure, similar in principle, if not in degree, to earlier ones in 1927 and 1928. To bring about lasting changes that would safeguard industrialisation plans, Stalin (having defeated the right at the Sixteenth Party Congress in April) launched a programme of collectivisation in November and December 1929, calling for the *kulaks* to be 'liquidated as a class'. Action was taken first against *kulaks* who resisted the grain collections. *Kulaks* were defined by Stalin as those peasants who had two horses and four cows; 'identification' of who was a *kulak* often went beyond this.

Mass collectivisation, 1930

Action against *kulaks* was stepped up after January 1930 when brigades of urban workers and Komsomol members, with the support of police and soldiers, went into the countryside to organise the setting up of collectives. Initially, persuasion was the main method used, but as Stalin pressed for rapid results violence was frequently used. This was especially true after a decree in February gave local committees power to apply 'necessary measures' against the *kulaks*. It also divided them into three categories. Two groups – 'counter-revolutionaries' and 'exploiters' – were to be harshly punished with execution or deportation respectively.

Richer peasants often destroyed their crops and livestock rather than hand them over to the local *kolkhoz*, or raided the *kolkhozes* to reclaim their property. Local parties were given targets of the number of households to be collectivised. Officials, who were either ambitious for promotion or fearful of being denounced as Rightists, increasingly resorted to force. Official figures set about 4 per cent of households as those of *kulaks*, but some 15 per cent of households were collectivised. Many peasants were imprisoned or executed for their resistance, and around 150,000 were forcibly moved to poorer land in the north and east.

By March 1930, it was reported that 58 per cent of peasant households had been collectivised. The process provoked serious resistance, including arson, riots and armed rebellions which often resulted in the killing of Communist officials. The situation was especially serious in the Ukraine, North Caucasus and Kazakhstan. This chaos and violence worried the Politburo; apart from the political dangers of rebellion, the spring sowing was being jeopardised. In March 1930, Stalin was pressurised by other Communist leaders into calling a halt. Official policy returned to voluntary collectivisation and many peasants who had been wrongly classified as *kulaks* had their property restored. By October 1930, only about 20 per cent of households were still collectivised (the figure in October 1929 had been 40 per cent).

Collectivisation, 1930–37

This retreat was only temporary. Once the 1930 harvest had been secured, collectivisation resumed in earnest. By 1931, 50 per cent of households were in collective farms; by 1934 the figure was 70 per cent, by 1935 75 per cent and by 1937 90 per cent. Each collective (usually around 70 households) was headed by a farm manager who took control of the harvest and ensured all taxes (in kind or money) were duly paid to the government. Machine Tractor Stations (MTS) were established to supply seed and to hire out machinery to local *kolkhozes*, for which payment was made in grain. Between 1929 and 1932, over 2,500 MTSs were built.

These statistics hid the great upheaval and confusion of collectivisation, which resulted in a dreadful famine in the years 1932–33. The first sign of problems came in October 1931, when it was revealed that many agricultural areas had been affected by drought. Famine first appeared in the Ukraine in the spring of 1932. With occasional slight improvements, it spread to several more areas, especially in parts of the North Caucasus. In the end, it became the worst famine in Russia's history. Though the worst was over by 1933, some areas were still affected by serious food shortages in 1934. Despite increasing warning signs of this rural catastrophe, Stalin persisted with forced collectivisation and high state grain procurements. In all, it is clear that millions died, although historians are still not agreed on the total numbers. This is partly because the Great Purge and the Great Terror of the second half of the 1930s have confused matters (pp. 86–90).

Agriculture did revive after 1933, although grain production increased slowly. It finally surpassed the pre-collectivisation figure of 75 million tonnes in 1935; it dropped to 56 million tonnes in 1936, then increased again in 1937 to 97 million tonnes. Livestock numbers increased even more slowly and did not exceed pre-collectivisation levels until 1953. However, the drive to collectivise continued and state procurement quotas were constantly raised. As a result, life on the collectives remained very hard for most of the 1930s.

The political result of collectivisation was that, for the first time since 1917, the party was able to establish a firm control over the countryside. The 25 million individual private farms had been replaced by about 250,000 collective farms, each of which was run by a chairman who was a Communist appointed by the state. Under Gorbachev and his policy of *glasnost*, many criticisms were made of Stalin's methods and the immediate results of collectivisation, with some historians describing his methods as a 'distortion of socialism'. However, some of the same historians also pointed out that collective farming contributed to the survival of the USSR during the Second World War.

Industrialisation

As industrialisation was the key to the creation of a communist society, the early economic emphasis was on increasing the Soviet Union's industrial base and productive capacity, not only for political and social reasons but also to build up military defences. This factor became increasingly important in the years following Hitler's assumption of power in 1933.

The First Five-Year Plan, 1928–32

The First Five-Year Plan began on 1 October 1928. It concentrated on heavy industry – coal, iron, steel, oil and machine-production – and overall production was planned to increase by 300 per cent. Light industry, too, was to double its output and, in order to ensure that sufficient energy was available, electricity production was to increase by 600 per cent. Many workers were enthused by the vision of creating a planned socialist economy and worked hard to fulfil each year's targets. Soon reports – mostly unreliable – began to arrive in Moscow of how targets were being exceeded. In 1929 talk began of fulfilling the plan in four years, not five. Stalin officially backed this in June 1930 and posters appeared proclaiming '2 + 2 = 5'. Stalin urged Communist and Komsomol members to form 'shock work' and socialist emulation brigades. These groups made special efforts to achieve high production targets, to encourage other workers and set the right example.

There were significant achievements which fundamentally transformed the Soviet economy. Hundreds of new factories and mines were set up in many regions, some of which had no industrial developments before 1928. New industrial complexes, such as Magnitogorsk, were built, as were new rail links and hydroelectric schemes. However, Stalin's announcement that the First Five-

Year Plan had been fulfilled was an exaggeration. Despite tremendous growth, no major targets had actually been met. Part of the reason for Stalin's push for rapid industrialisation was the uncertainty of the international situation. In 1931, he pointed out the USSR's relative economic backwardness (it was 50 or 100 years behind Western countries) and said that it had to make this up in 10 years: 'Either we do it, or they crush us.'

The crisis year, 1932–33
Ironically, the very success and too-rapid implementation of the first plan created problems in the period 1932–33 which delayed the drafting and implementation of the second plan. Implementation costs had been much greater than had been allowed for by Gosplan and the large increases in coal, iron and industrial goods proved too much for the railway system to cope with. At the same time, the rapidly expanding urban populations soon led to housing shortages, while the effects of forced collectivisation led to food shortages and rationing. This situation caused many workers to change jobs frequently, and managers, desperate to retain skilled workers so they could complete their plan targets, had to increase wages and offer additional, unofficial, perks. Moves away from egalitarianism and towards increasing wage differentials, piece-rates and bonuses exacerbated the problem as workers exploited the situation by playing managers off one against another for higher wages and better perks.

The Second Five-Year Plan, 1933–37
Nonetheless, Gosplan drew up the Second Five-Year Plan. Its intention was to create a fully socialist economy, with the disappearance of money, between 1933 and 1937. However, nothing was finally approved until the Seventeenth Party Congress in January 1934. The delay was the result of the economic crisis, which forced Gosplan to continually modify cost calculations and targets. The final draft simply called for increased production and improved living standards and recognised the need to build on the achievements of the first plan.

Between 1934 and 1936, there were many successes – in particular, machine-production and iron and steel output grew rapidly, making the Soviet Union practically self-sufficient in these areas. Many of the new industrial plants began producing, while the number of new enterprises opened was nearly 5,000 (compared to almost 2,000 under the first plan).

The Stakhanovite Movement
Part of the reason for the success of the Second Five-Year Plan was the big increase in labour productivity. The Stakhanovite Movement was set up to encourage workers to follow the example of Stakhanov, a miner in the Donbas mining region, who dug out a massive 102 tonnes of coal in one shift (the normal figure was 7 tonnes) in August 1935. Most industries had their own model workers, who received higher bonuses and other material advantages (such as new flats) as well as medals for being 'Heroes of Socialist Labour'. However, as R. T. Manning and R. Thurston have pointed out, Stakhanovism contributed to anti-managerial resentment among the rank-and-file workers. This, in turn, has been

seen by some historians as an important aspect in the Great Purge which took place during the late 1930s.

By this time, the worst effects of forced collectivisation were over, allowing rationing to be abandoned in 1935.

The Third Five-Year Plan, 1938–42

Once again, despite significant achievements and successes under the second plan, the industrialisation programme was hit by problems in 1937. The severe winter of 1937–38 caused serious fuel shortages which, in turn, hit factory production and the transportation of goods and raw materials by rail. Industrial planning was also affected by the growing impact of the purges, which saw thousands of managers and experts either imprisoned or executed (see pp. 86–90), and by the worsening international situation, which meant that funds were increasingly diverted to defence (see pp. 73–75).

Planning began in February 1936, but the purging of Gosplan specialists created confusion and delays and the Third Five-Year Plan was not formally approved until the Eighteenth Party Congress in March 1939. By then, earlier proposals to develop light industry and to increase the production of consumer goods were already being undermined by a new emphasis on heavy industry and defence. Nonetheless, huge increases in production were planned (92 per cent) and Molotov claimed that, because the first two plans had laid the foundation for a socialist economy, this third plan would complete the process and enable the USSR to begin the transition to communism. The already distorted Third Five-Year Plan was totally disrupted in June 1941, however, when Nazi Germany launched its invasion.

How successful were Stalin's economic policies?

Did Stalin plan his 'revolution from above'?

Many historians have suggested that Stalin did not have a master plan for the measures he implemented in 1928. They point to the fact that changes came about in both agriculture and industry because of unforeseen problems arising from the NEP. It can also be argued that Stalin's constant interference – especially by increasing the targets – prevented the plans from being coherently and successfully implemented.

In particular, Stalin's initial response to the grain crisis can be seen as an emergency short-term measure which triggered off a sequence of developments that led to more and more radical decisions being taken. M. Lewin, for example, argues that Stalin did not really know where his policies might take the Soviet Union.

Others, such as R. Tucker, argue that Stalin clearly intended to modernise the Soviet Union, and adopted deliberate agricultural and industrial policies to do so, once he considered that political factors enabled him to begin. Others go on to argue that Stalin was deliberately attempting to complete the Bolshevik Revolution of 1917. Once he felt politically secure, he consciously launched his own second 'revolution from above'.

How reliable are the statistics?

Official statistics, produced during and after Stalin's rule, about the increases in productivity achieved by the five-year plans, are highly suspect: for the period 1928–40, the official figure for increased industrial production is 852 per cent. Similar doubts apply to figures for specific industries. However, by applying stricter criteria, most historians, such as A. Nove, accept that there were tremendous increases in production, especially in heavy industry. According to most Western estimates, the actual increase in the output of civilian industries between 1928 and 1940 was 260 per cent.

One problem with these official statistics is that many factory managers, fearful of being punished for non-fulfilment of targets, either deliberately underestimated production capacity or claimed production figures higher than those actually achieved. An associated problem was the lack of skill of many of the industrial workers in state enterprises – numbers rose from 1.4 million in 1928 to 6.4 million in 1932, 7.9 million in 1937 and 8.3 million in 1940. Many were ex-peasants: 9 million alone joined the ranks of industrial workers under the First Five-Year Plan. They had little basic training and no experience of factory discipline; most were under 29, and fewer than 20 per cent had five years' experience of factory work. Such workers, used to seasonal working, found factory discipline hard to accept.

Production was not helped by 'storming', which involved workers and machines working for 24 hours or more at a time, in order to meet or surpass targets. Machines frequently broke down, disrupting production. The pace demanded by Moscow was too fast to sustain and by the late 1930s many projects were incomplete and the resources to finish them were often not available.

	Production in 1928	First Five-Year Plan		Second Five-Year Plan	
		Real	Planned	Real	Planned
Electricity (million Kwhs)	5.0	13.4	17.0	36.2	38.0
Coal (million tonnes)	35.4	64.3	75.0	128.0	152.5
Oil (million tonnes)	11.7	21.4	22.0	28.5	46.8
Pig iron (million tonnes)	3.3	6.2	8.0	14.5	16.0
Steel (million tonnes)	4.0	5.9	10.4	17.7	17.0

Source: Allan Todd, *The modern world*, Oxford, 2001.

Production figures for the first two five-year plans. What are the problems with statistics such as these?

The impact on workers

In order to meet the high targets, new work practices were introduced. In 1929, the 'uninterrupted' week was introduced, with shift work organised so that factories were not idle at the weekend. Absenteeism and late arrival for work were punished, either by the loss of the job and factory housing or, after 1931 when such offences were criminalised, by imprisonment or sentence to a labour camp. This strict discipline led many to change jobs frequently, especially once the five-year plans had ended unemployment and created extra employment.

Overall, most historians agree that the rushed pace of industrialisation – especially during the first plan – drastically reduced living standards, especially through food shortages, rising prices and continued housing shortages. Even recovery during the mid-1930s did not, according to J. Barber, restore living standards to pre-1928 levels. However, the plans did end the high unemployment of the 1920s, while the huge increase in the numbers of workers (including many women) enabled joint family incomes to increase. Those peasants who became industrial workers also experienced improvements in living standards, while many younger women who might have become domestic servants under the old system increasingly found employment in offices. Many workers also benefited from the opening-up and expansion of education from 1929, especially technical colleges and universities, designed to increase the skills and hence the productivity of the workforce.

The Gulag

As early as 1929, the OGPU were instructed to establish timber camps in the remoter regions in order to overcome immediate labour shortages so that targets could be met (initially to earn foreign currency via the export of timber). In 1930, OGPU set up the Chief Administration of Camps (Gulag) to run them. Previously, some historians estimated that the numbers in such forced labour camps grew from about 30,000 prisoners in 1928, to about 2 million in 1932 and to an estimated 8 million by 1938. These prisoners (*zeks*) comprised about 8 per cent of the total workforce. They were increasingly used to undertake huge construction projects, such as canals and railways. Many of them were deported ex-*kulaks* or workers who had committed labour discipline offences and many more came from those purged during the 1930s. From 1934, all prisons, camps and colonies were under Gulag control. Conditions were hard and food was often scarce, particularly so in the Kolyma camps, where prisoners worked the goldfields under extremely primitive conditions.

However, since *glasnost* and the subsequent collapse of the Soviet Union, historians such as R. W. Davies and S. Wheatcroft have used newly available evidence to estimate that by 1939 the total number of prisoners detained in such camps was just under 3 million. A similar debate surrounds the numbers who perished in the Gulag.

Collectivisation

The move to collectivisation was intended to solve a serious shortfall in the amount of grain needed to feed the urban population. However, the destructive resistance by *kulaks* and the disruption caused by deporting about 2.5 million people to the Gulag in the years 1930–31 led to a serious and sudden drop in food production by 1931. As we have seen, this led to famine in 1932–33, especially in the Ukraine and the North Caucasus.

Historians do not agree on the total number of people who died in the famine. Estimates vary from S. Wheatcroft's 3.5 million to R. Conquest's 7 million. However, these deaths are only some of the deaths that can be attributed to the process of collectivisation in general. Again, historians are divided, with total estimates (including the famine) ranging from S. Wheatcroft's 6 million to S. Rosefield's 20 million.

The economic results of collectivisation are also an area of controversy, although historians agree that, after 1928, grain deliveries to the state did increase, despite total agricultural production suffering a serious decline in the 1930s. One group of historians supports the orthodox standard model, which argues that despite the decline in agricultural output collectivisation did shift resources and funds from rural to urban areas and so allowed rapid industrial-isation to succeed. M. Ellman, for example, claims that collectivisation provided food, labour and funds (via foreign currency from increased grain exports) for the First Five-Year Plan, while others argue that if the NEP had continued industrial growth rates would have been much lower than those achieved by the five-year plans. However, historians such as J. Millar and H. Hunter offer a revisionist argument, claiming that collectivisation was an economic disaster which consequently made little contribution to the industrialisation programme.

Soviet foreign policy under Stalin

While the Soviet Union's internal policies were linked to Stalin's attempt to build socialism in one country, foreign policy was based on Soviet isolation. This resulted in a growing belief that the cause of international revolution was best served by the survival of the Soviet state. For this reason what was judged to be in the interests of the Soviet Union was imposed on the Comintern and its Communist members.

Isolation of the Soviet republic

The Bolshevik Revolution in November 1917 alarmed most European states and consequently Soviet Russia was increasingly boycotted. As we have seen there was considerable foreign involvement in the Russian Civil War (see pp. 22–27).

Soviet Russia had not been invited to help negotiate the peace treaties of 1919–20 and was not allowed to join the League of Nations. After most foreign troops were withdrawn from Soviet Russia in 1920 (the last Japanese troops did not leave until 1925), many European states placed restrictions on trade and economic relations with the new workers' state. It was hoped that this would bring down the Soviet government or at least encircle the Soviet Union with a *cordon sanitaire* made up of the successor states (these were the small independent states, such as Czechoslovakia, formed after the collapse of the Austro-Hungarian empire at the end of the First World War).

To begin with, the Communists were neither too bothered nor too surprised and hoped that the Comintern would help assist existing (in Germany, Hungary and Italy) and future revolutionary socialist outbreaks to succeed. These new workers' states would help economic recovery and growth in the Soviet Union. However, these revolutionary movements were repressed and, as we have seen, by the end of the early 1920s it was clear that the Soviet state would have to survive on its own.

Relations with Germany

With hopes of immediate revolution in Europe dashed, Lenin's government was desperate for foreign financial and technical assistance. Shunned by the USA, the west European democracies and the increasingly authoritarian regimes in central and eastern Europe, Soviet Russia turned to the other outcast in Europe: Germany. In 1922, they signed the Treaty of Rapallo with Germany: in return for allowing secret German military training and arms manufacture in the Soviet Union, Germany provided economic assistance and established trade links. The 1930 Treaty of Berlin continued and developed these arrangements.

Diplomatic tensions in the 1920s

By the end of 1924, as the economic and political situation improved, the intense hostility of the post-war years declined and the Soviet Union was able to establish diplomatic links with all major states except the USA, which remained extremely anti-communist. However, certain diplomatic develop-ments such as the 1925 Treaty of Locarno and the admission of Germany to the League of Nations in 1926 led Stalin to suspect that Britain and France were moving towards the creation of a new west European alliance against the Soviet Union.

The five-year neutrality pact that the Soviet Union signed with Germany in 1926 led the British Conservative government to break off diplomatic relations with the USSR in 1927 and to the deterioration of its relationship with France. These events led to a 'war scare' in the Soviet Union in 1927, based on fears that Britain was encouraging a Franco-Polish invasion of the USSR. Particularly worrying for Stalin was the fact that Soviet attempts to sign neutrality pacts with France – in 1927 and 1928 – were totally rejected.

The Great Depression

However, when the depression began to hit the USA in 1929 and the rest of the world by the early 1930s, even US firms were keen to do business with the USSR which, with its non-capitalist planned economy, was the only major country to remain unaffected. Nonetheless, Stalin remained deeply suspicious of all capitalist countries. This was partly due to his fear of imminent war, which led him to believe that the USSR needed to catch up quickly. This was one impetus for the five-year plans and the drive for rapid industrialisation.

By 1932, with Germany moving increasingly to the right under the impact of the depression, France began to be concerned and started to see that the Soviet Union's Red Army might be a powerful bloc in the east to rising German militarism. Consequently, in November 1932, a Franco-Soviet non-aggression pact was finally concluded. By then, the Soviet Union had signed similar pacts with Poland, Finland and the three Baltic republics, in an attempt to safeguard its western borders from any German expansionism.

The Nazi threat

When Hitler and the Nazis came to power in Germany in 1933, Soviet fears were rekindled. At first, Stalin and his supporters believed that the Nazis would soon be swept away by a communist-led revolution: in the November 1932 German elections, the Nazis had lost a large number of seats while the German Communist Party had continued its steady rise. However, after the suppression of the German Communist and Social Democratic parties by the summer of 1933, it soon became clear that the Nazis would be secure for some time to come.

Nazi ideology was violently anti-communist; in addition, one of Hitler's stated aims was the desire to take 'living space' in the east, especially from the USSR and its 'inferior' Slavic population. Once Nazi Germany left the World Disarmament Conference and withdrew from the League of Nations, Germany's relations with the Soviet Union began to deteriorate. In response, Stalin cancelled all military co-operation with Germany and took up French offers of joint military discussions and assistance. In November 1933, the USA – which, like the Soviet Union, was becoming alarmed at Japanese aggression (first shown by Japan's invasion of Manchuria in 1931) – finally asked the Soviet Union to establish diplomatic relations. Soviet fears also led Stalin to apply for League membership, which was finally granted in 1934.

The Soviet Union and 'collective security'

As early as December 1933, Litvinov, the Soviet commissar for foreign affairs, began to argue that, because of the threats from Japan and especially Germany, the Soviet Union's best defence lay in approaching Britain, France and the USA to seek an alliance to uphold the peace settlements of 1919–20 against threats from Nazi Germany.

In 1934 the Soviet Union and France began to draft a treaty whereby the Soviet Union would help guarantee France's borders with Germany in return for French military help if Germany attacked the Soviet Union. They also discussed the possibility of involving Nazi Germany in an agreement to guarantee the security and independence of the successor states and the three Baltic republics. However, the proposals to guarantee Germany's eastern frontiers foundered: the eastern European states distrusted the motives of the USSR, Nazi Germany was totally opposed to the idea and Britain was not really interested. Despite these disappointments, when the Soviet Union attended its first League of Nations meeting in September 1934, it began to make real efforts to strengthen the League's 'collective security' role. However, events in 1935 and 1936 soon led Stalin to return to direct diplomacy.

The search for an anti-fascist alliance

By 1935, Stalin had ordered the Comintern to pursue a new policy of seeking to form popular fronts with any party prepared to join the anti-fascist struggle. In May France signed a new treaty with the Soviet Union which agreed to the mutual protection of Czechoslovakia from any attack by Nazi Germany. However, France specifically avoided making any definite military commitment as it was afraid to commit itself without British support. When Italy invaded Abyssinia in October 1935, Stalin was disturbed by the lack of any effective response from the League. He was further unsettled by the League's weakness over Hitler's reoccupation of the Rhineland in March 1936 and, later in the year, over German and Italian involvement in the Spanish Civil War.

Despite keeping his options open by making periodic attempts to achieve some kind of non-aggression agreement with both Germany and Japan, the main thrust of Stalin's policy in 1936 was aimed towards achieving an anti-Nazi alliance between the USSR, Britain and France. However, Britain's National (but essentially Conservative) government was strongly anti-communist and saw Nazi Germany as a useful block against the spread of communism. In addition, many in Britain believed that aspects of the Versailles settlement should be revised to take account of Germany's 'legitimate' grievances. Thus, Britain saw appeasement of Nazi Germany as preferable to strengthening the League or forming an alliance with the USSR. Britain's attitude played a large part in France's 1935 decision to avoid specific military promises in the Franco-Soviet treaty to protect Czechoslovakia.

Meanwhile, events in Asia continued to worry the Soviet Union. Jiang Jieshi, the leader of Nationalist China, still refused to launch an attack on the Japanese invaders in Manchuria, preferring instead to try and destroy the Chinese Communist Party. Stalin tried to reach an accommodation with the Japanese, by agreeing to the sale of the Eastern Railway to Manchukuo (the new name given by Japan to Manchuria). Japan's foreign policy was still undecided as regards expansion at the expense of the Soviet Union – one faction favoured this option, while the other wanted to expand in the Pacific and south-east Asia.

Then in November 1936 Japan signed the Anti-Comintern Pact with Germany and in 1937 so did Fascist Italy. This was followed in July 1937 by a full-scale Japanese invasion of China. These events led Stalin to fear that the USSR might have to face a combined two-front attack from both Nazi Germany and Japan. Consequently, in a new treaty with China, signed in August 1937, the Soviet Union sent military aid to the Guomindang (the Chinese National Party, led by Jiang Jieshi) and, in August 1939, the Red Army inflicted a serious defeat on Manchukuo forces at the Battle of Khalkin-Gol.

The Nazi–Soviet Non-Aggression Pact, August 1939

While events were unfolding in Asia, the Soviet Union's diplomatic approach to western European states was beginning to falter. Litvinov still believed an agreement with Britain and France was possible, in view of Germany's ongoing breaches of the Versailles settlement. However, in March 1938, neither Britain nor France opposed Hitler's *Anschluss* with Austria. More worrying for the USSR was the growing crisis over the Sudetenland in Czechoslovakia.

As Hitler's demands for land increased during September 1938, the Soviet Union offered to act on the Franco-Soviet Pact of 1935, designed to protect Czechoslovakia. France, however, was not prepared to act without Britain – and Britain refused to become involved. Poland also refused to give permission for the Red Army to cross Polish territory. Soviet offers of further talks were also ignored and, instead, Britain, France and Italy agreed in Munich on 29 September 1938 that Czechoslovakia should hand over the Sudetenland to Germany.

Then, in March 1939, Nazi Germany invaded the rest of Czechoslovakia, with Britain and France once again refusing to take any action. However, Britain finally decided that Poland, Hitler's next likely target, should be protected and in April it initiated talks with the Soviet Union about the possibility of joint action between Britain, France and the USSR to 'guarantee' Poland against Nazi aggression. At this point France's Popular Front government collapsed and was replaced by a right-of-centre government which was more hostile to the Soviet Union. At the same time, the majority of the British cabinet began to have second thoughts about allying with the Soviet Union, so the talks faltered.

Stalin had become increasingly suspicious of the real motives behind British and French foreign policy. In 1939 he decided that, in order to avoid war, more serious approaches should be made to Germany and Japan to sign non-aggression pacts. Consequently, in May 1939 Litvinov was replaced as commissar for foreign affairs by Molotov, who was instructed to pursue a new diplomatic policy. Evidence released since the collapse of the Soviet Union in 1991 suggests that a definite military alliance with Britain and France was still the favoured option.

Britain, however, was still continuing to drag out the negotiations in a half-hearted way when, on 23 August 1939, it was announced that Molotov and von Ribbentrop, Germany's foreign minister, had signed a non-aggression pact. Secret clauses in this pact divided Poland and large parts of eastern Europe between the two signatories – Germany was to have western Poland, while the USSR would get eastern Poland, Finland, the three Baltic republics and the part of Romania (Bessarabia) that had been part of Tsarist Russia. Shortly afterwards, on 1 September 1939, Germany invaded 'its' part of Poland and on 3 September – to both Hitler's and Stalin's surprise – Britain and France declared war on Germany.

Soviet motives and the historical debate

Historians are divided as to the real aims and motives of Soviet foreign policy in the 1930s. Beginning with A. J. P. Taylor's *The origins of the Second World War*, many (such as G. Roberts) have argued that Stalin's policy, as pursued by Litvinov, was genuine. These 'collective security' historians argue that even after the Munich Crisis in September 1938 Stalin still hoped for an alliance with Britain and France. Only when he came to the conclusion that Britain and France were encouraging Hitler 'to go east' was the approach to the western European democracies downgraded. The new approach, via a non-aggression pact, was designed to buy the Soviet Union time to build up its defences. Even then, it is argued, negotiations with Britain were continued in the increasingly weak hope that success might be achieved.

Opposed to this view are historians such as R. Tucker who argue that the approach to the West was a screen behind which the Soviet Union followed its main policy of maintaining the close links with Germany that were established in the 1920s by the Treaty of Rapallo. These 'Germanist' historians believe negotiations with the West were just a ploy to put pressure on Nazi Germany to sign an agreement with the USSR. A third group of historians, however, stress the importance of 'internal politics' in understanding the two different strands of foreign policy pursued by Stalin from 1933 to 1939. J. Haslam and C. Kennedy-Pipe, for instance, have pointed out the genuine policy differences which existed between the pro-Western Litvinov (his wife was English) and Molotov, who placed his faith in the independent strength of the Soviet Union, and the fact that Stalin wavered between these two options.

However, as G. Roberts has pointed out, recently released Soviet archives show that the infrequent Soviet contacts with Nazi Germany from 1935 to 1939 were made only in response to German approaches (which were intended to block any agreement between Britain, France and the Soviet Union) and that internal policy differences regarding Soviet security were not great. More importantly, France's – and especially Britain's – reluctance to negotiate seriously with the Soviet Union (borne out by the fact that Britain sent only low-ranking officials to the USSR for diplomatic and military discussions in the summer of 1939 and made no indication that these were urgent; one official took six days to arrive in Moscow) meant that by the summer of 1939 the Western foreign policy option had practically ceased to exist. This left the Soviet Union with no choice, if war was to be avoided, but to opt for an isolationist policy and buy time with a temporary insurance deal with Nazi Germany. This was especially necessary as the Red Army, seriously affected by the Great Purge in 1937–38, was already involved in fighting in Manchuria and was in no state to fight Germany.

The Soviet Union at war, 1941–45

After Britain and France declared war on Germany in September 1939, Stalin believed the danger of an imminent German attack had passed. He did not believe Hitler would attack (and so risk a two-front war) until Britain and France had been defeated in the west. In this interval before the Nazi attack on the Soviet Union, however, Soviet military action did take place. Though some historians see these conflicts and occupations as a continuation of Tsarist imperialism or proof of Soviet intentions to 'export' revolution by conquest, many others (such as C. Ward) see these as essentially defensive steps, given Western inaction over the open aggression displayed by the Nazi Third Reich and Japan.

The Red Army had been involved in military actions in Manchukuo since 1937. This was seen as essential if the Soviet Union was to prevent a clearly aggressive Japan from invading Siberia for the fourth time in 50 years (the Sino-Japanese War, 1894–95; the Russo-Japanese War, 1904–05; and the civil war, 1918–20).

Despite declaring war on Germany over its invasion of Poland, Britain and France at first did nothing (the so-called 'phoney war'). This confirmed Stalin's suspicions about their real intentions. He therefore decided to invade the 'Soviet half' of Poland on 17 September.

At the end of November, the Soviet Union attacked Finland in what became known as the 'winter war'. In earlier attempts to obtain better protection for Leningrad (where there were important armaments factories) and Murmansk (the USSR's only northern ice-free port), Stalin had tried to negotiate exchanges of territory and the lease of some strategic islands from Finland. When Finland refused, Stalin ordered an invasion, even though he was concerned about Finland's good relationship with Nazi Germany.

The Red Army, still adversely affected by the Great Purge and not prepared for a winter offensive, did badly against Finnish troops. This, and Soviet fears that Britain might become involved, led to the conclusion of a lenient treaty in March 1940. The Red Army's poor performance persuaded many – especially Hitler – that it was a weak fighting machine.

While the fighting in Finland was taking place, Stalin was also involved in taking over the Baltic states. In 1939 military agreements were signed which allowed Soviet troops to be stationed on their territories. In June 1940 Lithuania, and Bessarabia and northern Bukovina in Romania, were taken over. In July 1940 all three Baltic states became republics of the USSR.

By the summer of 1940, therefore, the Soviet Union had, via a mixture of border wars and diplomacy based on the threat of military aggression, extended its frontiers in the west and south. As a result, any German attack could now be resisted by the Red Army on non-Russian territory. By then the 'phoney war' had ended – in fact, France had already been defeated in May 1940. However, Britain remained undefeated, which allowed Stalin to feel reasonably confident that Germany would not be able to attack in the near future.

Early defeats, 1941–42

Despite the signing of the Nazi–Soviet Non-Aggression Pact in August 1939, Stalin still expected a German attack at some point. As a result, measures were rushed through to improve the Soviet Union's military defences. However, when the Battle of Britain prevented a further German victory, Stalin began to think that Britain and Germany might exhaust each other in war. Consequently, military preparations in the Soviet Union were slowed down, despite warnings from Soviet and British intelligence that Hitler was planning an attack. Stalin believed the latter was a trick designed to make him break the non-aggression pact.

In fact, Hitler had been preparing for an invasion of the USSR since December 1940. Britain's continuing resistance, Italy's poor performance in Greece, bad weather and delays in building airfields near the post-1939 Soviet border delayed the start of the offensive (known as Operation Barbarossa) until 22 June 1941. Immediately prior to this, there had been open and massive German military preparations along its eastern frontiers as well as several *Luftwaffe* incursions over the Soviet borders. Stalin and several senior NKVD officials dismissed reports from NKVD agents that an invasion was imminent; instead, they believed these actions were just manoeuvres to extract some concessions. Even warnings by Schulenberg, the non-Nazi German ambassador in Moscow, two weeks earlier were dismissed as attempts to provoke war. As a result, Stalin issued orders against mobilisation and for all provocations to be ignored where possible. Though many units quietly ignored these orders, many others did not and Stalin's signal to expect imminent attack came too late for them.

The German invasion in June 1941, which began what the Soviets called the Great Patriotic War, was massive and swift – over 5 million Axis troops (over 3 million Germans initially and, later, units from Italy, Hungary, Finland, Bulgaria, Romania, Slovakia and Spain) were involved, along with over 3,000 tanks, 50,000 pieces of artillery and 5,000 war planes.

Using the tried-and-tested *Blitzkrieg* methods, the *Wehrmacht* invasion forces advanced quickly and deeply into western Russia. Although the Soviet troops outnumbered the Axis forces in men and equipment in places, the Soviet Union lacked the economic strength of Germany, which also had the resources of occupied Europe at its disposal. Within a week, the Red Army's defences had been smashed, vast quantities of equipment and supplies had been destroyed or captured and a third of the airforce had been eliminated before it could even take off, and over 500,000 had been taken prisoner.

Stalin lost his nerve and, for the first few days of the invasion, Molotov took effective charge of the country. The system of military command was altered. Stavka was set up to take charge of all land, air and sea operations and the State Committee of Defence (GKO) was set up a few days later to oversee not just the military but also the political and economic aspects of the war.

On 3 July, Stalin announced that, because of the tremendous German advances, a 'scorched earth' policy was to be adopted. At the same time, partisan and sabotage units, mainly controlled by the NKVD, were set up to operate behind enemy lines. This was particularly important as the rapid German advance was increasingly stretching their supply lines.

By August, the Baltic republics had been lost and much of the important agricultural areas of Belorussia and the Ukraine were occupied. In September, the German forces began Operation Typhoon; this massive attack on Moscow took Stavka by surprise. The Red Army suffered heavy losses and was forced to retreat. Initially deeply shocked, Stalin considered the possibility of seeking peace terms (similar to the Treaty of Brest-Litovsk), while many government offices were moved from Moscow to Kuibyshev in the east. As government offices in the Kremlin began to close, panic swept the city. A train was prepared to take Stalin and other government officials to the east. However, in the end, Stalin decided to stay and fight.

Moscow and the Soviet Union were saved by a combination of factors. First, the serious defeats suffered by the Red Army led to Marshal Zhukov taking command of the whole western front on 19 October 1941. In addition to his abilities, his forces for the defence of Moscow were strengthened by Siberian troops moved from the Far East. This move was possible because Soviet spies had discovered that the debate within the Japanese army about whether to attack the Soviet Union or to expand in the Pacific had been won by the latter group. Even before the Japanese launched their attack on Pearl Harbor in December 1941, about half the troops protecting Siberia had been moved west. Second, the Russian weather began to hit German troops and equipment, neither of which had been prepared for a winter war.

As the German advance slowed down, Zhukov began to plan a counter-offensive. This was launched in December 1941, initially to save Moscow. Early success here led to further counteroffensives in the north, the Ukraine and the Crimea. Although these were not as successful as the Moscow offensive, the Germans suffered high casualties and were pushed back several hundred kilometres in places. Soviet tanks proved superior to German ones and the Katyusha rocket launcher (nicknamed 'Stalin's organ') proved effective.

Nonetheless, by the end of 1941, the Soviet Union's position seemed desperate: about 4 million soldiers were either dead or captured and the Red Army had lost huge amounts of equipment. This was due, in part, to low morale following the purge of the Red Army (which had included many of its generals) and Stalin's orders that Red Army units should not retreat, which led to heavy losses and many being surrounded and taken prisoner.

In early 1942 Stalin planned a new offensive, as the Red Army had been strengthened by equipment (mostly jeeps and lorries) from the USA under the terms of a lend-lease agreement made with the Soviet Union in November 1941. Prior to that, in July 1941, Britain and the Soviet Union had signed a mutual assistance pact for equipment and supplies with the possibility of troops being supplied later. Soviet requests for troops, however, were ignored, although after the USA had declared war on Germany in December 1941 the flow of equipment increased.

Stalingrad

In August 1942 the Germans began their attempt to take Stalingrad – heavy bombing was followed by a fresh offensive. At times, the Germans held most of Stalingrad, but there was strong Soviet resistance for over a month of bitter close-quarter fighting over every street and building. While Soviet defenders held on, Stalin and Zhukov clashed over what to do. Finally, Stalin agreed to Zhukov's plan for a counteroffensive. Known as 'Operation Uranus', it began in September and, by November, the German Sixth Army was surrounded. However, the savage fighting continued until February 1943, when the remnants of von Paulus's Sixth Army finally surrendered, much to Hitler's fury.

The battle for Stalingrad was an important turning point in the war – according to Churchill, the Soviet victory there 'tore the guts out of the German army'. With the exception of lend-lease aid from the US, Allied bombing of Germany and the North African and Italian campaigns in 1942 and 1943, the Soviet Union had faced the bulk of the German forces on their own. At least 75 per cent of all German troops and military equipment was sent to the Russian front (*Ostfront* or eastern front). By June 1944, when the Allies finally opened up a second front (via the D-Day landings in Normandy), there were 228 German and Axis divisions fighting the Russians, compared to 61 divisions in western Europe.

Victory, 1943–45

During 1943 the Red Army slowly pushed the *Wehrmacht* westwards, but Soviet losses continued to be heavy. In July 1943, Hitler ordered another offensive, intended to surround the Soviet armies in the Ukraine. The fighting centred on Kursk, in what was to become the biggest tank battle in history, involving over 6,000 tanks, 5,000 aircraft, 30,000 pieces of artillery and over 2 million soldiers. The Soviet T34 tank proved its superiority: the Germans were surrounded and suffered heavy losses.

From September 1943, the Soviet offensive was stepped up – by the end of the year, over 60 per cent of the territory lost since 1941 had been recaptured. During 1944, the victories continued: in January the long siege of Leningrad was ended and Smolensk and Kiev were retaken; in May and June, the Crimea and Belorussia were recaptured and, by August 1944, all German forces had been expelled from the Soviet Union. The Red Army then began to invade Germany's Axis partners in eastern Europe; by early January 1945, the Red Army crossed into Germany, reached the River Elbe in April and entered Berlin in May.

The historical debate

Ever since the end of the war, historians have argued about the reasons behind the final victory of the Soviet Union, focusing on the various military, political and economic factors. Overall, however, as noted by C. Ward, these differing viewpoints can be divided into negative and positive interpretations.

The negative argument essentially explains the Soviet victory by pointing to Nazi Germany's weaknesses and mistakes and tends to reject the idea of Soviet strengths. R. Medvedev, for example, points out how Stalin's trust of Hitler after the pact of 1939 brought the USSR close to total collapse in 1941. Reasons for this include Stalin's belief in offence, the lack of preparations to defend the new territories acquired in 1939–40 and his failure to reorganise the Red Army after the purges and its poor performance in Finland. Operation Barbarossa took the Soviet Union by surprise and the Red Army was unable to stop the swift advance of the Germans in the summer of 1941. Furthermore, there is evidence to suggest that, until 3 July 1941, Stalin gave way to panic.

What saved the USSR, according to this view, was a combination of Axis errors and Soviet luck. The errors include Hitler's decision not to press on with the capture of Moscow, but instead to divert part of his forces to the important oil regions of the Caucasus. Especially important was his refusal to put Germany on a total war footing until 1944, which was really too late as the USSR was outproducing Germany in the replacement of destroyed military equipment. In addition, Nazi ideology and the barbarism it produced lost Germany the support of many Soviet citizens in some areas (especially the Ukraine and the Baltic republics) who, in the beginning, had been willing to aid the German invaders. Some historians estimate that over 2 million Russians (the willing and the unwilling) fought with the Axis powers against the USSR, the most well-known group being Vlasov's 'Russian Liberation Army'. However, Nazi racial theories meant Hitler was reluctant to make full use of these Slavic *Untermenschen* (they had to be redefined as Cossacks). Hitler also ignored German army intelligence advice which, from the autumn of 1941, was that in order to defeat the USSR a civil war should be encouraged by treating Soviet citizens leniently. This, it was believed, would encourage them to rise up against Stalin.

The USSR was also saved by the weather – first the autumn rains which turned Soviet roads into quagmires and then the winter frosts and snow. The *Wehrmacht* was not well prepared for this, as Hitler had predicted that the Soviet Union would collapse in a few months – many of the troops rushed from the Balkans to the *Ostfront* were still in summer uniforms. Thus, the German army got bogged down outside Moscow, which finally gave the Soviet forces the chance to counter-attack.

Other historians, however, emphasise the positive features of the Soviet Union's ability to respond to the German invasion. These include the expertise of its military leaders and the underlying strengths of the Soviet system. On the military side, Stavka soon began to operate on the principles of 'superior force' and 'defence in depth'. This approach led to the many victories in 1943, such as Kursk. There was also an intelligent use of guerrilla warfare. The partisan movement, with widespread popular support, was often co-ordinated by the NKVD so that its raids coincided with Red Army offensives. Also, despite occasional interference, Stalin (unlike Hitler) tended to let his general staff make most of the operational decisions. Military successes – and the heroic survival of Leningrad and Stalingrad – appear to have genuinely raised Soviet morale, over and above the efforts of official propaganda. Popular patriotism and heroism were widespread and went beyond the ranks of party members and officials, who wished to emulate the heroes of the revolution and the civil war. Many ordinary industrial workers and members of collective farms took pride in the achievements of socialist construction in the 1930s, while others were determined to defend the USSR from the hated invaders.

In addition, the Soviet administrative and economic systems proved resilient. Despite early setbacks, which included the loss of important agricultural land, collective farms kept military personnel and industrial workers from starvation. As part of the pre-war five-year plans many new factories had been built in and behind the Ural mountains, which allowed Soviet production to recover rapidly from the initial destructive impact of the Nazi invasion. The administrative structure, too, showed a great ability to improvise and adapt to changing circumstances, shown, for example, in the evacuation of the state and party apparatuses from Moscow. Between 1941 and 1945, over 10 million people were evacuated to the east, while vast new industrial areas were built in the Urals, Siberia and Central Asia. As a result, by 1944, industrial production was 4 per cent higher than it had been in 1941 and, by 1945, the USSR had more operative railway lines than ever. According to R. Overy, 'Soviet planning displayed a flexibility and organisational power which belied its bureaucratic image.'

The immediate consequences of the Great Patriotic War

The human cost

Overall, the Second World War resulted in some 50–60 million deaths – of these, about 25 million were Soviet citizens. Some estimates of Soviet deaths put the figure as high as 28 million, but it is impossible to be exact, as there were no published censuses in the 20 years from 1939 to 1959. Of these deaths, about 9 million were Soviet military personnel – approximately half of these died after being captured, from various causes, including hunger (in some makeshift POW camps, Soviet soldiers were reduced to cannibalism), exposure, disease, forced labour and execution. This figure also includes those killed or executed by the Soviet authorities at critical times (for instance, at Stalingrad); units of the NKVD's special department operated on the front lines to prevent desertion, either by shooting deserters in battle or executing them later. This special department dated back to 1919; in April 1943, it became known as Smersh ('Death to Spies'). Axis military losses were also high on the *Ostfront*, accounting for approximately 8 million soldiers in all.

Civilians, however, suffered even more. At least 15 million Soviet civilians also died, from bombing, hunger, exposure, forced labour, reprisals for partisan actions and from 'special actions' carried out by SS units (though these were often aided by regular *Wehrmacht* forces). At first, in some areas (such as the Ukraine, which had particularly suffered under Stalin's collectivisation policy) many Soviet citizens had welcomed German troops as 'liberators' and many had volunteered to fight for the Germans. Such volunteers were known by the Germans as *Hiwis* (*Hilfswillige*) and they included large numbers of former Red Army troops, some of whom had deserted or been forced into such units after being captured. The Soviet authorities generally took a very severe line with such 'former Russians', both during and immediately after the war.

However, Hitler and the Nazis believed Slavs were racially inferior and, like Jewish people, should be exterminated. Before the start of Operation Barbarossa in June 1944, the *Wehrmacht*'s senior officers had been informed of the 'special orders' and 'special tasks' to be carried out in captured Soviet territory. As well as 'collective measures of force' against villages where partisans were active, and the 'commissar order' which stated the army was to hand over all communist officials, partisans and Jews to the SS or Secret Field Police, army officers were told of the need to co-operate with the SS *Sonderkommando* and security police.

A 'jurisdiction order' effectively gave German soldiers *carte blanche* to loot, rape and murder. This was justified on the grounds that, for Hitler and the Nazis, this was no ordinary war, but a war of annihilation between Nazi ideology and communism and, at the same time, a *Rassenkampf* (race war). Not all *Wehrmacht* officers agreed with this and some were clearly disgusted. However, very few protested and many did co-operate. The Sixth Army, for example, provided troops to help the SS round up the Jewish population of Kiev and to transport them to Babi Yar, where 100,000 were massacred.

Economic devastation

The Great Patriotic War (first described as such by Stalin in 1943 in a comparison with the struggle against Napoleon's invasion in 1812) was immensely destructive. Between what was destroyed by the Germans or looted and sent back to Germany and what the Russians themselves destroyed by their 'scorched earth' policy, much of the gains of the five-year plans had been wiped out. In all, about 25 per cent of all factories, mines and transport facilities were lost – in some of the occupied areas, the percentage was more than double this. By 1942, almost 80 per cent of productive capacity was devoted solely to the war effort. Though the Soviet armaments industry managed to produce more than was destroyed, so enabling final victory, it was a tremendous waste of resources.

From Grand Alliance to Cold War

Since December 1941 Britain and the Soviet Union had been partners in the 'Grand Alliance', which aimed to defeat both Germany and Japan. However, desperate Soviet requests for the opening of a second front in Europe were unsuccessful for several years. Though Roosevelt and Molotov reached an agreement in May 1942 on the urgent need to open up 'a second front in Europe in 1942', Churchill refused to give his support, insisting instead on the primacy of the North African campaign and stating that there could be no second front until 1943. Though Soviet fears of a separate Anglo-American peace with the Axis powers were partially calmed by Roosevelt's Casablanca declaration in January 1943, which promised that neither Britain nor the USA would negotiate with the Axis powers, Stalin became increasingly suspicious about the continual delays in opening up a second front.

By the time the Big Three met at the Tehran conference in November 1943 to discuss the post-war settlement of Europe, the victories of Stalingrad and Kursk had made it clear that the Red Army was already winning on the eastern front, without Allied assistance. Now Stalin at last received assurances of an Allied invasion of France, to take place in the spring of 1944.

By the time the war ended in 1945, disputes between the Allies were already emerging over what to do with Germany and eastern Europe. The tremendous destruction suffered by the USSR left the Soviets feeling very vulnerable and played an important part in Stalin's desire to control eastern Europe. Furthermore, Stalin – acutely aware of Soviet losses and economic destruction – feared the newly enriched USA, which had, since August 1945, possessed a monopoly of nuclear weaponry. These disagreements and mistrust laid the groundwork for what became known as the Cold War.

4 The Stalinist state, 1929–39

Stalin's insecurities, 1930–34

Although Stalin had defeated the Left, the United and the Right Oppositions by 1929, dissent still existed within the Communist Party. Signs of this became apparent at the Sixteenth Party Congress in June 1930 and on several occasions in the years 1930–34 Stalin found he could not always get his policies adopted. This undercurrent of dissent, which involved the most important leaders of the Communist Party in the Politburo and the Central Committee, led Stalin to fear that he might be replaced, especially as his old opponents and defeated rivals were still around. While this opposition was not overt, Stalin came to feel that, in order to maintain the party's – and his own – power, drastic action was required. Although some historians have explained Stalin's Terror as the result of madness (he was certainly deeply disturbed by the suicide of his second wife and he never accepted the fact that many of his colleagues had been closer to Lenin than he had been) there are several objective reasons why Stalin did not feel secure in his power.

While it is true that on occasion Lenin and the Bolsheviks had been prepared to use limited terror against opponents, Stalin pushed terror way beyond the limits set by Lenin. In this, Stalin was like other twentieth-century dictators, who realised that control over the media and effective propaganda are often not enough to establish and secure total power; coercion and violence, or at least the threat of them, are also necessary weapons.

Purges before 1930

Purges had taken place in the Communist Party before Stalin's rise to power. They had, however, only been used to 'purify' the party and the Soviet administration by expelling those judged to be unsuitable, such as drunkards, careerists and those who were hostile to Bolshevik aims. During the power struggle of the 1920s, many of Stalin's opponents to the left and right lost senior posts or were expelled from the party. However, these purges were not violent, nor were they as extensive as those of the 1930s. Up until this time, the majority of Gulag prisoners were ex-*kulaks* or workers who had breached labour discipline; from the mid-1930s, the vast majority of Gulag inmates were the victims of Stalin's purges.

Though Stalin had defeated his main opponents by 1929, he was not totally dominant. In the late 1920s, his calls for stricter action against defeated opponents were not always supported by members of the Politburo and his lack of complete control meant he had to accept compromises. Furthermore, though removed from high office, Bukharin, Rykov and Tomsky (leaders of the defeated Right Opposition) still had sympathisers and supporters in the party. At the Sixteenth Party Congress in June 1930 these three were re-elected to the Central Committee. In addition, the early problems arising from mass collectivisation and rapid industrialisation began to create doubts and political division even within the Politburo, where only Molotov and Kaganovich were uncritical supporters of Stalin. In December 1930, Syrtsov and others were expelled from the Central Committee for criticising the excesses being committed in the name of collectivisation – significantly, they had previously supported Stalin in the struggle against Bukharin and the right.

The Shakhty Affair, 1928

Almost from the beginning, however, Stalin's purges included an anti-managerial, anti-expert aspect. This began when setbacks started to occur in the early years of the First Five-Year Plan. The first significant example of this was the Shakhty Affair in the spring of 1928, when 55 mining engineers in the Shakhty area of the Donbass were accused of sabotage on behalf of 'international capital'. Between 2,000 and 7,000 specialists are thought to have been removed from their posts in the aftermath of the Shakhty Affair. In 1930, 'counter-revolution-aries' were said to be operating in the gold and food-processing industries and, in 1931, there was the 'Industrial Party' trial, in which white-collar workers in Vesenkha and Gosplan were accused of working with White emigrés in order to undermine the five-year plan. After 1933, though, purging of specialists began to lessen.

The Ryutin Affair, 1932

A more serious indication of the extent of opposition to aspects of Stalin's policies came in 1932 when Ryutin, a Rightist and a senior figure in the party, wrote a document calling for the end of forced collectivisation, the rehabilitation of the defeated Oppositionists (including Trotsky) and the dismissal of Stalin. Ryutin's document also accused Stalin of destroying the communist revolution and was signed by several prominent Communists. They were put on trial in September and Ryutin, Zinoviev, Kamenev and 17 others were then expelled from the Central Committee. Although Stalin wanted Ryutin executed, the Politburo refused to go that far, thus underlining the fact that Stalin did not yet have complete control and that the party could still restrain him from exercising arbitrary power. One of those who spoke against Stalin in this affair was Kirov, the powerful and popular head of the party in Leningrad and one of Stalin's appointees to the Politburo. Nonetheless, during the next two years, nearly a million members were expelled from the party for being 'Ryutinites'.

The Seventeenth Party Congress, 1934

Despite these expulsions, however, opposition to Stalin continued. In January 1933, Smirnov (another leading Communist) was expelled for forming an 'anti-party group' to remove Stalin. A major turning point seems to have been the Seventeenth Party Congress (the 'congress of victors'), which took place in February 1934 (the economic chaos and the unrest generated by collectivisation and industrialisation meant no congress was called between 1930 and 1934).

Evidence suggests that before the congress began Kirov might have been asked by some leading local officials to replace Stalin, but he refused. However, this congress did abolish the post of general secretary – this meant that, in principle, Stalin was now no more important than the three other newly elected secretaries of the Communist Party: Kirov, Kaganovich and Zhdanov. Although it is possible that Stalin himself desired this, in order to share responsibility for the economic crisis, the Central Committee elected by the congress indicates that not all in the Communist Party approved of Stalin's leadership. In particular, it appears that Kirov received votes from almost all the 1,225 delegates who voted for seats on the Central Committee, while about 300 did not vote for Stalin at all.

The Kirov Affair, 1934

Kirov was known to have doubts about the pace of industrialisation and Stalin's methods of disciplining the party, and Stalin had not forgotten that Kirov had criticised him during the Ryutin Affair. Although there is no firm evidence that Kirov's assassination in December 1934 was ordered by Stalin, most historians accept he was behind it. Stalin immediately claimed that Kirov's assassination was part of a plot to overthrow him and the rule of the Communist Party, supposedly by a 'Leningrad Opposition Centre' which had links with Trotsky's Left Opposition and the United Opposition. The recently reorganised NKVD (in July 1934, it had absorbed the OGPU), headed by Yagoda, was given sweeping powers of arrest, trial and execution under a special terrorist decree passed the day after Kirov's assassination.

In the next few weeks, over 100 party members were shot and thousands of Trotskyists and Zinovievists were arrested, including Zinoviev and Kamenev. Trotsky himself was abroad, having been deported in 1929. In January 1935, Zinoviev, Kamenev and 17 others were tried and imprisoned for 5 to 10 years. A few days later, 12 important NKVD members in Leningrad were also tried and imprisoned, and several thousand 'bourgeois elements' were rounded up and imprisoned.

The Great Purge

By mid-1935, the purges described above had begun to come to a halt, in part because of the improving economic situation. In this relatively calm period, the drafting of a new constitution, taking account of the Soviet Union's advance to socialism, went ahead. Known as the Stalin constitution, it was approved and came into effect in December 1936. However, a new purge had begun in the summer of 1936. The first show trial signalled the start of what became known as the Great Purge.

The Trial of the Sixteen, August 1936

In early 1936 the NKVD claimed to have uncovered a Trotskyist–Zinovievist counter-revolutionary conspiracy, in league with capitalist states, White Guards and *kulaks*. Although in prison, Zinoviev and Kamenev as well as Smirnov, Syrtsov and 12 others were accused of organising this conspiracy and plotting to kill Stalin and other Politburo members. NKVD interrogations (based on the 'conveyor system' of sleep deprivation, continued questioning and beatings) resulted in 14 of them admitting their 'guilt'. All 16 were found guilty and then executed. At the same time, 43 other leading communists disappeared without trial. Some of the 'confessions' implicated the former Right Opposition leaders, Bukharin, Rykov and Tomsky. They and others (including Radek and Piatakov) were questioned but were not arrested. Tomsky subsequently committed suicide. Eventually Yagoda dropped the investigations, possibly because Bukharin and Rykov refused to confess or possibly because of disagreements within the Politburo. As a result, Stalin had Yagoda replaced by Yezhov, on the grounds that Yagoda had not been active enough in exposing the full scope of the 'conspiracy'.

The Trial of the Seventeen, January 1937

In January 1937 a second show trial of 17 communist leaders took place. They were accused of plotting with Trotsky (who was said to be in league with Nazi Germany and Japan) to carry out assassinations, terrorist activities, sabotage of industry and spying. Those accused again included Radek and Piatakov and once again NKVD interrogations produced 'confessions'. These provided Vyshinsky, the prosecutor-general, with his main 'evidence'. This time, 13 were sentenced to death, including Piatakov (who was deputy commissar for heavy industry, under Ordjonikidze). Ordjonikidze contacted both Yezhov and Stalin to plead for Piatakov's life; the next day, Ordjonikidze's death was announced. Officially he died from a heart attack, though evidence exists which points to either voluntary or forced suicide.

Following this second show trial and the subsequent executions, the Central Committee met during February and March 1937. Its main business was to consider stepping up the exposure and destruction of the 'Trotskyist conspiracy', as revealed by Stalin and Molotov. Yezhov, recently appointed general commissar for state security, took his cue from Stalin and accused Bukharin of having known of Trotsky's plans. Bukharin refused to confess to this and a special sub-committee expelled both him and Rykov from the party. They were immediately arrested and taken to the Lubianka, the NKVD headquarters. After the last Central Committee meeting in early March, Bukharin, Rykov, Tomsky (already dead) and Yagoda were charged with having links with Trotsky and his supporters.

The Trial of the Twenty-one, March 1938

This, the last and biggest of the show trials, focused on Bukharin, Rykov and Rakovsky (who had been expelled from the party in 1927 for his support of Trotsky) and 18 others. They were accused of membership of a Trotskyist–

This is an OGPU poster produced in 1930. The lightning spells out 'OGPU' and is striking a character labelled 'counter-revolutionary wrecker'.

Rightist bloc which was supposedly responsible for, among other things, industrial sabotage, weakening the Red Army, spying for foreign enemies and attempting to restore capitalism. Once again, most of the accused 'confessed' to their 'crimes', though Bukharin refused to admit his guilt. Vyshinsky called for them to be found guilty and shot. The court returned the desired verdict and all but Rakovsky and two others were shot.

The Great Terror

By the time of the last important show trial, the Great Purge had begun to transform into the Great Terror – or Yezhovshchina – as the number of denunciations, expulsions, trials, imprisonments and executions multiplied. Initially, the purges had affected mainly party members; by mid-1937 they had widened to include large numbers of administrators and specialists, including engineers and railway workers. In the years 1937–38, many important officials were arrested and shot, all of the Leningrad party's Central Committee was removed and almost the entire party structure in the Ukraine, from the Politburo downwards, was purged. In most of the other republics, high-ranking party officials were purged of 'nationalists'. Moscow even set quotas for each region as to the number of 'wreckers' (those accused of industrial sabotage) they should find. Many ended up in the Gulag, while others were simply executed by the NKVD.

This purge also spread to the Red Army. Some officers or former officers had been implicated in the first or second show trials in 1936–37, including Muralov, a high-ranking commander in the 1920s who had been expelled for Trotskyism in 1927. In May 1937, Marshal Tukhachevsky, chief of the general staff and a deputy commissar for defence, and Gamarnik, head of the Red Army's political commissars and also a deputy commissar for defence, were arrested and accused of plotting with Trotsky and foreign enemies to assassinate Soviet leaders. On 12 June 1937, Tukhachevsky and some other leading commanders were executed. Gamarnik, like Tomsky, committed suicide once sentence had been passed. The Great Terror then spread down to the lower ranks of the Red Army so that, by the end of 1938, the list of those executed included 3 of the 5 Red Army marshals, 14 of the 16 top commanders, all 8 admirals, 60 of the 67 corps commanders, 136 of the 199 divisional commanders and 221 out of the 397 brigade commanders. Also badly hit were the airforce officers and the military intelligence service. In all, about 35,000 of the entire officer corps (about 50 per cent) were either executed or imprisoned; all 11 deputy commissars for defence and 75 of the 80 members of the Supreme Military Council were also executed.

This 1937 photo shows (left to right) Marshals Budenny, Kalinin and Voroshilov. The marshals whose faces have been blacked out were some of the Red Army victims of the Great Terror.

The Great Terror also began to affect large numbers of ordinary people – many, keen to avoid suspicion falling on themselves, tried to prove their loyalty to Stalin by denouncing others. Some saw it as a way of settling scores or securing for themselves the jobs of those purged. More recent studies have pointed out the pressures felt by local officials to show their loyalty by discovering 'traitors'. Many ordinary people went along with the purges, seeing them as part of a policy directed against arrogant party officials and factory managers, and one which would benefit rank-and-file workers by creating job opportunities. By the end of 1938, though, most Russians were in a state of terror, reluctant to talk openly to anyone. It was at that point that the Great Terror began to diminish.

The end of the Great Terror

As early as October 1937 Stalin began to raise doubts about the purging of industrial workers. In January 1938 the Central Committee decided that a party recruitment drive was necessary to replace those purged as a result of false denunciations. In December of that year Beria replaced Yezhov as general commissar for state security and at the Eighteenth Party Congress in March 1939 Stalin and Zhdanov announced that 'mass cleansings' were no longer needed and even admitted mistakes had been made. Later in 1939, Yezhov was accused of being a British agent and was executed. As a result, the mass arrests ended, several thousand Gulag prisoners were released and many more who had been expelled from the party and had lost their jobs were rehabilitated – this time is sometimes referred to as the 'spring of liberalism'. However, it is important to note that people continued to be arrested and imprisoned or executed, albeit on a much smaller scale.

Power and the Stalinist state

Historians are undecided about the extent of Stalin's popularity and support, and about the nature and distribution of power in the Soviet Union following the Great Purge and the Great Terror. There is also disagreement about whether the USSR can properly be called a totalitarian state.

The 'Stalinists' and Stalin's power

One important effect of the Great Terror was that by 1941 Stalin had created a new caste of administrative bureaucrats and party officials who owed both their position and their survival to him alone. Even the more powerful, like Beria and Molotov, were forced to go along with Stalin's decisions. Nevertheless, Stalin had still not created a totally monolithic, subservient and loyal party machine – evidence suggests that factional and personality clashes had not been eliminated. Zhdanov, for example, was more prepared to allow debate and appears to have favoured a more moderate approach than either Molotov or Yezhov. The administrative confusion and even chaos that existed in some places as a result of the purges allowed local party leaders to take drastic measures without referring to Moscow.

Stalin's tyranny

Several historians, such as T. H. Rigby, argue that during the 1930s Stalin established a system of one-man rule by the use of systematic terror. By 1937 this had effectively atomised Soviet society and destroyed any mutual trust among leading communists (both nationally and locally), leaving the party powerless to oppose Stalin's plans. This individual power was enhanced by the fact that both Stalin and the state controlled the means of mass communication, while the cult of personality (see p. 92) ensured public support. Stalin's 1936 constitution, for example, allowed people to vote on various policies. This one-man rule is seen as a significant qualitative break from the collective oligarchical method of rule (by which a large number of bureaucracies shared power and influence) which had been established by the Communist Party after 1918 and which was re-adopted by the party after Stalin's death in 1953.

If totalitarianism is defined as a state in which a dictator or a single political party or group suppresses all opposition, destroys all individual political freedoms and demands total loyalty from its subjects, then the USSR at the end of the 1930s seems to fit this description.

Stalinist pluralism

Other historians argue that the division of power was not so clear cut and stress instead that there was a significant amount of conflict at the top levels of the party-state machine. This resulted in several of the heads of the large bureaucracies wielding considerable influence. Studies by historians such as S. Fitzpatrick and J. Harris show how powerful Stalinists accepted the official party line, but responded to central policies in their own way, even using them in their own interests. R. H. McNeal has pointed to a clash in the years 1934–39 between those who favoured the rule of law and those who wanted to use arbitrary terror and coercion. In this contest, Yezhov was able at first to defeat the 'soft liners' led by Zhdanov, but by 1939 Zhdanov succeeded in ending the mass purges favoured by the hardliners.

Central power and the regions

Other historians place more emphasis on the division of power and thus the conflict between the centre and the localities. In this scenario, 'mini-Stalins' were able to take control of the party-state machine. They used their positions and the great distances from Moscow to ignore the law and to use patronage as a way of establishing loyal networks of supporters who could protect their power. Historians such as G. Rittersporn point out that, although Stalin and the Politburo were partially aware of this state of affairs, their attempts to retake control – by mass purging, for example – were largely ineffective. The end of the purges can be seen as a victory over Stalin and his attempts to establish total control over the party. The historian M. Fainsod thus refers to the Stalinist state as 'inefficient totalitarianism'.

At the same time, however, evidence suggests that Stalin's power did not rest solely on terror and coercion. The caste of bureaucrats appointed and promoted under his leadership seems to have supported his party and government directives loyally. In addition, many ordinary citizens of Soviet Russia, relatively unaffected by the Great Terror, seem to have had great respect for Stalin, even when life was hard.

The impact of the Great Purge

The numbers debate

Before Gorbachev and *glasnost* and, later, the collapse of the Soviet Union in 1991, estimates of total victims of the purges who were imprisoned, sent to the Gulag or executed varied from 5 million to 18 million. Historians who try to come up with an accurate total face the problem of having to separate deaths that resulted from the 'liquidation' of the *kulaks* and the famine from deaths connected to the Great Terror.

In 1990, however, KGB archives were made public and these showed that the figure was the much lower one of just under 2 million victims. Many historians accept that these lower figures which support the lower estimates given in the past by, among others, J. F. Hough, M. Fainsod and T. H. Rigby are fairly reliable.

The cult of personality

Beginning as early as December 1929 and Stalin's fiftieth birthday, the party and the media consciously began to build up Stalin as a hero and to equate his political thinking with that of Marx and, especially, Lenin. *Pravda* called on the party and the people to unite around 'Lenin's most faithful and dedicated pupil and associate'. Elements of this had already emerged during the power struggle, when Stalin portrayed himself as Lenin's true disciple while branding all his opponents as 'anti-Leninists'. During the upheavals of collectivisation, the five-year plans and the purges, references were made to a 'Lenin–Stalin partnership' and it was claimed that 'Stalin is the Lenin of today'.

Increasingly during the 1930s, Stalin was portrayed as the 'father of the nation', who had saved the Soviet Union from its enemies, and as an expert in science and culture. Posters, paintings and statues of him appeared everywhere, in streets, factories, offices, schools and even homes. The media referred to him in glowing terms, such as 'universal genius' and 'shining sun of humanity'. He was credited with having made the Soviet Union the envy of the world through the achievements of the five-year plans. Artists, writers and film directors were ordered to produce work in praise of Stalin and his achievements. Propaganda aimed at children was disseminated through the schools and the Komsomol.

Explaining the Great Purge and the Great Terror

Both contemporaries and later historians have puzzled over why Stalin initiated and followed such destructive policies. There are several different interpretations and explanations, but this issue – like so many surrounding the history of twentieth-century Russia – was made more complicated by the impact of the Cold War from 1945 to 1991, with historians from the left, centre and right often taking diametrically opposed positions.

Totalitarian theories

The orthodox or traditional views on the causes of the Great Purge centre on the role of Stalin and are based on his position as dictator of the Soviet Union, which was clearly established by the time the purges ended. Some historians, such as R. Tucker, have argued that Stalin launched the purges because he was suffering from some form of mental illness, or at least paranoia, that led to irrational and extreme action. Others, while accepting Stalin's responsibility for and planning of the Great Terror, argue that it should be seen, at least in part, as a rational response to the circumstances of the 1930s.

While continuing to attack Stalin, Trotsky himself saw the Great Terror as a way of providing scapegoats to explain away Soviet Russia's economic problems. He also believed that they were caused by the inevitable paranoia Stalin experienced as a result of his increasing isolation and the bureaucratisation of Soviet society. The historian I. Deutscher (who, as a Polish communist, had initially supported Trotsky during the power struggle, until the formation of the Trotskyist Fourth International in 1938) linked the Great Terror to Stalin's fear that, with the increasingly threatening international situation of the 1930s, the outbreak of war might lead opponents in the party and/or the army to attempt to overthrow him. R. Medvedev has connected Stalin's 'lust for power' and his 'measureless ambition' to the huge support given to Kirov at the 1934 party congress. Thus the Great Purge can be seen as a deliberate action, designed to strengthen the regime and Stalin's position within it.

Revisionist theories

More recently, several historians have turned their attention away from Stalin himself and on to other factors, such as the existence of genuine opposition that posed a potential threat to Stalin's position. Echoing the structuralist–intentionalist debate over the nature and distribution of power in Nazi Germany, some historians, such as G. Rittersporn, have argued that although Stalin made crucial appointments (especially replacing Yagoda with Yezhov as head of the NKVD) the NKVD and local party bosses were often out of control in the chaos of the 1930s and frequently took matters well beyond Stalin's intentions. At times, the Great Terror was an opportunity for rival local leaders to settle old scores.

Other historians, such as J. Arch Getty, have also suggested that there is evidence to prove that Stalin's belief in a Trotskyist–Zinovievist plot was based, at least in part, on fact. While the allegations about links with foreign agents and sabotage were false, between 1930 and 1932 middle-ranking communist officials did contact Trotsky (by that time in exile abroad) about forming a new opposition bloc, and proposals for a Trotsky–Zinoviev alliance were made. Getty has also suggested that the Yezhovshchina can be seen as a radical measure that was intended to remove entire layers of bureaucracy. Others have linked it to pressure from below from young party radicals and workers who saw the collectivisation and industrialisation programmes as part of a wider cultural revolution, and seized the opportunity presented by the Shakhty Affair to drive out specialists and other 'bourgeois elements'. Thus the Great Terror can be seen as part of an anti-managerial, anti-expert movement by rank-and-file workers, and so revolutionary in social terms.

Structuralists have tended to dismiss ideological, personal and social factors as explanations, and have focused instead on institutional causes. They point out that from 1931 to 1933, following the 1928–30 *chistka* (not a political witch-hunt so much as a purge of those guilty of misconduct and inefficiency), almost 1.5 million new recruits flocked to join the party. On top of this influx of careerists and hangers-on, there were signs that local party bosses were safeguarding regional interests and their 'own people'. Therefore, the purges are seen by the structuralists as an attempt from the centre to reimpose control over the local parties.

Stalin and Leninism

Trotsky only joined Lenin's Bolshevik Party in August 1917 after almost 14 years of intermittent differences about party organisation and the likely course of the revolution when it came to Russia. By 1917, both Lenin and Trotsky had moved closer to the other's position. Trotsky's reasons for not joining the Bolshevik faction when the RSDLP split in 1903 were based mainly on his fears concerning Lenin's insistence that the party should be run on the basis of democratic centralism. Given the lack of democracy in Tsarist Russia, Trotsky believed that it would lead to 'substitutionism', with the party organisation substituting for the party as a whole, then the Central Committee for the party organisation, until 'finally a single "dictator" substitute himself for the Central Committee' (see pp. 37–40).

Historians such as R. Conquest have thus argued that the rise of Stalin and the Great Terror can be traced to the Marxist roots of early Bolshevism and particularly to Leninism. They point out that Lenin and the Bolsheviks frequently portrayed those who had different ideas as 'traitors' and 'class enemies' and to the fact that in the 1920s the Bolsheviks resorted to purges of the party membership. Purges also took place during the civil war and as the NEP was introduced, both of which threatened the survival of the new revolutionary Bolshevik government. In 1919 and 1921, about 15 per cent and 25 per cent respectively of party members lost their party cards. These expulsion rates were much higher than those of the 1930s: 11 per cent of members were expelled in 1929 and 18 per cent in 1933 and only 9 per cent in 1935. The Cheka also used terror against opponents in the civil war. In 1921, Lenin banned factions in the Communist Party as well as all opposition parties.

However, Trotsky always rejected the argument that Stalin and Stalinism were a logical outcome of Lenin's ideas and methods of rule. Historians such as

I. Deutscher and R. Medvedev have also portrayed Stalinism as being quite distinct from Leninism, pointing to the fact that terror was not used against Communist Party members before Stalin. In addition, at several points in the 1930s, the Communist Party leadership tried to limit actions taken against various opponents. They point out that Lenin never tried to force defeated political opponents to recant their views or make preposterous 'confessions' – such methods were used only by Stalin. Several historians also point out that the early purges had much more to do with expelling the many careerists and politically immature for personal deficiencies than with attempting to create an ideologically 'pure' and monolithic party. The historian A. Wood comments that there is nothing in Lenin's writings or actions which points to, let alone condones, the use of terror on such a great scale, and makes an important distinction between the use of terror in an extreme revolutionary or military situation and the mass murder of people in relatively peaceful situations.

The Stalinist state after the Great Patriotic War

The Second World War exposed both the strengths and the weaknesses of the Stalinist state. Though historians still debate the extent to which the USSR's survival and eventual victory can be said to have been because of or in spite of Stalin himself, there is no doubt about the fact that Stalin emerged from the war in an even more powerful position, both nationally and internationally. This came about even though the war devastated the Soviet Union and wiped out many of the gains made under Stalin's five-year plans.

Victory

Against all expectations, Stalin and the Soviet Union survived the Great Patriotic War. The Generalissimo (Stalin promoted himself to this position in June 1945), whose policies of forced collectivisation and the Great Terror had rendered both himself and his Stalinist state hugely unpopular with large numbers of Soviet citizens, was now seen by many as a national hero. While final victory owed much to the determination and ruthlessness of the Soviet state, millions of Soviet citizens and soldiers had shown genuine bravery and patriotism, without the need for NKVD intimidation.

After the war, those who survived felt proud of their system, which they believed had saved not only the Soviet Union but also the rest of Europe from Nazi domination. This pride was increased by the fact that most of this had been achieved by their own efforts, with little more than material help, in the years 1941–44. However, many of these same people hoped for some political relaxation now that the war was over. Such hopes were quickly dashed as Stalin, fearing the growing antagonism building up between the Soviet Union and the Western powers, was determined to maintain tight control.

НАШ КРАЙ ПОКЛИКАВ ЛЕНІН ДО ЖИТТЯ
І СТАЛІН НАС ПОВІВ НА ВЕРХОВИНИ,

This portrait was produced at the end of the Second World War to
show Stalin as the architect of the victory over fascism. It appeared
on the front cover of a book entitled *Glory to the great Stalin*.

The armed forces

Stalin was determined to reassert political control over the armed forces after the
war. He became increasingly suspicious of the Red Army's generals, whose
prestige had been tremendously boosted by their recent victories. Stavka and
then the GKO were abolished in September 1945 and the system of political
commissars in the army was reintroduced in August 1946. In March 1947
Bulganin (a political general who had replaced Voroshilov as the chief armed
forces' representative on the GKO in November 1944) took Stalin's place as
minister of defence and from 1946 to 1948 also sat on the Politburo. At the same
time, Marshal Zhukov lost his place on the Central Committee and other high-
ranking officers also lost their influence and positions. From 1945 until Stalin's
death in 1953, there were virtually no promotions to the higher ranks in the
armed forces. In this period, Stalin also continued with his cult of personality.

The party

In order to reassert political control the Politburo met fortnightly from December 1945. However, Stalin was also suspicious of potential rivals within the Communist Party. For this reason Stalin decided to exclude leading party members from the decision-making processes. From 1947, he thus dispensed with both the Politburo and the Central Committee and instead relied on small sub-committees composed of those he trusted at any particular time. The full Central Committee did not meet again until the Nineteenth Party Congress in October 1952. Party affairs were now supervised by a new Orgburo which, along with a new Politburo and secretariat, had been elected by the Central Committee in March 1946.

Beria, who was made a marshal in 1945, still headed the NKVD (which from 1943 to 1946 included the secret police) and aided Stalin in his efforts to remain in total control. Soon Stalin began resorting to his old methods of the 1930s, including purges, as he became increasingly suspicious of everyone, even his old allies. In January 1946, for example, Beria lost control of the secret police, which was handed over to a new ministry of state security (MGB).

Thus, within a couple of years after the end of the war, Stalin had emerged as the undisputed and unchallengeable leader of the USSR, with his power enhanced. This was a very different fate from that experienced by Mussolini and Hitler, the two fascist dictators whose regimes will be examined in the following chapters.

The rise of Italian Fascism, 1918–24

Italy was the first state in both Europe and the world in which a fascist party developed and which later had a fascist dictator. Even the term 'fascist' derives from the Italian word *fascio* (pl. *fasci*), meaning 'group' or 'band'. In Sicily in 1893 radical groups of mostly socialist workers formed *fasci* to organise demonstrations and strikes against low wages and high rents. They were banned by the government in 1894 and many of their leading members were arrested or deported to the Italian mainland. In the following years several other Italian political organisations also used the term before it was adopted in 1919 by Mussolini for his political movement.

The impact of the First World War and the peace treaties, 1914–19

Although Italy had been a member of the Triple Alliance (along with Germany and Austro-Hungary) since 1882, it did not join the First World War when it began in 1914. Instead Italy announced that it had decided to stay neutral because Austria had broken the terms of the alliance by declaring war on Serbia without first informing Italy. Most Italians, especially the socialists but most Catholics and liberals as well, were neutralists and so welcomed this decision, but the nationalists demanded that Italy should become involved as they believed that the war would offer Italy an opportunity to grab more land and make its mark as a great power.

At the same time, the Liberal government began to think that, in view of its ambitions in Europe, it might be prudent to see which side would offer the best terms for Italy's participation in the war. Negotiations with the Triple Alliance in 1914–15 soon revealed that Austria would never concede Trentino or Trieste (part of the *terra irredenta* or unredeemed land in Europe that Italian nationalists wanted to reclaim from Austro-Hungary); the Triple Entente (consisting of Britain, France and Russia), however, promised these, along with other Austrian territory in the south Tyrol and Istria, and northern Dalmatia on the Adriatic coast. Consequently, the Italian government signed the Treaty of London in May 1915 promising to join in the war on the side of the Triple Entente. While the Italian parliament was debating the issues, interventionists set up the *Fasci di Azione Rivoluzionaria*, which organised many street demonstrations to demand Italian involvement in the war. These became known as the 'radiant days of May'.

The members of the *Fasci*, a mixture of anarcho-syndicalists and national socialists who believed war would hasten revolution, were joined by the right-wing members of the Italian Nationalist Association (*Associazione Nazionalista Italiana* or ANI), which had previously pushed for the conquest of Libya. Irrespective of the many demonstrations, however, the leading Liberal politicians had already decided on Italy's participation in the war.

Italy at war

Despite the interventionists' hopes that the war would lead to national regeneration and the creation of strong national unity, the war did not go well for Italy. Over 5 million Italians were conscripted; although most of them fought bravely, they were often badly equipped and supplied. The military leadership was often poor and the Italian army was soon bogged down in a costly war of attrition. Officers often sacrificed thousands of lives needlessly; in all, over 600,000 men were killed, about 450,000 were permanently disabled and a further 500,000 were seriously wounded. November 1917 was an especially low point in the war: the Italians suffered a terrible defeat at the hands of the Austrians at the battle of Caporetto – over 40,000 Italian soldiers were killed and about 300,000 were taken prisoner. The army's commander-in-chief blamed the defeat on the alleged cowardice of his troops and had several thousand executed. The Liberal government blamed the commander-in-chief and sacked him, while the nationalists blamed the government for being inefficient and failing to supply the troops with enough equipment. Though a costly victory was won over Austro-Hungary at Vittorio Veneto in October 1918, many Italians only remembered the defeats and the high casualties of the war. It also had clearly failed to unite Italians as the socialists had remained implacably opposed to the war throughout.

The First World War had a tremendous effect on the relatively weak Italian economy. In order to finance its involvement in the war, the Liberal government had borrowed heavily from Britain and the USA. As a result, the national debt had risen from 16 billion lire to 85 billion lire. When the loans proved inadequate, the government had printed more banknotes, resulting in rapid inflation, with prices increasing by over 400 per cent in the period 1915–18. This inflation destroyed much of the savings of the middle classes, reduced the rent incomes of many landowners and resulted in the real wages of many workers dropping by over 25 per cent. At the end of the war, the situation for many was made much worse by high unemployment, which had resulted from the closure of the war industries and the demobilisation of over 2.5 million soldiers.

The war also deepened the economic divisions between north and south Italy. Those industries linked to war production (especially the steel, chemicals, motor vehicles, rubber and woollen industries) had done extremely well, as they were guaranteed big state contracts. When inflation began to hit, industrialists simply passed on the increases to the government. Companies such as Pirelli (tyres) and Montecatini (chemicals) made huge profits, while Fiat continued to expand and by 1918 was the largest motor manufacturer in Europe. However, the end of the war meant the loss of lucrative state contracts as the government began to cut back expenditure in order to cope with its mounting debts. The south, still predominantly agricultural, had not shared in this prosperity and farming had been badly affected by the large numbers of peasants and farm labourers conscripted for the war. However, during the last years of the war, in an attempt to limit the attraction of socialism and the Russian Bolsheviks, the government had promised a programme of land reform when the war ended.

The 'mutilated victory'

When the war ended in November 1918, many Italians clearly thought their sacrifices would be rewarded by substantial territorial gains and that Italy would be acknowledged as one of the great powers. These hopes were to be largely disappointed. Prime minister Orlando went to the Paris peace conferences in January 1919 expecting to receive all that had been promised by the Treaty of London. Under pressure from the nationalists, he also demanded the port of Fiume, on the border of Istria, as it contained a large Italian-speaking population. Orlando also wanted Italy to receive a share of the former German colonies in Africa.

Although Italy eventually received most of what it wanted, there were some important exceptions: not only would Italy gain no territory in Africa, but Britain and the USA also refused to grant Italy Fiume and northern Dalmatia, arguing that these were vital for the new state of Yugoslavia. Despite the fact that Austro-Hungary, Italy's long-term opponent, had been defeated and no longer even existed and that Italy now clearly dominated the Adriatic, Italian nationalists were disgusted at the terms of the agreement and accused the Liberal government of allowing Italy to be humiliated and cheated. Gabriele D'Annunzio, the popular nationalist poet and war hero, spoke for many Italians (especially war veterans) when he called it a 'mutilated victory'. Many ex-officers, in particular, believed their sacrifices to create a strong and expansionist Italy had been betrayed by the weak Liberal government.

The rise of Fascism, 1919–22

By 1919 it was thus clear that the Liberal regime would face many problems in post-war Italy. In addition to the growing dissatisfaction of the nationalists, the Liberals now faced increased political opposition from other quarters. When the papacy finally lifted its ban on the formation of a Catholic party in January 1919, the Italian Popular Party (*Partito Populari Italiano* or PPI) was formed. This political party was a coalition of conservative and liberal Catholics who wanted to defend Catholic interests and improve life for the peasants. Though it was prepared to give some support to the Liberals and was reluctant to play a major role in government, the PPI was generally suspicious of liberalism because of the latter's history of anti-clericalism. However, the Italian Socialist Party (*Partito Socialista Italiano* or PSI) posed a more serious threat to the government.

The socialist threat and the *biennio rosso*, 1919–20

The economic problems resulting from the First World War produced great discontent among industrial and rural workers. In 1917, inspired by the Bolshevik Revolution in Russia, the Socialist Party called for the overthrow of the Liberal state and the establishment of a socialist republic. Industrial workers, who had resented the imposition of wartime discipline in the factories as it had benefited employers' profits but had only increased their hours of work and removed their right to strike, began to join the Socialist Party in large numbers. With only about 50,000 members in 1914, the Socialist Party had increased its membership to over 200,000 by 1919. At its congress in that year, delegates talked of the need to use force in order to achieve 'the conquest of power over the bourgeoisie'.

As the situation worsened – unemployment rose to over 2 million in 1919 – industrial workers began a wave of militant action, which lasted from early 1919 to November 1920. These years became known as the *biennio rosso* ('the two red years'). During 1919, a wave of strikes and factory and land occupations, organised by trade unions and peasant leagues and involving over a million workers, swept across Italy. By the end of 1919, socialist trade unions had over 2 million members, compared to about 250,000 at the beginning of the year. In many areas, especially in the north, socialists took control of local government. To many industrialists and landowners, and to the middle classes in general, it seemed that a communist revolution was about to begin. Yet the government, headed by Giolitti, did little: working on the premise that the workers were less dangerous in the factories than they would be on the streets and that their militancy would soon decline, they urged employers and landowners to make some concessions. Their response to the riots against the high price of food was to set up food committees to control distribution and prices. This inaction (rather than the tough repression favoured by the industrialists and landowners) led many in the middle and upper classes to view the government as dangerously incompetent.

Mussolini and the 'third way'

It was during this wave of socialist militancy that Mussolini, who was to become the Fascist prime minister of Italy in a mere three years' time, founded his political movement. Benito Mussolini was 36 in 1919 and had followed an inconsistent political path in the preceding years. Initially, more influenced by his father (a blacksmith with revolutionary socialist views) than by his mother (a schoolteacher and a devout Catholic), Mussolini drifted into socialist politics and journalism and, from 1904 to 1910, he gained a reputation as a militant as a result of articles in which he expounded traditional socialist views. He frequently attacked the Catholic Church and repeatedly called for a deepening of the class struggle. He also opposed Italian imperialism: in 1911 he was imprisoned for his part in attempting to provoke an insurrection against the war in Libya. When he was released in 1912 he was made editor of the Socialist Party's newspaper *Avanti*, in which he continued to advocate revolutionary violence against the Liberal state. In 1914, he was involved in the 'Red week', when socialists seized control of some towns and local government in order to bring about the revolutionary overthrow of the Liberal state.

However, the outbreak of the First World War led Mussolini to make a dramatic political U-turn. Like the Russian Bolsheviks, the Socialist Party stuck to the principles of revolutionary internationalism and condemned the war as an inter-imperialist conflict. They urged the working class and the Italian government to stay neutral. One result of this was that Mussolini abandoned the idea of class struggle and moved rapidly towards an extreme nationalist position that advocated Italian involvement in the war. In November 1914, he was sacked as editor of *Avanti* and set up his own newspaper, *Il popolo d'Italia* ('The people of Italy'); shortly afterwards, he was expelled from the Socialist Party. His newspaper was financed by wealthy Italian companies, such as Fiat, which expected to gain lucrative war contracts, and by the French government, who wanted to persuade the Italians to join the war on their side. Not surprisingly, the paper was a strong advocate of Italian involvement in the war and Mussolini's articles demanding this contributed to the rioting in May 1915.

Despite his views, Mussolini did not volunteer for the army, but was conscripted in September 1915. In 1917, having only reached the rank of corporal, he was invalided out of the army after an accident during a training exercise. He then resumed his role as editor of *Il popolo* and ran articles which blamed the Liberal government for military incompetence and called for a dictator to take charge of the war effort. Though he still advocated social reform, in particular demanding that Italian soldiers should not have to return to their pre-war poverty, he was rapidly moving away from a socialist position. In July 1918 he formally renounced socialism, claiming that his paper was for 'combatants and producers' instead.

'Fascists of the first hour'

Mussolini was not alone in his attempts to find a 'third way' between revolutionary socialism on the one hand and capitalism on the other. Many others were also moving towards a form of reactionary ultranationalism. Apart from the *Fasci di Azione Rivoluzionaria* (which, as we have seen, was made up of a mixture of national syndicalists and ex-socialists who wanted revolutionary upheaval to bring about the birth of a new society), there were also the Futurists. This group of artists, led by Filippo Marinetti, also wanted a drastic renewal of Italian culture and society. Far more right-wing than these groups was the extremely nationalist and imperialist Italian Nationalist Association. Beyond them were a great many dissatisfied nationalists and frightened conservatives who wanted to return to a more glorious Italian past and who feared the growth of socialism and the threat of communist revolution. Such views were widespread among the upper and middle classes in Italy, not just among the industrial, financial and landowning elites but also among shopkeepers, small farmers and clerical workers. Many despised the weak Liberal coalitions and wanted a stronger, more authoritarian government that would defend their interests.

After the war, these militant and disaffected groups were joined by another group demanding change. These were the demobilised unemployed officers and troops who found it hard to accept many aspects of post-war Italian society. In particular, the black-shirted crack commando troops of the Italian army (known as the *Arditi*) hated the Liberal political system which, in their eyes, betrayed their wartime sacrifices by not gaining the land which had been promised to Italy and by doing little to crush the revolutionary left. In early 1919, the *Arditi* formed themselves into organised groups. The first *Arditi* Association was set up in January in Rome, while Marinetti established one in Milan. During February, many other *Arditi* groups were set up across Italy. As more groups were established, they started their own newspaper. These groups increasingly used weapons in their attacks on Socialists and trade unionists, who they saw as the enemies of the Italian nation.

In March 1919 Mussolini (himself a member of an *Arditi* group) tried to bring these disparate groups together. On 23 March 118 people, representing various political groups, met in Milan and formed a *Fascio di Combattimento* (Combat Group). These founding members later became known as 'Fascists of the first hour'. This group was supposed to bring together nationalists and socialists. On 6 June 1919 they published a far-reaching and militant-sounding Fascist Programme which combined various left- and right-wing demands. Overall, however, the force that bound these nationalists, syndicalists, artists and ex-servicemen together was a strong hatred of the Liberal state.

Though *Fasci di Combattimento* were established in about 70 other towns, Mussolini's tiny group of militant agitators were soon overshadowed by the actions of Gabriele D'Annunzio, who in March led 2,000 armed men to the city of Fiume, one of the areas not awarded to Italy by the peace treaties. D'Annunzio's force quickly took control and, in open defiance of the Liberal government and the Allies, ruled the city for the next 15 months. This bold action made him a hero to Italian nationalists and acted as an inspiration to Mussolini. He adopted the theatrical trappings used by D'Annunzio, especially the black shirts of the *Arditi*, the ancient Roman salute and the many parades and balcony speeches.

The relative weakness of Mussolini's group was underlined by the results of the November 1919 elections which, for the first time, used a system of proportional representation. Each local *fascio* was allowed to decide its own election manifesto but, despite this, not a single Fascist candidate was elected. Mussolini himself won only 5,000 votes out of 270,000 in Milan. He was so disappointed he contemplated emigrating to the USA. In all, there were probably only about 4,000 committed Fascist supporters in the entire country.

However, the unrest of the *biennio rosso* boosted Mussolini's group. He offered to send in *squadre d'azione* (action squads) to end the factory and land occupations that had been organised by trade unions and peasant leagues. Industrialists in the north and landowners in the Po Valley and Tuscany, frustrated and angered by the Liberal government's stance of concessions and inaction, were only too pleased to give money to Mussolini's group in return for the *squadristi*'s violent actions against the left's strikes and occupations. As well

A group of blackshirts from a *squadra d'azione* – note that several are carrying truncheons known as *manganelli*.

as attacking strikers, the *squadristi* also burnt down the offices and newspaper printing works of the Socialists and trade unions in many parts of north and central Italy and tried to destroy the influence of the peasant leagues encouraged by the more liberal elements of the Roman Catholic PPI. These action squads were controlled by local Fascist leaders known as *ras* (an Ethiopian word meaning 'chieftain'), who often had a large degree of independence.

Although the growing alliance between industrialists, bankers and landowners began to build a mass base for Mussolini's *Fasci di Combattimento* among the middle and lower-middle classes who feared socialist revolution, it increasingly alienated the more left-wing elements (such as Marinetti and the syndicalists). As time went by, these action squads consisted mainly of disaffected demobilised army officers and NCOs, and middle-class students, who were united by their hatred of socialists and their belief in violent action rather than any coherent political ideology.

The practical appeal of the Fascist *squadristi* grew after September 1920, when a wave of factory occupations, involving over 400,000 workers, hit the industrial factories of the north, while agrarian strikes and land occupations continued to spread in central Italy. In the local elections, the Socialists won control of 26 out of Italy's 69 provinces, mostly in northern and central Italy. All this greatly increased the fears of the upper and middle classes and the action squads were used more and more. As they proved effective, their numbers were swelled by recruits from the ranks of small farmers, estate managers and sharecroppers.

Although the factory and land occupations had started to decline by the end of 1920, *squadristi* violence had not. Initially, Mussolini had not ordered the violence – it had been adopted by powerful *ras* leaders in the regions, such as Italo Balbo in Ferrara and Dino Grandi in Bologna. However, Mussolini quickly grasped the political – and financial – opportunities which could result from a more organised use of violence against his opponents. The appeal of Mussolini's group was increased when government military action against D'Annunzio finally forced him to surrender control of Fiume in January 1921. For Mussolini this action also removed a potentially powerful rival force from the political landscape. Slowly, with much initial resistance, Mussolini began to assert central control over regional Fascist leaders, arguing that without his leadership and newspaper the various groupings would fall apart. He stressed the need to depict Fascist violence as necessary to prevent the victory of a Bolshevik-style revolution in Italy.

The first step towards making the *Fasci* a national movement was taken in April 1921 when Mussolini made it clear that he saw Fascist violence as a necessary part of the anti-socialist crusade to 'break up the Bolshevist state'. Despite his attacks on the Liberal state, Mussolini began to make it clear to Giolitti and other Liberal politicians that talk of Fascist revolution was not to be taken seriously. He wanted to reassure the wealthy that their property would not be confiscated under a Fascist government. Giolitti then offered to form an anti-socialist national bloc with the Fascists for the national elections due in May 1921. Fascist squads continued their violence during the campaign, killing about 100 Socialists. Despite this, the Socialists won 123 seats, thus remaining the largest party, and the PPI won 107 seats. Though Giolitti was disappointed by the results, Mussolini was pleased: his group had won 35 seats (7 per cent of the vote). He himself was now a deputy (member of parliament); significantly, all 35 Fascist deputies represented were from the right of the movement. More importantly, the Fascists had gained an image of respectability and a foothold in national politics. Having achieved this success, Mussolini announced that the Fascists would not support Giolitti's coalition government after all.

The attitude of the elites

From May 1921 Mussolini hoped to achieve real power and he was determined to make full use of the new opportunities. He now realised that he had to convince the industrialists, landowners and the middle classes of three things: that the Liberals were finished as an effective political force, that there was a real threat of socialist revolution and that only the Fascists were strong enough and determined enough to take the necessary action and restore order and dignity to Italy.

Denied the support of the Fascist deputies, Giolitti managed to form a coalition with the PPI. This collapsed within a month, however, when Giolitti tried to introduce a tax that would have affected, among other things, Vatican investments. From then on, weak coalition governments staggered along (there were three between May 1921 and October 1922), but they were unable to take effective action against industrial struggles and political violence. Matters were not helped by the fact that the Liberals themselves were still divided into opposing factions of rival politicians.

The attitude of the elites now became increasingly crucial to the prospects of Fascist success. During the *biennio rosso*, the police and army leaders had often turned a blind eye to Fascist violence against Socialists and industrial and agrarian militants. In fact, in many areas, some commanders had even provided transport to take action squads to Socialist demonstrations and congresses. In the first half of 1921 over 200 Socialists were killed and over 800 wounded by these action squads, and Emilia and Tuscany had become Fascist strongholds. However, as *squadristi* violence continued into the summer of 1921 and law and order declined, Mussolini began to worry that this might alienate the conservative elites and encourage anti-Fascist unity. His concerns were increased on 31 July when 12 *carabinieri* were able to disperse over 500 Fascists at Saranza; this was hardly a sign of a party able to impose law and order.

So on 2 August Mussolini surprised the opposition – and angered the *ras* – by signing a peace deal, known as the 'pact of pacification', with moderate socialists and the General Confederation of Workers (CGL), the main trade union organisation. In an attempt to outmanoeuvre the *ras*, he then resigned from the Fascist Central Committee. This ploy was successful and in October 1921 he was able to persuade members to transform the *Fasci di Combattimento* into a formal political party, to be known as the National Fascist Party (*Partito Nazionale Fascista* or PNF). Mussolini was able to follow up this victory in November 1921 by convincing the Fascist National Congress to elect him as leader. In return, he agreed to end the truce with the Socialists and immediately ordered all branches to organise action squads. Mussolini then formed a strong central party organisation staffed mainly by his supporters in Milan. Though the local *ras* still had considerable influence and some autonomy, he could now present himself as the clear and undisputed leader of an organised, united political party.

His growing control of the new party now allowed him to drop what remained of the more left-wing aspects of the original 1919 Fascist Programme, especially those that were hostile to the Roman Catholic Church. This was intended to increase Fascist support among the conservatives and was especially important as Pius XI, the new pope, did not support the leader of the PPI and had, as archbishop of Milan, formally blessed the Fascists' banners. Mussolini now concentrated on keeping Fascist statements of policy deliberately vague, declaring his party to be against socialism and liberalism and for a strong and ordered Italy. By the end of 1921 the Fascist Party claimed a membership of over 200,000, many of whom were the shopkeepers and clerical workers who had previously supported the Liberals.

The Fascists' 'creeping insurrection'

Despite Mussolini's growing control over the Fascist Party and its increased attraction for conservatives, many of the local *ras*, such as Roberto Farinacci and Italo Balbo, still continued to use extreme violence. Mussolini was determined to avoid any split in his party so, during 1922, he followed a dual policy: while he encouraged the *ras* to continue their violent activities, he let the conservatives know that he had no intention of pushing for a violent seizure of power. During the spring of 1922 there was a concerted campaign of *squadristi* violence in northern and central Italy. In May 1922 Balbo led a force of over 60,000 Fascists and unemployed into Ferrara, took over the city and forced the local government to fund a massive programme of public works. In Bologna, the Fascists forced the town council to resign. By July serious street fighting was common in most northern towns; soon, Cremona, Rimini and Ravenna were under Fascist control. Once again, the police either stood by or even intervened on the side of the Fascists. In some areas, they even loaned them weapons if it looked as if the Socialists were gaining the upper hand. The weak coalition government lacked the political will to order police action against the Fascists, especially as it seemed increasingly likely that there would have to be some sort of parliamentary deal with the Fascists in the near future.

The Socialists and their trade unions responded by calling for a general strike on 31 July to force the government to take action against Fascist violence. Mussolini took this as an opportunity to prove that the Socialists were still a threat and, more importantly, that only the Fascists could stop a socialist revolution. Fascists immediately began to break the strike, taking over public transport and the postal service and using violence against strikers. The general strike, which had been hastily organised, collapsed after only a few days and was called off by the Socialists on 3 August. This was followed by further Fascist takeovers in Ancona, Livorno and Genoa. This series of events not only impressed the conservative middle classes, it also led to renewed contacts between Mussolini and Liberal ex-prime ministers such as Salandra, Orlando, Nitti and Giolitti to discuss the possibility of the Fascists entering a coalition government. These talks even progressed to the point where it was decided which government posts would be held by Fascists. In September, to increase Fascist respectability, Mussolini declared he was no longer opposed to the monarchy. By October, Trento and Bolzano were also under Fascist control.

The March on Rome, October 1922

Now that they had gained considerable control of northern and central Italy, the *ras* wanted to make the move from local to national power. After the collapse of the general strike many of them had urged a coup and Mussolini had struggled to restrain them. In early October 1922 this pressure from the *ras* was renewed; Balbo is said to have told Mussolini that they intended to march on Rome and seize power with or without him. In an attempt to appease his more militant supporters, and to intimidate the Liberal government into making concessions,

Mussolini agreed to organise a march on Rome and announced it to a meeting of Fascist *squadristi* in Naples on 24 October.

The local action squads were organised into a national militia, under Balbo and Grandi, and Mussolini and other Fascist leaders drew up a plan which involved four *ras* – Balbo, Bianchi, Cesare de Vecchi and General de Bono – seizing control of the major towns and cities in northern and central Italy. Once this had been achieved, some 40,000 Fascists would converge on Rome. On the night of 27 October, Fascist squads seized control of town halls, railway stations and telephone exchanges across northern Italy, The prime minister, Luigi Facta, finally decided to act on 28 October and persuaded the king, who was commander-in-chief of the army, to declare a state of emergency so that the government could use the army as well as the police to stop the Fascist columns which were apparently converging on Rome. Initially, roads and railways were blocked and troops met little Fascist resistance as they began to retake control of some buildings seized by the Fascists. De Vecchi, among others, began to waver and the prefect (governor) of Milan was instructed to arrest Mussolini (who was in Milan in order to be able to escape into Switzerland should things go wrong).

However, the prefect, Alfredo Lusignoli, was persuaded not to act by the promise of a seat in a coalition government containing Fascists, and Mussolini was not arrested. Later in the morning, the king changed his mind and refused to sign the necessary papers declaring a state of emergency. Facta resigned in protest. The king then asked Salandra to form a government. Mussolini rejected the offer of four cabinet posts for Fascists – he wanted to be prime minister himself. Salandra then advised the king to appoint Mussolini as prime minister; Mussolini accepted on 29 October 1922. It is not clear why Salandra acted in this way, but he was a political rival of Facta and was sympathetic to the Fascists' anti-communist stance.

In the end, the actual March on Rome was more myth than reality. Mussolini did not march at the head of the Fascist columns, instead reaching Rome by train. Significantly, he had accepted the post of prime minister while in Milan. The Fascist militia did not reach Rome until 30 October, when about 70,000 Blackshirts celebrated their victory in the streets. Mussolini thus owed his success more to the king than to the strength of his Fascist militia.

Historians are still undecided why the king acted as he did. Some argue that he was uncertain of the reaction of the military, others that he had little faith in the Liberal politicians and that he genuinely feared civil war might break out, or that his cousin, the Duke of Aosta, would replace him as the latter was a known Fascist supporter. Others have pointed out how leading industrialists, landowners and senior churchmen favoured compromise with the Fascists and that even Margherita, the Queen Mother, was a fervent Fascist. They also argue that the king saw the Fascists as a bulwark against the threat of a communist revolution. Whatever his motives, Mussolini had become prime minister by legal, constitutional means, even if Fascist violence was the starting point.

Mussolini's consolidation of power, 1922–23

Although Italy's prime minister was a Fascist, Italy was not yet a Fascist state. In order to bring this about, Mussolini would have to change the constitution. He set out to win new political allies by doing all he could to widen the political appeal of Fascism. This was essential as his coalition government only had four Fascists in the cabinet. The government was essentially a Nationalist – PPI – Liberal coalition, which could fall at any time if one of these parties withdrew. In addition, the king had the power to dismiss Mussolini (both he and the other political leaders believed Mussolini could be tamed, transformed and used).

First steps

Mussolini, however, had no intention of being tamed. He intended to establish a one-party Fascist state, with himself as dictator. In his first speech to parliament on 16 November 1922, he made a veiled threat about the strength of the Fascist Party (he claimed 300,000 armed and obedient members), spoke of his desire to create a united and strong Italy and asked for emergency powers to deal with Italy's economic and political problems. The deputies – including ex-prime ministers Giolitti, Salandra and Facta – gave him an enormous vote of confidence and emergency powers for a year.

The elites and the party

In order to increase his support amongst the conservative elites, Mussolini appointed the Liberal Alberto de Stefani as finance minister. Although his economic policies (reducing government controls on industry and trade and cutting taxation) pleased the industrialists and shopkeepers, many on the left of the Fascist Party were angered, as they wanted significant social reforms instead.

In an attempt to increase his control over the Fascist Party, Mussolini established a Fascist Grand Council in December. This was declared the supreme decision-making body within the Fascist Party. It could discuss proposals for government action, but Mussolini insisted on sole power over appointments to the council. In effect, he was attempting to establish total control over Fascist policy-making. In January 1923 Mussolini succeeded in persuading the Fascist Grand Council to agree that the regional Fascist action squads should be formed into a national Fascist militia, funded by government money. This militia, called the National Security Guards (MVSN), swore an oath of loyalty to Mussolini, not to the king. This gave him a paramilitary organisation of over 30,000 which continued to use violence against anti-Fascists and, at the same time, considerably reduced the power of the provincial *ras*. The Fascist Grand Council also worked alongside the government's Council of Ministers: the Fascist ministers in the government made important decisions which were then passed on to the council for official approval. Mussolini also acted as interior and foreign minister.

During 1923 Mussolini continued to strengthen his position. In early 1923 he announced that no serious measures would be taken against tax evasion, which was widely practised by wealthy companies and individuals, with the result that the employers' organisation, the *Confindustria*, gave him their support. Partly as a result of this step, the small Nationalist Party (a member of the coalition government with close links to big business and the army) merged with the Fascists in March 1923. Not only did this bring the Fascists additional paramilitary forces in the form of the Nationalists' Blueshirts, it also confirmed Mussolini's increasing shift to the right and the conservative elites. This move disturbed the more militant Fascists. Ex-Nationalists such as Corradini, Federzoni and Rocco also brought with them their desire for an authoritarian government and a much-enlarged Italian empire.

The Catholic Church

From April to June 1923 Mussolini worked to increase support from the Catholic hierarchy in order to widen the Fascists' political base and, at the same time, to weaken the position of the PPI, the other key member of the coalition government. Mussolini announced various measures, including renouncing atheism, making religious education compulsory, banning contraception and punishing swearing in public places. The pope, Pius XI, already a Fascist sympathiser, signalled his willingness to withdraw support from the PPI. In April, Mussolini sacked all PPI ministers from his government, claiming that they had refused to give him full support. Then in June, the pope forced the PPI leader, the priest Don Luigi Sturzo, to resign. The result was that conservative Catholics ceased supporting the PPI, which meant that, by the summer of 1923, it had lost most of its political importance.

Mussolini and his ministers meeting with leading members of the Catholic Church in the Vatican.

The Acerbo law

Now that he felt more secure, Mussolini announced his intention to reform the electoral system in a way which he hoped would strengthen his position even further. On his instructions, Giacomo Acerbo, the under-secretary of state, outlined a new electoral law designed to give the party (or alliance) which won most votes two-thirds of the seats in parliament, provided they obtained at least 25 per cent of the votes cast. This, according to Mussolini, would give Italy the stable and strong government it needed. In fact, given the likely intimidation and violence that could be expected from the Fascists and the fact that, as minister of the interior, Mussolini could order the police not to intervene, this law was clearly intended to give the Fascists total, but legally acquired, control over Italian politics. It also meant that there would be little likelihood of their opponents ever being able to vote them out of office. To ensure the passage of this law, Mussolini overcame the opposition (who greatly outnumbered the 35 Fascist deputies) by threatening to abolish parliament and by having armed Fascists guard the doors and intimidate the deputies. Liberal leaders such as Giolitti and Salandra advised their supporters to vote for this law and it was finally passed by parliament by a large majority in July 1923, although most PPI deputies abstained from voting.

The Corfu Incident

Having secured the passage of the Acerbo law, Mussolini now needed to ensure his party would win most votes in the next election. He was helped by the events of August 1923. When an Italian general was murdered on Greek soil while making maps of a disputed area on behalf of the Conference of Ambassadors, Mussolini took advantage of this opportunity. He demanded that Greece pay 50 million lire as compensation and make a full apology. When Greece refused to pay (as they were not responsible), Mussolini ordered Italian marines to invade the Greek island of Corfu. Even though the Greek government eventually paid the fine, they made no official apology. Mussolini was criticised by the League of Nations and was forced to withdraw by the Conference of Ambassadors. Nevertheless, the Corfu Incident (as it became known) led many Italians to view Mussolini as a national hero.

The April 1924 election

However, Mussolini did not hold new elections until April 1924. Prior to that, in January, he set up a secret gang of thugs and gangsters to terrorise anti-Fascists in Italy and abroad. Known as the Ceka, they were led by Amerigo Dumini, who had his own office inside the ministry of the interior. Once the elections were announced in March, Dumini's gang unleashed a wave of terror against anti-Fascists in which over 100 people were killed. During the election, voting certificates were seized, Fascists voted on behalf of dead people and ballot boxes were stolen in areas where Fascists thought they might have lost. As a result, the Fascists (and the right-wing Liberals, including Salandra and Orlando, who had formed an electoral alliance with the Fascists) won almost 65 per cent of the vote and the number of Fascists in the 535-seat chamber rose from 35 to 374. Despite the intimidation and vote-rigging, over 2.5 million people voted for opposition parties, mainly the Socialist and Communist parties.

The Matteotti Crisis

When the new parliament met for the first time on 30 May, Giacomo Matteotti, the Socialist leader, strongly condemned Fascist violence and corruption during the election. He actually dared to produce corroborating evidence and called the results a fraud. On 10 June, he was abducted in Rome. Although there was no hard proof, many assumed he had been murdered by Dumini's Fascist thugs and many began to distance themselves from Mussolini's regime. For a time, it seemed as though the revulsion at Matteotti's murder might actually bring down Mussolini, who was sufficiently worried to suspend parliament in order to prevent a debate.

Mussolini ordered the arrest of Dumini and his gang on 15 June; shortly after Matteotti's body was found on 18 August, Dumini was found guilty of his murder and imprisoned. Then some newspapers began to print evidence of Mussolini's involvement. This led most of the opposition deputies (mainly Socialists, Communists and radical PPI), under the lead of the Liberal Giovanni Amendola, to boycott parliament in protest. This became known as the Aventine Secession (based on a similar action in Ancient Roman history) and was intended to force the king to dismiss Mussolini.

However, the king refused to consider such an action and instead accused the opposition, who had set up their own alternative assembly, of unconstitutional behaviour. The pope gave his support to Mussolini by condemning the PPI deputies who had participated in the Aventine Secession. They were joined by Giolitti and Salandra and other leading Liberals and conservatives, who saw this as a way of reasserting influence over a now weakened Mussolini. They also feared that Mussolini's fall might be followed by a revival of the strength of the revolutionary left-wing parties. In July they supported his law on press censorship and in August his ban on meetings by opposition parties. When more evidence of Fascist violence emerged, Mussolini felt it necessary to promise to get rid of the thugs in the Fascist Party and sacked three Fascist ministers from the government. By November, however, some leading Liberals had joined the opposition in criticising the continued press censorship.

Mussolini's actions provoked a revolt by leading *ras* and some 50 senior officers of the MVSN in December 1924. They presented Mussolini with a clear choice: either he put a stop to any further investigations of Fascist violence and become dictator of Italy or they would overthrow him and replace him with a more hardline Fascist.

The rise of Fascism in Italy

5.1 Intellectual origins and content of fascism

We allow ourselves the luxury of being aristocrats and democrats; conservatives and progressives; reactionaries and revolutionaries; legalitarians and illegalitarians, according to the circumstances of the time.

Source: Mussolini commenting on fascist ideology in 1919, in R. Pearce, *Fascism and Nazism*, London, 1997, p. 7

5.2 The Fascist *squadristi*, according to a member of the Italian Communist Party

In the Po valley, the towns were on the whole less red than the country, being full of landowners, garrison officers, university students, rentiers, professional men, and trades people. These were the classes from which Fascism drew its recruits and which formed the first armed squads.

Source: Angelo Tasca, 'The rise of Italian Fascism', in H. Macdonald, *Mussolini and Italian Fascism*, Cheltenham, 1999, p. 17

5.3 The Communist International's view on the purpose of fascism, December 1933

Born in the womb of bourgeois democracy, fascism in the eyes of the capitalists is a means of saving capitalism from collapse. It is only for the purpose of deceiving and disarming the workers that social democracy denies the fascistisation of bourgeois democratic countries and the countries of the fascist dictatorship.

Source: Extract from the plenum on fascism of the Communist International, in R. Griffin (ed), *Fascism: a reader*, Oxford, 1995, p. 263

5.4 Fascist violence

And, however much violence may be deplored, it is evident that we, in order to make our ideas understood, must beat refractory skulls with resounding blows . . . We are violent because it is necessary to be so . . .

Our punitive expeditions, all those acts of violence which figure in the papers, must always have the character of the just retort and legitimate reprisal; because we are the first to recognise that it is sad, after having fought the external enemy, to have to fight the enemy within . . . and for this reason that which we are causing today is a revolution to break up the Bolshevist State, while waiting to settle our account with the Liberal State which remains.

Source: Extracts from a speech by Mussolini to the Fascists of Bologna, April 1921, in M. Robson, *Italy: liberalism and Fascism 1870–1945*, London, 1992, p. 51

5.5 Support for Fascism: a historian's view

Finally, there were sectors who assisted Fascism indirectly: although they could not bring themselves to support Fascism openly they were at least prepared to tolerate it in a way which would have been out of the question with, for example, socialism. One of these groups was the political establishment . . . Another was the aristocratic class, who were appeased by Mussolini's willingness to end his attacks on the monarchy. In fact, the Queen Mother, Margherita, and the king's cousin, the Duke of Aosta, were admirers of Fascism. A third sector was the Catholic Church, taking its cue from Pope Pius XI who, from the time of his election in 1922, remained on good terms with Mussolini. The Church undoubtedly considered a Communist revolution to be the main threat.

Source: S. Lee, *The European dictatorships, 1918–1945*, London, 1987, p. 95

Document case-study questions

1 What does document 5.1 tell us about the importance of ideology in the Italian Fascist Party?

2 Explain, *briefly*, the references to 'red' and 'armed squads' in document 5.2.

3 How useful are documents 5.2 and 5.3 as historical evidence of those sections of Italian society which supported Fascism?

4 Assess the reliability of document 5.4 as evidence of the reasons for Fascist violence in Italy during the 1920s.

5 Comment on the reference in document 5.5 to 'Mussolini's willingness to end his attacks on the monarchy'.

6 To what extent do these five documents, and any other evidence known to you, support the view that Fascism was based on the defence of capitalism?

The Fascist state, 1925–45

Mussolini hesitated before deciding to establish a Fascist dictatorship. He was determined that it would be a personal dictatorship and that he would be independent of the *ras*.

The establishment of the dictatorship, 1925–28

Increased violence

On 3 January 1925, Mussolini addressed the chamber of deputies. He denied setting up the Ceka and condemned the actions of Dumini's gang, but he went on to assume responsibility for Matteotti's murder, as prime minister and leader of the Fascist Party. However, he made it clear that he would not resign; he would continue to rule Italy, by force 'if necessary'. When Mussolini became seriously ill in February, Italy was ruled by Farinacci, the notorious *ras* of Cremona and newly appointed party secretary, who launched a new campaign of *squadristi* violence against the Socialist and Communist parties and the more radical sections of the PPI. As a result, several people were killed and many others decided to go into exile. Farinacci also supervised a purge of Fascist Party members, especially local leaders who were seen as insufficiently loyal to Mussolini.

The press

The first step in establishing a Fascist dictatorship was taken in July 1925 when Mussolini, now recovered, imposed a series of laws to control the press. Anti-Fascist newspapers were closed down and those remaining were only allowed to print articles approved by the government. From December 1925 all journalists had to be registered with the Fascist Party.

Central and local government

In August 1925 Mussolini took the next step in establishing his dictatorship. This time he focused on local and central government. Elected mayors and councils of towns and cities in the 93 provinces were replaced by appointed Fascist officials known as *podesta*. Although they were party members, they were mainly conservative and were drawn from the traditional landowning and military elites. In this way, Mussolini tried to ensure that the more militant Fascists were excluded from real power in the provinces. Fascist political control was further established on 3 August, when all meetings by opposition parties were banned.

Mussolini also moved to increase his personal power in central government. On 24 December 1925 Mussolini made himself head of government and in January 1926 he increased his powers to allow him to issue decrees without parliamentary approval and made himself responsible only to the king. The new law also stated that the king needed his agreement before anyone could be appointed as minister. Soon, Mussolini insisted on being called *Il Duce* (the leader). By 1929, he held eight ministerial posts himself, which excluded many other Fascist leaders from power. In practice, these state departments were run by the traditional conservative civil servants, which meant that little change was made to the status quo.

The parties

However, Mussolini's position was still not totally secure. The king and the chamber of deputies still existed, as did the increasingly harassed opposition parties. In October 1926, after yet another assassination attempt on Mussolini, all parties other than the Fascist Party were banned and their deputies were expelled from the chamber. At the same time, trade unions were outlawed and a new law court was set up to deal with political offences, some of which carried the death penalty. In 1927 Mussolini formed a secret police force, known as the OVRA, to suppress any political opponents. This was not, however, a specifically Fascist organisation, as it was essentially an adaptation of the interior ministry's secret police section. The OVRA was thus not the equivalent of the Nazi SS or Gestapo, as it was under state, not party, control.

In May 1928, when new elections were due, Mussolini took further measures to ensure that Italy would remain a one-party state. These included changes to the electoral system so that only men aged 21 or over who belonged to Fascist syndicates (see p. 118) could vote. The Fascist Grand Council then drew up a list of 400 candidates from lists approved by confederations of employers and employees; voters then had to vote 'for' or 'against' those on this list. Fear of Fascist violence meant that most Italians voted for, as Fascist officials in the polling stations were able to identify those who voted against as this required a white voting slip as opposed to the coloured one used by those voting for. Mussolini secured a clear electoral victory which made him the dictator of Italy. The king's power was drastically reduced.

The Fascist Party

However, this authoritarian regime was not a Fascist Party dictatorship, in that Mussolini deliberately restricted the influence of the party by retaining members of the traditional conservative elites in the police, the judicial system, the civil service and the army. Mussolini made no serious attempt to 'fascistise' the system of government by only appointing leading Fascists to positions of power. In 1927, only about 15 per cent of the civil service were said to be Fascists and both the interior minister, Luigi Federzoni, and the justice minister, Alfredo Rocco, were conservative ex-Nationalists. In the 1930s civil servants tended to join the Fascist Party merely to retain their jobs.

There was, however, a purge of the judiciary, in which many judges were sacked for lack of loyalty or for following too-independent a line. Mussolini frequently intervened in cases and imprisonment without trial became common, as Mussolini destroyed what impartiality the Italian legal system had had. The chief of police was another position that was filled by career politicians, not Fascists.

In January 1927 Mussolini issued instructions that all Italians – including Fascists – should be totally obedient to the prefects (the senior civil servants who ran the provinces and controlled the police). In the provinces, the prefects appointed the *podesta*. Once Farinacci had been dismissed in October 1926 (ostensibly for another outburst of *squadristi* violence, but really because he had begun to push for a 'second wave' of Fascist revolution), the prefects and the *podesta* set about stamping out *squadristi* violence.

The new party secretary, Augusto Turati, purged the party of more militant Fascists and allowed people to join who merely wanted to further their careers. Soon, there were very few 'Fascists of the first hour' left in important positions. This policy was expanded in the 1930s under Turati's successors, when the Fascist Party became a mass party with almost 5 million (mainly inactive) members by 1943. Most of its members were white-collar employees; the workers and peasants, who had once made up 30 per cent of the party's membership, had become a small minority. The Fascist Party was thus increasingly turned into a tame and loyal support base for Mussolini. At the same time, party posts were now to be filled by appointment from above, not through election by party members. The influence of the latter was further reduced in 1928, when the Fascist Grand Council was made part of the state machinery of government.

This gradual weakening of the Fascist Party, which resulted in it becoming the servant rather than the master of the state, was due in part to the divisions and disunity which had existed from its foundation. According to R. Thurlow, it had at least five different factions, including the militant *ras*, who sought a 'second wave' of Fascist revolution to replace state institutions with Fascist ones, and the 'left' Fascists, who wanted to establish a corporate or national syndicalist state – this latter group was led by Edmondo Rossoni, among others. Opposed to these two factions were the Fascist 'revisionists', led by Dino Grandi, Massimo Rocca and Giuseppe Bottai, who were prepared to co-operate and merge with the existing political system. Mussolini was able to play off these various factions against each other in order to enhance his own personal power. At the same time, he also played off different sectors of state personnel to ensure that no-one was able to challenge his power. One result of this, however, was to cause administrative confusion and weakness.

The corporate state

Those Fascists who believed that Fascism was a 'third way' between capitalism and communism favoured the creation of a corporate state. The corporate state would replace the traditional parliamentary democracy with a political system of corporations that represented the nation's various economic sectors. Along with state appointees, these corporations, each with equal representation for employers and employees, would enable class conflict to be overcome (thus avoiding strikes and other labour disputes) and instead give prime consideration to the interests of the nation. Although this system would increase state influence, there was no thought of eradicating private ownership.

The Fascist syndicates

During their rise to power in the years 1920–22, the Fascists had closed down the traditional labour movement trade unions in the areas they controlled and replaced them with Fascist-controlled syndicates which, theoretically, were still supposed to represent workers' interests. By 1922 a Confederation of Fascist Syndicates, headed by Rossoni, had been set up. Its aim was to create corporations (see below) that would force industrialists to make some concessions to workers' demands. However, this Fascist aspiration, coming from the left of the party, was not popular with the *Confindustria*, the organisation representing the main industrialists. In December 1923, when Mussolini had been prime minister for 14 months, the Chigi Palace Pact, in which industrialists promised to co-operate with the Confederation of Fascist Syndicates, was concluded. The industrialists nevertheless insisted on maintaining their own independent organisations.

Despite this agreement, many employers were not prepared to make any significant concessions to workers. Their intransigence resulted in a series of strikes in 1925. This was resolved by the Vidoni Palace Pact, which confirmed that the *Confindustria* and the Confederation of Fascist Syndicates were the only organisations that could represent, respectively, employers and employees. It was also made clear that workers were not to challenge the authority of employers and managers; all workers' factory councils were then closed down and all non-Fascist trade unions were abolished. This was followed up in 1926 by Alfredo Rocco's law which made all strikes illegal and stated that all industrial disputes had to be settled in special labour courts. It also made it illegal for there to be more than one organisation of workers and employers in each branch of industry and identified seven main areas of economic activity.

The corporations

In July 1926 Mussolini established a ministry of corporations, with himself as minister. Each corporation consisted of representatives of employers and workers from the same economic or industrial sector (e.g. mining) and three representatives from the government, who acted as referees and final adjudicators. In practice, this new ministry was mainly run by Giuseppe Bottai, the under-secretary. In April 1927 he produced the Charter of Labour, which promised not only fair judgements in labour disputes, but also social reforms such as improved health and accident insurance schemes.

However, the existence of corporations tended to weaken the Fascist syndicates and in 1928 the Confederation of Fascist Syndicates was abolished and Rossoni was dismissed. In 1929 Bottai took over as minister of corporations and in March 1930 he set up the National Council of Corporations (NCC) to represent the seven largest corporations. In 1932 Mussolini again resumed control of the ministry of corporations. The number of corporations grew slowly until, by 1934, there were 22 in total. These sent delegates to the General Assembly of Corporations (also headed by Mussolini), which was supposed to make important decisions about economic policy, including setting wage and price levels. In practice, Mussolini usually ignored the general assembly and made the important decisions himself. Most of the decisions that were made to deal with the effects of the Great Depression were not made by the corporations but by the government and employers, including the decision to cut wages. It should also be noted that most of the trade unionists experienced in industrial negotiations and disputes were socialists or communists and they were, therefore, dead, in prison or in exile. For this reason, employers had undue influence within the corporations, especially as the workers' representatives were usually selected by the Fascist Party or the ministry of corporations, rather than being chosen directly by the workers. Many of the representatives were, in fact, tame members of the Fascist syndicates or even middle-class careerists. In addition, the employers were nearly always supported by the three government representatives, who were Fascist Party members, even though they were supposed to be neutral.

In 1938, in a belated attempt to give more credibility to the corporate state, Mussolini decided to abolish the chamber of deputies and replace it with the chamber of *fasci* and corporations. The corporate state was supposed to be a new form of politics in which people were given a voice according to their economic function or occupation, rather than their geographical location. In reality, however, it had too little substance or power as it was dominated by Fascists appointed from above.

Economic policy

In many respects, Mussolini's main concern was not so much to create Fascism as a viable 'third way', as it was to make Italy a rich and great power. To do this, he believed it was necessary to make Italy economically self-sufficient in food and in raw materials for industry. This not only included overcoming problems of poverty and improving agriculture, but also conquering a large empire.

Mussolini's 'battles'

To achieve economic greatness – and in keeping with Fascist methods – Mussolini decided to launch a series of initiatives he called 'battles'. The first battle was announced in 1924 and was directed at trying to overcome the long-term poverty that existed in southern Italy. Called 'the battle over the southern problem', it promised to build thousands of new villages in Sicily and the south to wipe out the poverty suffered by so many.

In 1925 a much more serious campaign known as 'the battle for grain' was launched in response to a poor harvest and a consequent increase in grain imports. The aim was to get Italian farmers to grow more cereals, especially wheat, in order to reduce foreign imports. Import controls were imposed, which helped the inefficient farmers in the south to continue farming without having to modernise, and more land for grain growing was made available. This was done by ploughing up pasture land, olive and citrus orchards, and vineyards. In addition, medals were awarded to farmers who grew the most and their stories were reported in the newspapers. In the more prosperous north, farmers shifted from maize to wheat and also became more mechanised. This greater use of tractors and fertilisers also benefited industrial firms such as Fiat, Pirelli (rubber) and Montecatini (chemicals).

In 1926 'the battle for land' was begun. Its aim was to further increase the amount of available farming land. Marshes and swamps were drained, in particular the Pontine Marshes near Rome. This created many small farms and work for the unemployed, which was financed from public funds. Attempts were also made to farm on cleared woodland sites and on hillsides.

When the value of the lira dropped, 'the battle for the lira' was announced on 18 August 1926. In order to restore its value abroad and help stop price rises and to increase and maintain Italian prestige, the lira was revalued (by the application of 'quota 90') at just over 92 lire to the pound – a much more realistic exchange rate would have been 150 lire. This allowed Italy to continue importing coal and iron for armaments and shipbuilding.

In 1927 Mussolini launched 'the battle for births' in order to increase the Italian population. His intention was to build up a large army which would enable Italy to conquer a large empire, seen as being essential for both raw materials and national pride. His aim was to increase Italy's population from 40 million to 60 million by 1950 – Mussolini claimed that the ideal family size was 12. It was believed that this would be achieved by encouraging early marriages, giving maternity benefits, encouraging women not to take paid employment, giving jobs to married fathers in preference over single men and giving prizes to the 93 women, one from each of Italy's 93 provinces, who gave birth to the most children. By 1934, the total number of children produced by these 93 women was 1,300! Taxation was also used: bachelors (especially those between the ages of 35 and 50) had to pay extra taxes, while couples with 6 or more children paid none. Newlyweds were given cheap railway tickets to help them to go on honeymoon. Homosexuality was outlawed in 1931, new laws against abortion and divorce were imposed and attempts were made to exclude women from paid employment.

Success and failure

Most of Mussolini's economic 'battles' were far from successful, however, often because they were inconsistent. None of the new villages promised by 'the battle over the southern problem' was built. The 'battle for grain' succeeded in almost doubling cereal production by 1939, thus making Italy self-sufficient in wheat. However, it also involved the misallocation of resources and resulted in Italy having to import olive oil. Fruit and wine exports dropped, as did the numbers of cattle and sheep. The 'battle for land' resulted in only one area – the Pontine Marshes – being effectively reclaimed. (As it was near Rome, Mussolini saw this as a way of impressing visitors and tourists.)

The 'battle for the lira', which had involved artificially overvaluing the lira, resulted in Italian goods becoming more expensive and a consequent decline in exports and increase in unemployment – car exports, in particular, were badly hit. The revaluation also undermined the free trade and traditional financial policies Mussolini had adopted in the period 1922–25. It led to a recession in Italy, made worse by the Great Depression. The 'battle for births' was particularly disastrous. Despite all Mussolini's initiatives, the number of births actually declined throughout the 1930s and by 1940 the birth rate had dropped to 23.1 per 1,000 from 29.9 per 1,000 in 1925. In addition, nearly one-third of Italy's paid workforce continued to be female. This was partly due to the fact that Mussolini's military adventures led to the conscription of large numbers of men. Most of Mussolini's battles, which were intended to achieve autarky (self-sufficiency), tended to cause at least as many problems as they solved. This tendency was worsened by the effects of the depression.

State intervention

Before the depression, Mussolini had not interfered with private enterprise and had favoured the large companies and heavy industry. Once the depression began to take effect, Mussolini began to intervene. At first, this took the form of encouraging job-sharing schemes. By 1933, however, unemployment had risen to over 2 million, while millions more still suffered from underemployment, especially in the rural south. At its peak, over 30 per cent of labouring jobs in agriculture were lost and many women were forced to give up their jobs to unemployed men. The situation in the countryside was made worse by controls on migration from rural areas to the larger urban and industrial areas. This was designed to keep the problem of unemployment hidden in rural areas where the population was less concentrated.

In 1931, in an attempt to deal with these problems, Mussolini's government decided to use public money to help prevent the collapse of banks and industries hit by the depression. Then in April 1933 the *Institute per la Reconstruzione Industriale* (Institute of Industrial Reconstruction or IRI) was set up. Initially, it took over various unprofitable industries on behalf of the state. By 1939, the IRI had become a massive state company, controlling many industries, including most of the iron and steel industries, merchant shipping, the electrical industry and even the telephone system. However, the intention was never that these industries should be permanently nationalised. Parts were regularly sold off to the relevant larger industries still under private ownership, thus helping the formation of huge capitalist monopolies. Examples of this are the two giant firms of Montecatini and SINA Viscasa, which ended up owning the chemical industry.

Autarky

The effects of the depression led Mussolini to adopt increasingly protectionist measures and to push for autarky. This increased after 1935 when many member countries of the League of Nations imposed some economic sanctions on Italy following its invasion of Abyssinia (now Ethiopia) (see pp. 132–33). Once Mussolini began to involve Italy in further military adventures and wars, the push for autarky – and the problems it caused – increased accordingly. Nonetheless, there were some moderate achievements: by 1940, industrial production had increased by 9 per cent, resulting in industry overtaking agriculture as the largest proportion of GNP for the first time in Italy's history. In addition, between 1928 and 1939, imports of raw materials and industrial goods dropped significantly. Overall, however, the end result of Fascist economic policy was not a significant modernisation of the economy or even increased levels of productivity, and Italy recovered much more slowly from the depression than most other European states. Once Italy was involved in the Second World War, these economic and industrial weaknesses became increasingly apparent.

The social impact of Fascism

According to the 'third way' ideal, fascism was supposed to replace class conflict with class harmony. It was intended to bring equal benefits to employers and employees as they worked in partnership for the good of the nation, the state and the Italian people. It claimed that workers would no longer be exploited and that they would have a new, improved status under the corporate state.

The classes

In the first years of Mussolini's rule (between 1922 and 1925), male workers had experienced a drop in unemployment and an improvement in living standards. This was due partly to the orthodox and cautious economic policies followed by de Stefani, but was mainly the result of the general economic revival in Europe that took place in the early 1920s. (De Stefani, a Liberal, was appointed finance minister by Mussolini as part of his attempt to show the elites that Fascism was not a threat to them.) By 1939, however, it had become clear that only a small minority of people had gained any significant benefits from Fascist rule. Most Italians, especially the working classes, saw their standard of living and general quality of life decline under Fascism.

During 1925–26, workers lost their independent trade unions and their right to strike, and the promises made about the corporate state failed to materialise. Instead of ending class conflict, Mussolini's Fascist state merely suppressed the workers' ability to defend their interests, while employers were able to manage their companies without interference from the state or opposition from their workers. For example, as the economy began to experience problems in the second half of the 1920s, employers and the Fascist representatives on the corporations were able to extend the working week and cut wages at the same time (from 1925 to 1938, the level of real wages declined by over 10 per cent). As unemployment began to rise during the Great Depression, even the various public work schemes had little effect. In addition the relatively high level of unemployment also tended to intimidate workers into moderating their efforts to improve their conditions. For many, foods such as meat, vegetables, fruit, wine, sugar and coffee became so expensive they were unable to afford them and this was exacerbated by the effects of the 'battle for grain'. Social welfare legislation, including old age pensions and unemployment and health insurance, and a significant increase in expenditure on education, did not make up the tremendous decline in real wages and working conditions.

Despite Mussolini's claim to love the countryside and his promises to return Italy to a mythical rural innocence, the situation there worsened, if anything, under the corporate state. In general the north–south divide continued. Mussolini's policies benefited the large landowners more than the small farmers and agricultural labourers. A law introduced in 1922 to break up the large estates and redistribute the land was never acted on and agricultural wages were reduced by well over 30 per cent during the 1930s. Not surprisingly, many rural workers ignored the various government decrees intended to stop migration to the towns. They usually ended up in the slums of Milan, Turin and Rome. Rural poverty was made even worse when the USA drastically reduced immigration quotas, as over 200,000 Italians had already emigrated in the period 1900–29 in an attempt to escape Italy's rural poverty. Not surprisingly, therefore, many ordinary Italians did not develop a strong attachment to Fascism.

The lower middle classes, who formed the backbone of the Fascist Party, were affected in different ways. Many of those who had small businesses were quite hard hit by the impact of the depression and by Mussolini's various economic policies. However, those who worked for the administrative bureaucracy of the state or the Fascist Party experienced relative prosperity. They benefited from good wages and considerable fringe benefits as well as the opportunity to increase income via corruption, which was rife in Fascist Italy.

The classes who did very well in Fascist Italy were the large industrialists and landowners. The Vidoni Palace Pact of 1925 and the Charter of Labour of 1927 destroyed the ability of workers to defend, let alone improve, their living standards and increased the power of employers. Decisions made by the corporate state also benefited employers and worsened the conditions of workers. Even during the depression, the large firms benefited in many ways, either from large government contracts or from the financial assistance given by the IRI. This also helped in the creation of huge monopolies which, with no competition acting as a spur, militated against any significant modernisation.

The large landowners were another group that benefited during the depression, especially by the government's 1930 legislation that restricted the migration of rural workers to cities. The landowners benefited further in 1935 when special workbooks (*libretto di lavoro*) were introduced which had to be stamped by a Fascist official before a worker could leave an area to find work elsewhere. This helped to keep unemployment high in rural areas, a situation that was exploited by landowners in order to cut wages. There was certainly no attempt to redistribute land. By 1930, 0.5 per cent of the population owned 42 per cent of land, while 87 per cent of the rural population (mainly small landowners) owned only 13 per cent.

Women

Women suffered especially under Fascism as their status was deliberately and consistently reduced, particularly by the 'battle for births', which stressed the traditional role of women as housewives and mothers. This was reinforced by a series of decrees designed to restrict female employment; in 1938, for example, it was decreed that only 10 per cent of jobs should be held by women. Although this was intended to solve male unemployment, it also reflected Fascist attitudes towards women.

The Roman Catholic Church

Mussolini was a little more successful in widening the base of Fascist support in the Roman Catholic Church. Although he never really lost his early anti-religious views, Mussolini soon realised the need to reach an understanding with the Church. As early as 1921, even before he become prime minister, he was presenting the Fascist Party as an alternative to the traditionally anti-clerical Liberals and the atheism of the Communist and Socialist parties. The Church hierarchy was particularly pleased by the Fascists' destruction of the Socialists and Communists as a political force and recognised the benefits of ending the conflict between state and church, which had begun in 1870 with the reunification of Italy when the papacy lost most of its land. In fact, sporadic discussions with various Italian governments had been taking place since 1917.

Once installed as prime minister, Mussolini restored Catholic education in state primary schools. One result of this was that the papacy ended its support for the Catholic PPI. The real breakthrough came in 1929, following a series of secret negotiations with Cardinal Gasparri, a senior Vatican official. These resulted in the signing of the three Lateran Agreements in May, which finally ended the conflict and bitterness which had existed between the papacy and the Italian state since 1870. Mussolini accepted papal sovereignty over the Vatican City, which became an independent state, in return for which the pope formally recognised the Italian state and its possession of Rome and the former papal states in central Italy. In a separate but related agreement, the state paid the pope £30 million (1750 million lire) in cash and government bonds as compensation for the loss of Rome. Finally, they agreed that Roman Catholicism would be the official state religion of Italy, that there would be compulsory Catholic religious education in all state schools and that the state would therefore pay the salaries of the clergy. In return, the papacy agreed that the state could veto the appointment of politically hostile bishops and that the clergy would not join political parties. It was also agreed that there could be no divorce without the consent of the Church and that civil marriages were no longer necessary.

What this meant was that Catholicism was able to continue as a potential rival ideology to Fascism (thus blocking any chance of establishing a truly totalitarian dictatorship), but Mussolini was satisfied because the pope and the Catholic Church now officially backed him as *Il Duce*, which in turn pleased large numbers of Italian Catholics. However, relations between the state and church were not always smooth. In 1928 rivalry between Catholic and Fascist youth movements led to the banning of the Catholic scout organisation, which continued even after the Lateran Agreements. In 1931 government attempts to suppress the Church's Catholic Action youth organisation, which offered an alternative to the Fascist Party's youth and leisure organisations, provoked another brief conflict. Mussolini suspected that Catholic Action and the FUCI, the Catholic university students' organisation, were being used by ex-PPI activists to foment opposition to the Fascist regime. These suspicions were justified as both the FUCI and the Catholic *Movimento Laureati*, dedicated to creating a new political order, did offer some opposition to Fascist aims and, in the late 1930s, even began to form potential rival political centres around some leading members of the Church hierarchy. However, the dispute over Catholic Action was soon resolved by compromise: Catholic Action was allowed to continue, but was restricted to religious activities. It is significant that this compromise came after the pope publicly criticised the Fascist oath of loyalty and Fascist interference in educational and family matters as it shows that Mussolini lacked control over the Catholic Church. Despite this agreement, by 1939 Catholic Action had created several youth organisations which competed with Fascist paramilitary, social and cultural groups.

Although the Church was in agreement with several Fascist policies, such as the invasion of Abyssinia and involvement in the Spanish Civil War, which were seen as 'Christian crusades' against 'barbarism' and communism, as well as Mussolini's opposition to contraception and abortion, several other disagreements emerged. The creed of the *Opera Nazionale Balilla* (see p. 129), for instance, was opposed as it was seen as 'blasphemous'. Thus it is clear that the Church was never fully controlled by Mussolini.

Racism

While explicit racism was not part of the early Fascist movement, an underlying racist attitude was part of Mussolini's and the Fascist Party's imperialist expansionist plans. It was believed that the Italian 'race' was superior to those African 'races' in Libya and Abyssinia. The Abyssinian invasion raised race as a public issue and Mussolini had been angered by opposition to this invasion from, among others, some Jewish organisations. Racism was also a strong element in the Romanita movement (see p. 130).

However, anti-Semitism did not play a part in Fascist politics until the signing of the Rome–Berlin Axis in 1936. In fact, in the *Historical dictionary of Fascist Italy* Mussolini had dismissed anti-Semitism as unscientific. Furthermore, some leading Fascists were Jewish and almost 30 per cent of Italian Jews were members of the Fascist Party. Mussolini had previously appointed a Jewish minister of finance (Guido Jung) and at one point he had a Jewish mistress.

Mussolini's adoption of anti-Semitism, signalled by the issuing of the Charter of Race in July 1938, was in response to pressure from Hitler. It was drawn up by Mussolini and 10 'professors' and claimed to give a scientific explanation of Fascist racial doctrine. Their findings were based on the 'fact' that Italians were Aryans and that Jews, who were not, consequently did not belong to the Italian 'race'. This charter was followed up, between September and November, by a series of racial laws and decrees. These anti-Semitic laws excluded Jewish teachers and children from all state schools, banned Jewish people from marrying non-Jewish people and prevented them from owning large companies or landed estates.

Even though these laws were never fully implemented in the period 1938–43, in large part because Italians simply ignored them, they were strongly and publicly opposed by the pope. He criticised them for breaking the Concordat and for attempting to imitate Nazi Germany; in fact, these anti-Semitic laws contributed to the unravelling of the earlier alliance between Fascism and the Catholic Church. There were also several senior Fascists who were unhappy about the introduction of these racial laws, including Balboa, De Bono, Federzoni, Gentile and Marinetti.

Despite this opposition, extreme racial persecution began in 1943 in the Italian Social Republic (known as the Salò Republic), which was nominally ruled by Mussolini following his overthrow as prime minister (see pp. 137–38). The brutal persecution of the Jewish people living there was, in fact, carried out by the German Gestapo and SS operating in this northern part of Italy.

Ducismo: the cult of *Il Duce* and propaganda

Mussolini wanted Fascism to penetrate every aspect of Italian life and society, and to create a 'new Fascist man' who would be strong, aggressive and willing to do anything to protect the nation. He intended to achieve this by building up his own image as the epitome of this superman, and by publicising the achievements of Fascism.

Il Duce

As Mussolini began to establish his dictatorship, he quickly realised the importance of a good public image and good publicity. He established a press office to ensure that photographs and newspaper articles projected a positive image of him and his activities. He was portrayed as youthful, energetic and an expert in a wide range of specialist areas and pursuits. He also set up state radio in 1924 – by 1939, however, there were still only about 1 million radios in Italy, which meant that there was only 1 set for every 44 people (in Germany the ratio was 1:7 and in Britain 1:5). To deal with this, public address systems were set up in cafés, restaurants and public squares, so that more people could listen to his speeches, and free radios were given to schools.

Mussolini also made full use of film and the opportunities it presented. He insisted that the state-sponsored newsreel films, which had to be played in all cinemas as part of the programme from 1926, showed him addressing large crowds of enthusiastic supporters and that he was always filmed from below, to hide his lack of height.

Propaganda

In 1933, Galeazzo Ciano, Mussolini's son-in-law, took over the press office (renamed the ministry for press and propaganda in 1935). Two years later, it was expanded to ensure that all films, plays, radio programmes and books glorified Mussolini as a hero and a new Caesar, and the Fascists as the saviours of Italy, and was renamed the ministry of popular culture (Minculpop). These and other attempts to regulate the arts were not very successful as traditional liberal culture proved too strong.

At the same time, Achille Starace, appointed party secretary in 1930, worked tirelessly to project an image of Mussolini as hero. Lights were left on in his office to imply that he worked 20 hours a day for Italy, while photographs and posters of Mussolini appeared in public buildings, streets and workplaces. Great prominence was also given to various catchphrases that were supposed to reflect Fascist ideals, such as *Credere, Obbedere, Combattere* ('Believe, Obey, Fight') and 'Mussolini is always right'. At press conferences, Mussolini was always accompanied by Blackshirt bodyguards, while all public appearances were attended by what soon became known as the 'applause squad', who whipped up sufficient enthusiasm for Mussolini's speeches, even at times resorting to prompt cards.

Much as this was based on current theories of crowd psychology. All public events, such as mass rallies and meetings, were consciously turned into political theatre, with full use being made of lighting and music. Mussolini also borrowed from the techniques used by D'Annunzio and the artistic events favoured by Marinetti and the Futurists. These methods not only added to the theatrical impact of Fascist propaganda methods, but also helped create a modern image for them. Even Goebbels was impressed by the Fascist propaganda machine. Despite all these efforts, Mussolini never established a complete monopoly: the independent Vatican Radio, for example, continued to broadcast.

Education and indoctrination

Central to the cult of personality was the way in which Mussolini presented himself and the Fascist Party as the only forces able to unite all Italians and make Italy great. As well as this and the use of force to coerce opponents, Mussolini also adopted various other methods to control the public, including indoctrination. The younger generations were of prime importance but, as we have seen, the Church's influence over the young remained significant and led to conflict.

In infant schools, the day started with a prayer that began: 'I believe in the genius of Mussolini', while in primary schools children were taught that Mussolini and the Fascists had 'saved' Italy from communist revolution. In 1929, it was made compulsory for all teachers in state schools to swear an oath of loyalty to both the king and to Mussolini's Fascist regime. In 1931, this oath was

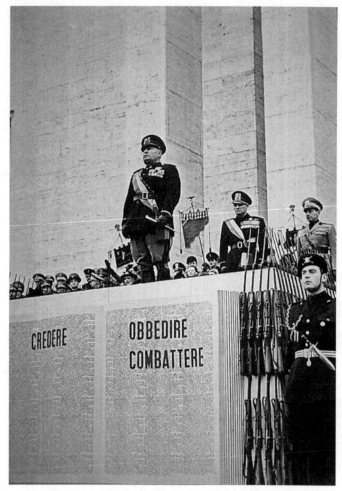

Mussolini at a typical public meeting. The Fascist slogan says: 'Believe, Obey, Fight'.

extended to university lecturers and only 11 resigned rather than take it. Mussolini was less successful in relation to secondary education as there were too many loopholes through which children could escape indoctrination. All school textbooks were examined and many were banned and replaced with new books, issued by the government, which emphasised the role of Mussolini and the Fascists. In 1926, for example, 101 out of 317 history textbooks were banned and, by 1936, there was only one official history textbook.

Fascist attempts to indoctrinate secondary school children were not helped by Giovanni Gentile, who, as the first Fascist minister of education, continued to concentrate on traditional academic education. Not only were classical courses (which allowed entrance to university) emphasised, but technical and vocational education was separated and downgraded. He also introduced exams which made it very difficult for most children to progress to secondary education itself; as a result, the numbers going to secondary school, and thus university, declined significantly. Protests from parents led to some modifications by his successor, Fedele, from 1925 onwards. Nonetheless, by the time Giuseppe Bottai became education minister and introduced the School Charter in 1939 (which promised to improve the status of practical subjects and vocational training), an important opportunity to help ordinary people and thus widen the Fascists' support base had been missed.

The Fascist Youth Movement

An important part of Mussolini's and the Fascists' indoctrination of the young was the setting-up of youth organisations. In 1926, all Fascist youth groups were made part of the *Opera Nazionale Balilla* (ONB). When the Boy Scouts movement was abolished in 1927, the ONB became the main youth group in Italy, apart from the Catholic groups. Boys aged 18–21 could joint the Fascist Levy (Young Fascists), after which they could apply to become members of the Fascist Party. In 1937, the ONB was merged with the Young Fascists to form the *Gioventù Italiana del Littorio* (GIL) and membership was made compulsory for all children aged 8–21. By then, the ONB's membership had risen to over 7 million.

All groups followed physical fitness programmes and attended summer camps, which included pre-military training, and older children also received political indoctrination. All members of the ONB and GUF (the Fascist University Groups) had to swear loyalty to Mussolini. However, the impact on school-children was not as great as was hoped – some 40 per cent of 4–18 year olds managed to avoid membership of these groups. Private and Catholic schools tended not to enforce ONB membership and many children, because of Gentile's entrance exams for secondary education, left school at the age of 11. In the universities, there was more contempt for Fascist ideals and even some resistance.

The indoctrination of adults

Mussolini also considered it important to influence the minds of adults and he attempted to achieve this by setting up organisations intended to control after-work activities. The *Opera Nazionale Dopolavoro* (OND) was set up in May 1925 to organise concerts, dancing and summer holiday activities in most towns and villages. It also established a vast network of clubs, libraries and sports grounds. By the 1930s, the OND controlled all of Italy's football clubs, along with 1,350 brass bands and 8,000 libraries. Membership had risen from about 300,000 in 1926 to over 4 million by 1939. Overall, about 40 per cent of industrial workers and 25 per cent of peasants were members. Sport was given particular emphasis and Italy began to do well in international motor racing, cycling, athletics and football competitions. Despite the fact that OND's main function was to increase acceptance of Fascist ideology and that its activities did result in some popular support, local organisers tended to ignore this aspect of the organisation, preferring instead to concentrate on the various sporting and cultural activities.

Between 1931 and 1939, a concerted attempt was made to expand membership of the party and its associated organisations to increase further Fascist influence among the masses. This process of uniting and incorporating the people was known as *l'inquadramento*. From 1931 to 1937, during the worst of the depression, the Fascist Party established its own welfare agencies to provide extra relief and also began to establish women's *fasci* to help run these agencies. Although these new networks and agencies led to increased party contact, surveillance and control, party membership did not increase dramatically: according to some historians, only about 6 per cent of the Italian population belonged to the party by 1939.

The Romanita movement

Another propaganda ploy to build up the prestige and popularity of Mussolini and the Fascists was to link them to the greatness of Ancient Rome and its emperors. This became known as the Romanita movement. Fascist writers, artists and scholars began to portray Fascism as a revival of Roman civilisation. From 1926, Mussolini was increasingly referred to as *Il Duce* and was portrayed as a new Caesar. Mussolini also adopted the *fasces* – the bundle of rods and the axe used by the lictor (speaker of the Roman Senate) to symbolise authority, discipline and punishment – as the Fascist emblem and had it incorporated into the national flag. He claimed that even the word 'Fascist' was derived from *fasces* and not from *fascio* (see p. 98). The Fascists' stress on establishing a second empire was part of this attempt to establish links with Ancient Rome and was reflected in the infant school prayer in which children prayed for 'the resurrection of the Empire'. According to those in the Romanita movement, the Fascist 'new man' was a modern version of the idealised Roman centurion.

Fascism and foreign policy

Although historians generally agree that Mussolini always wanted to make Italy a great Mediterranean power, with a large African empire, there are important disagreements about his actual conduct of foreign policy. While some see him as essentially opportunistic and inconsistent, others believe his policy unfolded and altered according to a systematic policy, not according to circumstances.

The pursuit of diplomacy, 1922–35

Initially, Mussolini was not in a strong enough military or political position to achieve his aims by force. The new state of Yugoslavia seemed to be a potential bloc to Italian ambitions along the Adriatic while, more importantly, Britain and France controlled strategically important areas in the Mediterranean (Cyprus, Malta, Gibraltar and Corsica) and in Africa and the Middle East (the Suez Canal, Egypt, Palestine, Morocco, Algeria and Tunisia). Although Mussolini's use of force in the Corfu Incident in 1923 (see p. 111) increased his support in Italy, it also showed him the relative weakness of Italy in the face of concerted Franco-British opposition.

For the next 11 years, Mussolini pursued a relatively passive foreign policy. He was often greatly influenced by the advice of traditional career diplomats. By April 1924, for example, he used a combination of diplomacy and unilateral action to force Yugoslavia to sign the Pact of Rome, which accepted Italian occupation of Fiume (a nationalist aim since 1919). At the time France, Yugoslavia's main ally, was too distracted by its occupation of the Ruhr to become involved. Mussolini continued to play the role of peaceful diplomat in 1925 by agreeing to the Locarno Pact in May and pursuing Italian interests in Albania by initially following a peaceful policy of economic penetration. In the following year, talks with Britain and France led to parts of Kenya and Egypt being handed over to the Italian colonies of Somaliland and Libya respectively.

Nevertheless, Mussolini was also using non-diplomatic methods to increase Italy's influence. He gave financial backing to an Albanian chieftain who seized power in 1929 and proclaimed himself King Zog; a treaty of friendship with Italy soon followed. He also increased his secret support of extreme nationalists in Germany, Bulgaria, Austria and Yugoslavia. Despite such activities, he signed the Kellogg–Briand Pact in 1928, which outlawed war. He signed the pact despite his growing dislike of French diplomatic moves in the Balkans (especially its alliance with Yugoslavia) which seemed, along with France's position in North Africa, to pose a threat to future Italian expansion. In particular, Mussolini objected to the Little Entente, which had been formed in 1927 by France, Yugoslavia, Czechoslovakia and Romania, as he wanted land that had been made part of Yugoslavia after the First World War but knew that France would make this difficult to achieve. By 1929 Mussolini had joined the calls for the 1919–20 peace treaties to be revised and was also plotting with Hungary to overthrow the king of Yugoslavia. At the 1930 international peace conference in London, his insistence that the Italian navy should be allowed to be as large as those possessed by Britain and France was not heeded.

In many ways, the period 1931–34 was a turning point. In 1931 Mussolini took particular note of the League of Nations' ineffectiveness in the face of Japanese aggression in Manchuria. Then in 1933 details of Italian arms deliveries to the right-wing *Heimwehr* in Austria and to the *Ustase* (a Croat terrorist group, based in Hungary, that wanted independence from Yugoslavia) came to light. These revelations disturbed Britain and France and caused the powers of the Little Entente to strengthen their ties with each other.

When Hitler became chancellor of Germany in 1933 Mussolini initially intended to play off Britain and France against Germany, despite Hitler being a fellow fascist. He tried to undermine the League of Nations by proposing a four-power pact between Italy, Germany, Britain and France. He put forward this proposal partly because he did not trust Hitler and his plans for expansion. He was particularly concerned over the Alto Adige area in north Italy because it contained many German-speakers; he also believed that Austria should be an Italian, not German, sphere of influence.

In September 1933 Mussolini signed a non-aggression pact with the USSR and in 1934 he attempted to establish closer relations with Austria and Hungary.

When Hitler attempted to take over Austria in July 1934 Mussolini acted swiftly to prevent this by placing Italian troops on the Austro-Italian border. In January 1935 he signed an accord with France and in April, alarmed by Hitler's attack on the disarmament clauses of the Treaty of Versailles and his introduction of conscription in March, he formed the Stresa Front with Britain and France in order to block the threat of German expansion.

Mussolini also calculated that siding with Britain and France against Germany might persuade them to take a more favourable attitude to his planned invasion of Abyssinia. Despite supporting Abyssinian membership of the League of Nations in 1923 and signing a treaty of friendship with that country in 1928, Mussolini had been making plans for this invasion since 1923. In fact, the Italians had made attempts to expand into disputed border areas on the fringes of Eritrea and Somaliland as early as 1929.

Aggression and Fascist 'crusades', 1935–39

Mussolini's first imperial war began on 2 October 1935 when 500,000 Italian troops invaded Abyssinia. Mussolini was determined to add Abyssinia (one of only two African states still retaining their independence) to Italy's two existing colonies in East Africa: Eritrea and Somaliland, both of which bordered Abyssinia. The invading forces met very little serious resistance as the

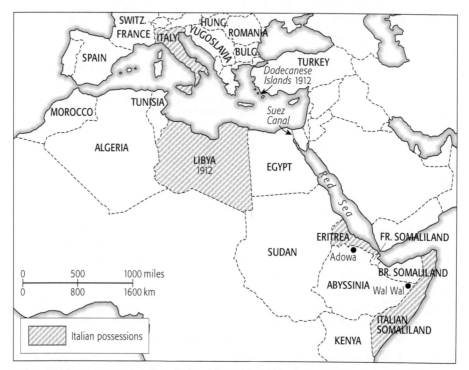

Italy's empire in 1914. Note the position of Abyssinia in relation to the two Italian colonies in the Horn of Africa.

Abyssinians were often only armed with spears, while the Italians had tanks and bombers, and used poison gas and mass executions to end resistance.

Mussolini's calculations about likely British and French reactions seemed confirmed when they drew up the Hoare–Laval Pact, which offered Italy two-thirds of Abyssinia. However, this deal collapsed as a result of hostile public opinion; instead, the League of Nations decided to impose sanctions on Italy. Up until then, Hitler had been supporting Abyssinia, but he changed his policy when Britain and France began to oppose Italy's invasion. He also took advantage of this crisis to reoccupy the Rhineland. This move put Austria under greater pressure, but Italy was now less able to prevent a German takeover as a rift had opened between it and its former allies, Britain and France.

The League's half-hearted protests against the invasion had little effect, especially as the limited sanctions specifically excluded vital war supplies such as oil, coal, iron and steel. In addition, Britain did not close the Suez Canal to Italian ships, while Germany totally ignored all sanctions and became a major supplier of essential raw materials. Consequently, Italian forces were able to capture the capital, Addis Ababa, by May 1936. Abyssinia was then merged with the other Italian colonies to form Italian East Africa. Thus, Mussolini's first steps in carving out a new Roman Empire were successful. Yet, despite boosting his popularity at home, the conquest brought little benefit to Italy. Abyssinia had poor agricultural land and not much in the way of raw materials. Mussolini's other priorities and lack of investment meant that he failed to develop the oil that existed in Libya. Furthermore, he had alienated Britain and France and made Italy increasingly dependent on a Nazi Germany that he still did not really trust.

By January 1936 Mussolini had informed Hitler that he would not object to a German *Anschluss* with Austria and had hinted that he would not support any League of Nations actions should Hitler reoccupy the Rhineland. Then on 6 March he followed Hitler's lead and took Italy out of the League of Nations. This shift to a pro-German policy was confirmed in June 1936 when, almost immediately after the end of the Abyssinian war and before Italy had recovered from its losses, he agreed to join Hitler in intervening in the Spanish Civil War. The signing of the Rome–Berlin Axis in October 1936 confirmed their joint opposition to communism and they agreed to divide Europe into spheres of influence, with Italy to have the Mediterranean and the Balkans.

Soon Mussolini had sent over 70,000 Italian troops to Spain to help the right-wing military, headed by General Franco, overthrow the democratically elected Popular Front government. As Franco was supported by the pope, Mussolini found it relatively easy to persuade Italians of the necessity for intervention. In fact, Mussolini made much more of a commitment to Spain than either Hitler or Stalin. The overall cost of Italy's intervention was over 10 billion lire: Mussolini provided over 600 planes and nearly 1,000 tanks as well as over 90 warships; some 6,000 Italian soldiers were killed in the war. Yet, as with Abyssinia, this military adventure brought very few tangible results, apart from the islands of Mallorca and Menorca. Mussolini was also angered and embarrassed by the fact that Italian exiles, fighting as volunteers for the Popular Front government, played a big part in the defeat of Italian troops at the battle of Guadalajara in March 1937. This victory encouraged anti-Fascists in Italy, which led to renewed efforts on the part of Mussolini's secret police to assassinate exiles abroad.

Mussolini noted the great reluctance of Britain and France to risk war over their intervention in Spain – to the extent that they refused to respond to the destruction of British and French merchant ships by Italian bombers and submarines. This led to a further widening of the breach between himself and his former Stresa Front allies. In contrast, Hitler was offering an alliance with Nazi Germany. The Rome–Berlin Axis between these two facist regimes, signed in October 1936, marked a significant turning point in Italy's foreign and diplomatic relations. The two fascist dictators moved even closer together in November 1937 when Mussolini joined Germany and Japan in their Anti-Comintern Pact (formed originally in November 1936), which was intended to oppose communism and the Soviet Union.

The following year, this new fascist alliance enabled Hitler finally to carry out *Anschluss* with Austria in March, in defiance of the Treaty of Versailles. This time Mussolini just stood aside, despite the fact that Hitler had not given Mussolini the advance notice he had promised for any such invasion. It was perhaps for this reason that Mussolini signed a pact of friendship with Britain in April 1938 and resisted strong pressure from Hitler to sign a firm military alliance with Nazi Germany throughout this year. Although he tried to act as peacemaker between Germany, Britain and France at the Munich conference in September 1938, he also ordered the Italian navy to prepare for war against Britain in the Mediterranean. This was partly because he had finally been convinced at this conference that Britain and France would never take any firm action to curb German expansion. This belief was confirmed by their lack of response to Hitler's takeover of the rest of Czechoslovakia in March 1939, following his occupation of the Sudetenland in 1938. Consequently Mussolini decided it was time to act: in April 1939 he annexed Albania and turned it into an Italian protectorate. Ominously, Italian troops had difficulty in conquering even this small state.

Any wavering on Mussolini's part was ended in May 1939, when Mussolini and Hitler finally signed a formal military alliance known as the Pact of Steel. This committed Italy to fight on Germany's side, should war break out. Mussolini warned Hitler that Italy needed at least three years of peace in order to recover sufficiently from the effects of the Abyssinian and Spanish wars before becoming involved in another conflict. Mussolini was thus again taken by surprise when Hitler invaded Poland on 1 September 1939, so beginning the Second World War.

The impact of the Second World War, 1940–45

Despite Mussolini's boasts that Fascist Italy had enough planes to blot out the sun and 8 million reservists as well as 150 army divisions well supplied with modern weapons, the reality of Italian military strength was very different. By September 1939, Italy only had 10 divisions (about 700,000 men) ready to fight. Although the army eventually numbered about 3 million men, only about half of them had rifles and many of these were old fashioned, as was their artillery. The army had about 1,500 armoured cars and light tanks, but fewer than 100 heavy tanks. Most of the airforce's 1,000 planes had unreliable radios and were generally inferior. In addition, Italy had no long-range bombers. Although the navy, which was supposed to control the Mediterranean, had new battleships, it had no aircraft carriers. Italy did have more submarines than Britain, but most of them were inferior and about 30 per cent were destroyed in the first three weeks of the war.

All of this was despite the fact that, between 1935 and 1939, the government had doubled its expenditure from 30 billion lire to 60 billion lire (increasing the national debt from 2 billion to 28 billion lire) and that about 30 per cent of this had been spent on the armed forces and the war industries. Italy's various wars from 1935 to 1939, including the recent invasion of Albania, had accounted for most of this spending. Overall, Italy had been spending about 11.8 per cent of its national income on the armed forces, compared to Germany's 12.9 per cent, France's 6.9 per cent and Britain's 5.5 per cent. There was also considerable lack of co-ordination between the armed forces, despite Mussolini being minister of all three of the branches and first marshal of the empire. Mussolini had allowed his generals to resist modernisation in order to retain their support for his regime.

Economic weaknesses

In addition to this lack of military preparedness, Italy lacked sufficient stocks of raw materials to sustain a major war. Mussolini's plans for autarky in coal, steel and oil had not been achieved. Because of Italy's weak economy – in 1939, Italy was only producing 2.4 million tonnes of steel, compared to Britain's 13.4 million tonnes and Germany's 22.5 million tonnes – Mussolini was dependent on Germany and the Axis-occupied territories for the coal, iron and steel needed to sustain the large armaments industry required for a major war. As the war began to go badly for Italy, Germany was increasingly reluctant to send these vital supplies to such an ineffective ally.

Economic planning was also weak: Italy's steel production actually declined by about 20 per cent in the period 1940–43, making it difficult to replace destroyed planes and tanks. Italy was unique in the fact that there was a general decrease of about 35 per cent in industrial production during the war. A similar problem existed with agriculture, which experienced a general decline in output of about 25 per cent. Wheat production declined by about 1.5 million tonnes as so many peasants were conscripted. This led to food shortages and a growing dissatisfaction with the Fascist regime. This failure, which meant that such items still needed to be imported, increased the pressure for conquests and empire, in order to gain *spazio vitale* (living space).

Early campaigns

Despite the various agreements signed between 1936 and 1939, Mussolini did not join Hitler in his attack on Poland. The commission on war production warned that Italy would not be ready to wage war until 1949. The king, who recognised the weakness of the Italian armed forces, argued forcefully that Italy should delay its entry into the war. As a result of these warnings, Mussolini demanded from Germany huge supplies of strategic resources and when these were not forthcoming he declared that Italy could not participate in the war. Instead, Mussolini sent agricultural and industrial labourers to Germany to help Hitler's war machine. In the event, Italy stayed out of the war until 10 June 1940, at which point, believing that France was about to surrender to Germany's armies, Mussolini sent troops to seize land along the French Riviera. Again, the Italian army did not do well in this Alpine War, despite France being near total defeat. Italian troops were forced to withdraw without obtaining any land. To make matters worse, Hitler (who had expected Mussolini to attack the British in Malta) refused to let Italy have France's North African colonies, allowing Vichy France to retain them instead.

A frustrated Mussolini then looked for another easy victim: with Britain seemingly near defeat, Italian forces grabbed British Somaliland in August 1940 and attacked Egypt in September. Then in October (in part to block German influence in the Balkans, following Hitler's occupation of Romania), he ordered an invasion of Greece. Determined Greek resistance meant that this campaign also went badly. In Africa, meanwhile, over 100,000 Italians were captured by British forces in Egypt. In November 1940 the Italian navy was beaten by the British at the battle of Taranto; a further defeat, at Matapan in March 1941, left Britain in control of the Mediterranean.

The following year was even more disastrous for Italy: in Africa, Italian forces were defeated by Britain at Tobruk, followed by an invasion of Italian East Africa. By May over 250,000 Italian soldiers had been captured and Haile Selassie was restored as ruler of Abyssinia. German troops (which had already invaded Greece and Yugoslavia in April 1941 in order to assist the Italians) had to be diverted to help Italy retain control of Libya, its last remaining colony. Mussolini, embarrassed by these failures and suspicious that Hitler might now ignore previous agreements about spheres of influence, decided to send Italian troops to help in the Nazi invasion of the USSR in June 1941. Initially, some 60,000 troops were provided, but the total soon rose to over 250,000. He also sent military equipment, which Italy could ill afford.

The emergence of opposition at home, 1941–43

One result of these setbacks was the first signs of internal opposition, marked by the outbreak of some strikes in 1941. By this time Germany was taking more from Italy than it was giving. About 50 per cent of the 350,000 workers sent to Germany by Mussolini were skilled and Italy was still supplying Germany with coal and iron. Food supplied to Germany had led to real food shortages in Italy. As a result, rationing was introduced in 1941 – the ration of 150 grams of bread per person was the lowest in Europe after the USSR and led to the growth of the black market. Despite all this, Mussolini was persuaded by Hitler to declare war on the USA in December 1941.

In 1942 Axis troops in Africa led by Rommel had some initial successes. After the battle of El Alamein in October 1942 and the Allied Operation Torch, however, Rommel was forced to retreat in the face of a combined force of British and US troops. Towards the end of 1942, Allied bombing of Italy was increased. Poor Italian anti-aircraft defences resulted in much destruction; as production was stepped up to compensate for these losses, hours of work and factory discipline were increased. This resulted in a great wave of strikes in March 1943.

The military situation also deteriorated during 1943. In Africa, Axis troops were forced to surrender in May (resulting in the loss of Libya), while in July the Allies invaded Sicily and began bombing Rome. The invading Allies met only token resistance as, by then, many Italians blamed Mussolini for the defeats and had also come to dislike the German armies that had begun moving into Italy. Many Italians, including the industrialists and the lower middle classes who had been the backbone of Fascism, had by now become disillusioned by the government's inefficiency and corruption and by nepotism involving the family of Mussolini's current mistress, Clara Petacci. Mussolini tried to deal with this disaffection between February and April 1943 by sacking or demoting several ministers and high-ranking members of the Fascist Party, including Grandi, Ciano and Bottai. However, this only led to plots against him, as many were critical of his strategy and especially of his closeness to Nazi Germany. These Fascists now wanted him removed from power. Another faction, which included Farinacci and Scorza, the new party secretary, wanted to forge closer links with Germany.

Mussolini's fall, July 1943

The setbacks of the summer of 1943 finally led to a coup against Mussolini on 24 July 1943, when the Fascist Grand Council voted 19 to 7 to remove him from power. On 25 July the king formally ordered Mussolini to resign. He was then arrested and imprisoned. The ease with which this happened underlines the fact that Mussolini had never been able to impose a totalitarian regime on Italy. Mussolini was replaced by Marshal Badoglio, who announced Italy's surrender to the Allies on 8 September 1943.

The Italian Social Republic

In September 1943, Mussolini was rescued by German paratroopers, who took him to Germany, where Hitler persuaded him to set up a new Fascist state in the north-east of Italy, which was not yet under Allied occupation. This Italian Social Republic (soon contemptuously known as the Salò Republic after the town in which Mussolini had his headquarters) was little more than a German puppet state, despite Mussolini's claims to be returning to the social idealism of his original fascism. He issued a Socialisation Law in February 1944, in which a form of nationalisation of firms (known as socialisation) replaced corporatism. In practice, as the German army and the SS controlled the area, the important decisions were taken by Rahn, the German ambassador, and by SS General Wolff. This area experienced much SS and Gestapo brutality – especially against

Jewish people – and thousands of Italian men were sent to Germany as forced labour. At the same time, Fascist extremists made a determined effort to round up the plotters of July 1943. Several were eventually captured and executed in the Salò Republic, including Ciano, Mussolini's son-in-law.

The end

During 1944 the Allies continued to push up into Italy and in April 1945, when they captured Bologna, the Germans decided to pull out of Italy. Mussolini tried to flee with them, but was recognised by a group of Italian partisans and was arrested on 27 April. The following day he was taken by another group of communist-led partisans and he and his mistress were shot. Fifteen other Fascist leaders and ministers, including Farinacci and Starace, were also executed. Their bodies were hung, upside down, outside a garage in Milan, where a group of partisans had been executed by the Germans for resistance activities.

7 Weimar Germany and the rise of Nazism, 1919–33

Russia and Italy were not the only countries to be adversely affected by the First World War and the subsequent peace treaties. Germany, too, suffered in several respects and, like Russia and Italy, had also experienced certain problems prior to 1914. The situations in Italy in the early 1920s and Germany in the 1920s and 1930s were quite similar: in both countries there was economic dislocation, dissatisfaction concerning the war and the peace treaties, growing support for communism, nationalist grievances and a relatively ineffective democratic system.

Germany's problems, 1918–20

War and the Weimar Republic, 1918–19

After four years of war, Germany was facing extreme difficulties: over 2 million troops had been killed and the Allied naval blockade had exacerbated the effects of the economic impact of total war and a series of bad harvests and severe winters. By 1918, many German civilians were suffering from serious shortages of food and fuel as well as the problems caused by inflation.

In early October 1918 the German High Command, led by von Ludendorff and von Hindenburg, realised that these problems – combined with the growing number of US troops joining the Allies on the western front – were bringing the German army near to total military collapse. In an attempt to avoid responsibility for the impending defeat of Germany, they advised Kaiser Wilhelm II to appoint Prince Max von Baden as chancellor and to instruct him to negotiate an armistice. US President Woodrow Wilson insisted that the authoritarian political structures of the Second Reich be replaced by a democratic system before real negotiations could take place. As a first step, Prince Max persuaded the kaiser to remove von Ludendorff as commander of the army.

In late October and early November these attempts to impose some democracy from above were overtaken by more revolutionary developments from below. After naval mutinies in Kiel and Wilhelmshaven, the collapse of military discipline spread to other centres, including Hamburg and Cologne, while in the monarchical state of Bavaria, socialists led by Kurt Eisner declared an independent republic. These events helped bring about the total collapse of the imperial regime. On 9 November Prince Max resigned and the kaiser, along with other local rulers, abdicated and fled. Philipp Scheidemann, a leading member of the Social Democratic Party (*Sozialdemokratische Partei Deutschlands* or SPD), declared Germany a republic and Friedrich Ebert, the leader of the SPD, became head of a provisional coalition government which also included the Independent Social Democratic Party (*Unabhängige Sozialdemokratische Partei Deutschlands* or USPD). One of its first acts was to sign an armistice with the Allies on 11 November.

Despite these developments, the political turmoil continued as the SPD came under pressure from more revolutionary groups, such as the Spartacists led by the Marxists Karl Liebknecht and Rosa Luxemburg. Inspired by the Bolshevik Revolution of November 1917, they wanted Germany to become a soviet-based republic. In December 1918, the USPD withdrew from the coalition government and began to work with the Spartacists. Their attempt to begin a workers' revolution in Berlin in January 1919 was bloodily suppressed by the army and the *Freikorps* (a right-wing paramilitary group of ex-soldiers). They had been called in by Ebert after they had threatened to suppress the revolt with or without his approval and to bring down his provisional government at the same time. Another attempt at revolution in March 1919 resulted in an even more bloody suppression. In April regular troops and the *Freikorps* carried out a brutal suppression of the Bavarian Soviet Republic which had recently been proclaimed by the Marxist Eugene Levine, following Eisner's assassination by a right-wing group. As a result, the revolutionary left – and especially the Spartacists, who renamed themselves the German Communist Party (*Kommunist-ische Partei Deutschlands* or KPD) – bore a bitter grudge against the new SPD government.

Meanwhile, elections for a new constituent assembly (*Reichstag*) were held in January 1919. The deputies decided to hold their initial meeting in the small town of Weimar because of the fighting in Berlin (hence Germany was often referred to as Weimar Germany in the years 1918–33). A coalition government was formed by the SPD, the Catholic Centre Party (*Zentrum* or ZP) and the German Democratic Party (*Deutsche Demokratische Partei* or DDP). With Ebert as president and Scheidemann as chancellor, a special committee was set up to draft a new constitution for Germany. This new government not only faced opposition from the USPD and KPD on the far left, but also from the Nationalists (*Deutsche Nationale Volkspartei* or DNVP) and the People's Party (*Deutsche Volkspartei* or DVP) on the right.

The weaknesses of Weimar

The right blamed all Germany's problems – especially Germany's defeat – on the new democratic Weimar government. In order to protect their reputations army leaders had helped to create the *Dolchstosslegende* ('stab in the back' myth) to explain Germany's defeat. They claimed that Germany had been destroyed by the revolutionary socialists and the Jews, just when it was on the point of winning the war. This seemed feasible to most Germans as they had been kept ignorant of many German defeats and Allied troops had never actually reached Germany's borders. Socialists and Jews were also blamed for the destruction of imperial Germany and for all the political upheavals in late 1918 and early 1919.

Weimar democracy was seen to be the result of Germany's defeat, interference by the Allies and the wicked plots of liberals and socialists.

Another factor that was to play a part in the future weakness of the Weimar republic was the new constitution itself, which was finally agreed in August 1919. The electoral system was based on a form of proportional representation which allowed even small parties to gain seats in the *Reichstag*. One consequence of this was that no one party was able to form a majority government, which led to a succession of coalition governments. In the 1919 elections the SPD, the ZP and the DDP gained 76 per cent of the vote between them (78 per cent of the seats in the *Reichstag*). In the 1920 election, however, their support dropped to 48 per cent and so led to minority coalition governments dependent on the support of some of the smaller parties. After Stresemann persuaded a section of the DVP to join the government in 1923, the SPD withdrew and remained an opposition party until 1928. As a result, some governments were forced to include members of the right-wing DNVP in order to govern with sufficient support in the *Reichstag*.

A more significant potential weakness of the new Weimar constitution was Article 48, which allowed the president (elected every seven years) to declare a state of emergency and to use special powers to rule by decree, thus by-passing the *Reichstag*. The president also appointed the chancellor, who was supposed to have majority support in the *Reichstag*.

In 1919 the new Weimar democracy suffered another political setback, which further undermined its support among most of the German population: this was the Treaty of Versailles, signed in June. The Germans had signed it under duress as the Allies had not negotiated with the representatives of the new democratic German state, but had merely presented them with the choice of signing it or resuming the war. The latter was not a realistic option, even according to the German military high command. The new government felt the terms were too harsh and did protest, and Chancellor Scheidemann even resigned, so strong were his feelings, but eventually his successor, Bauer, was compelled to sign the treaty.

The 'November Criminals' (as many nationalists described those politicians who signed the armistice) were blamed for accepting the terms of the Treaty of Versailles, especially for those clauses that imposed limitations on Germany's armed forces, took away all German colonies and some 13 per cent of its European land, and allowed Allied troops to occupy the Rhineland as a demilitarised zone for 15 years. They were also blamed for accepting the 'war guilt clause' and thus agreeing that Germany was liable to pay compensation or reparations for all the damage resulting from the war. In fact, most of the political leaders and parties of Weimar Germany were united in opposing many of the main items of the treaty.

Although the treaty was important in undermining public support for the Weimar republic, economic and political factors played the most important role in weakening it. Several of the terms of the treaty – especially the payment of reparations – helped to undermine the stability of the German currency and led to inflation. However, it is important to note that financial instability had already begun to appear in the closing stages of the war, leading to a devaluation of the mark, and this was made worse by the demobilisation of troops and the transition to a peacetime economy after 1918.

This dissatisfaction with the Weimar Republic resulted in an attempt by the right to overthrow the government in March 1920. Although Captain Wolfgang Kapp's right-wing *Putsch* failed after the Berlin workers called a general strike, it was ominous that the army – which had been all too keen to suppress revolts by the left – did nothing to help the government on this occasion.

Hitler and the Nazi Party, 1918–24

Adolf Hitler, the man who became dictator of Germany from 1933 to 1945, was born in Austria in 1889 to Austrian parents. In 1913 he moved to Munich in an attempt to avoid military service in the Austrian army. He was forced to return to Austria, where a military tribunal declared him unfit for military service in February 1914 after which he returned to Munich. However, when the First World War broke out in August 1914 he volunteered to fight in the German army and was recruited into a Bavarian regiment. During the war, he acted as a messenger, was twice wounded and twice decorated, and reached the rank of lance-corporal. It was while recovering from his second injury (temporary blindness resulting from a mustard gas attack) that he heard the news that Germany had surrendered.

The birth of the Nazi Party

Although there is no real evidence of Hitler having had any serious interest in politics before 1914, he had certainly started to develop an increasingly extreme form of German nationalism by this time. The signing of the armistice in November 1918 and the acceptance of the Treaty of Versailles in June 1919 seem to have been turning points in the development of his ideas. In common with a broad range of nationalist and conservative groups and individuals, Hitler blamed the new Weimar government, along with socialists and Jews, for 'stabbing Germany in the back'.

Although the war was over, Hitler remained in the army and returned to Munich to act as a political instructor. His main role initially was to combat the spread of socialist and communist ideas among the soldiers. This appointment was a reflection of the political turmoil that was developing in Bavaria and which, in late 1918 and early 1919, led to the creation of a short-lived socialist republic there. Although this was bloodily suppressed, the political atmosphere remained volatile. An extreme right-wing nationalist administration, headed by Gustav von Kahr, took over and was supported by the monarchists, national conservatives, the *Freikorps* and other right-wing paramilitary groups, and by the army.

It was in this atmosphere that Hitler was asked to act as an army spy to report on the various political groups still existing in Munich. The name of one group – the German Workers Party (*Deutsche Arbeiterpartei* or DAP) – seemed to indicate that it was plotting left-wing revolution. In fact, it was a right-wing group which had been formed by Anton Drexler in March 1919. Essentially an extreme nationalist party, it also included some vague socialist ideas intended to attract workers who might otherwise be tempted to support the socialists or the communists.

In many ways, the DAP was similar to many other *völkische* groups (nationalist groups which celebrated the 'purity' of the simple, folk community; they usually had racial overtones) that flourished in the early years of Weimar Germany – in fact, Drexler had taken the name DAP from a group set up in January 1919 in Berlin. In September 1919 Hitler was ordered to spy on this group, which by then had about 50 members. During one of its meetings Hitler spoke and then decided to join it. Significantly, several of its leading members were already linked to the army, including Ernst Röhm, who was a captain in the army's district command. This suggests that the military elites in Bavaria saw the DAP as a way of limiting the spread of Marxism among the workers.

The emergence of Hitler

Hitler soon became a prominent speaker and the propaganda officer for the DAP. In February 1920, with the support of some of his army colleagues, he was able to have the DAP renamed the National Socialist German Workers' Party (*Nazionalsozialistische Deutsche Arbeiterpartei* or NSDAP). It soon became known as the Nazi Party. The new party then adopted a new design, made by Hitler, which incorporated a black swastika on a white and red background. In April, Hitler left the army; nevertheless in December it gave him secret funds to help the NSDAP buy up a weekly newspaper in Munich. It was renamed the *People's observer* (*Völkischer Beobachter*). The rest of the money came from various leading Munich conservatives, especially Dietrich Eckart who, apart from financial help, gave Hitler many useful contacts among the Bavarian elites. The possession of a newspaper and the support of prominent people allowed the NSDAP to begin to set up branches elsewhere.

In July 1921 Hitler was elected party chairman in place of Drexler. Several important Nazis were associated with Hitler from the beginning. Apart from Röhm, there was Hermann Göring, a decorated *Luftwaffe* ace pilot, who had important contacts among the Bavarian upper classes. He was one of many leading army figures introduced to Hitler by Röhm. Also important from the early days was Alfred Rosenberg, who developed the NSDAP's anti-Semitic ideas, and Rudolf Hess. On becoming party leader in July, Hitler set up the Stormtroopers (*Sturmabteilung* or SA) with Röhm in command. Röhm recruited thousands of ex-soldiers and *Freikorps* members into the SA, which became a violent paramilitary group used by Hitler to disrupt the meetings and demonstrations of the Nazis' political opponents.

Ideology

In February 1920, the DAP gained more than just a new name and symbol. It also adopted a new 25-point party programme drawn up mainly by Gottfried Feder, who ran courses at Munich University on anti-Bolshevism for members of the army, which Hitler had attended in June 1919. However, Hitler had chaired the committee responsible for drafting the new programme. This programme was essentially a right-wing nationalist, corporativist and anti-Semitic one: it called for the overturning of the Treaty of Versailles, for all German speakers to be united in a greater German Reich and for Jewish people to be deprived of all rights of citizenship.

It also had a socialist element mixed up among the nationalism and racism which included calls for better pensions, profit-sharing in industry, helping small shopkeepers by restricting the large department stores, land reform and reducing the interest on loans. While many of the more militant members of the Nazi Party (especially among the SA) were genuinely behind these socialist-type policies, Hitler never saw them as anything but useful ploys with which to attract support from sections of the working class. This was vital if the Nazi Party was ever to become a mass party of extreme nationalism. It was this conflicting amalgam of nationalist, racist and socialist ideas which made the NSDAP unique among the many *völkische* groups.

Once Hitler had become leader of the party in July 1921, he began to push the leadership principle (the *Führerprinzip*). According to this, the leader should have complete authority and all members of the party should swear an oath of loyalty to the leader.

The Munich beer hall *Putsch*, November 1923

For some time, Hitler had been watching events in Italy with deep interest. His early admiration for Mussolini and his Fascist Party is shown by his decision to introduce the Nazi salute, brownshirt uniforms for the SA, and the greetings of *Heil* and *Sieg Heil*, all of which were based on Mussolini's propaganda techniques. He was particularly impressed by Mussolini's successful March on Rome in October 1922, which led to his appointment as prime minister of Italy.

Events in Germany in 1923 led Hitler to think that the time was ripe for a similarly bold initiative from the NSDAP. Despite surviving the right's failed attempt to overthrow it in March 1920, the Weimar government had continued to face hostility from the nationalists, conservatives and communists. Following the occupation of the Ruhr by French and Belgian troops in January 1923 when reparation payments were not made, this hostility increased. At this stage, the Nazi Party was still essentially restricted to Munich and Bavaria, although it had established groups in several south German towns. The occupation of the Ruhr was met by a campaign of passive resistance called by the German government, and a general strike by workers resulted in the French executing several Germans. In Germany the loss of resources from the Ruhr led to hyperinflation, which hit the middle classes or *Mittelstand* hard, especially those on fixed incomes – many went bankrupt or saw their pensions and savings wiped out. A large number of the *Mittelstand*, already unconvinced about the Weimar Republic, became deeply alienated from the new German democracy.

Although a new government, headed by Gustav Stresemann, began to stabilise the currency in September, many Germans were outraged when the campaign of passive resistance was called off and the government promised to resume payment of reparations. In November Hitler decided it was time for a March on Berlin, modelled on Mussolini's March on Rome, to overthrow the German government in a national revolution. Given his already close contacts with the political and military elites in Bavaria, Hitler believed he would be successful, especially as one of his supporters was General von Ludendorff. Hitler was also encouraged by the fact that the head of the police in Munich clearly tolerated the various right-wing gangs responsible for, among other things, murdering left-wingers.

On 8 November Hitler and a large group of SA members took over a meeting in a beer hall, which was being addressed by von Kahr, the head of the Bavarian government. Also present at the meeting were two other important members of the Bavarian administration: General von Lossow, commander of the army in Bavaria, and Colonel von Seisser, head of the state police force. Though these three were persuaded initially to support Hitler's plans (in large part because von Ludendorff later arrived to show his involvement), von Kahr and von Lossow later changed their minds. Despite now having no official support from the Bavarian government, army or police, Hitler decided to continue with his attempted *Putsch* on the following day. A group of about 600 armed SA men, led by Hitler and von Ludendorff, tried to take over government buildings. It turned out to be a fiasco: the police blocked their way and, in the fighting that broke out, 16 stormtroopers were killed and Hitler slipped and dislocated his collar bone as he ran from the scene.

Hitler was later arrested and, along with von Ludendorff, Röhm and other leading Nazis, was put on trial for high treason. The right-wing tendencies of the Bavarian judiciary were shown by the freedom given to Hitler to make long political speeches in which he tried to justify his actions. The trial was given plenty of newspaper coverage by sympathetic publishers, which gave the Nazis free publicity on a national scale. Though found guilty, Hitler received the lightest possible sentence of only five years. However, his plans of following in Mussolini's footsteps received another blow when the Nazi Party itself was banned.

The Nazis' 'lean years', 1924–28

With Hitler in Landsberg prison from January 1924 and his party banned, the Nazis began to disintegrate into warring factions. This was not altogether a disaster as far as Hitler was concerned as he began to make plans to increase his power over the party from his prison cell.

Party Führer

In prison Hitler began to write a definitive text which would contain all his beliefs on German unity and nationalism, anti-Semitism and foreign policy. By the time he was released early, in December 1924, this book – *My struggle* (*Mein Kampf*) – was virtually complete. It gave a reasonably clear view of the 'classless' folk community (*Volksgemeinschaft*) he wished to create, which would be ruled by a leader who would be known as the Führer, and a small elite group. Hitler also stressed the need to allow the strong to overcome the weak. He was deliberately vague about the populist, socialist elements in the Nazi 25-point programme drawn up in 1920; by this time the party had already become clearly nationalist with little real socialist content. He placed particular stress on the need to create a 'pure' Aryan master race (*Herrenvolk*) of supermen who would regenerate Germany and restore it to greatness. He also stated that the two main opposing groups to his plans were the Marxists and the Jews and in most of his book he deliberately attempted to make these two categories synonymous. Hitler presented Jewish people as an explanation of all Germany's problems and offered an easy solution: remove all of them from Germany.

The bulk of his book, however, focused on foreign policy, especially on overturning the Treaty of Versailles, uniting all German speakers (particularly those in Austria and parts of Czechoslovakia) in the same nation (Reich) and obtaining living space (*Lebensraum*) in eastern Europe. The latter aim would serve two purposes: destroy Communist Russia and make the greater German nation self-sufficient in food and raw materials.

Reorganisation of the party

When Hitler came out of prison in December 1924, he decided that the Nazi Party should declare its intention to seek power by legal and constitutional means. Nevertheless, he had no plans to abandon SA violence and was still determined to construct an authoritarian regime when he achieved power. As a result of this apparent change of heart, the ban on the Nazi Party was lifted and it was relaunched by Hitler in February 1925. It took Hitler over a year to re-establish his authority as Führer, because of strong opposition from some of the regional units of the NSDAP. This was especially true of the north German NSDAP, which was led by Gregor Strasser. They sought greater emphasis on the socialist parts of the 25-point programme, such as the nationalisation of main industries. It was not until February 1926, when Hitler was able to win over a majority to his views at the Bamberg conference, that he was able to assert his authority over Strasser and other similar populist units. This conference was also significant as it was then that he persuaded Josef Goebbels to desert the Nazi militants and come over to his side.

In order to strengthen his position, Hitler also drew up a new structure for the party in 1925. It was based on *Gauleiter*, who ran the party in each region and who were appointed by and were answerable to Hitler alone. He also set up various Nazi sub-groups for different sections of society such as the Nazi Teachers' Association, Hitler youth groups and, most significantly, the Protection or Security Squad (*Schutzstaffel* or SS). The SS was particularly important as it was seen as a potential counter to the growing power of Ernst Röhm and his SA, which contained many who still supported the 'socialist' elements in the party's programme.

All of this plus the use of very modern propaganda techniques (such as mass rallies, demonstrations and posters), which were deliberately aimed at specific sections of the population, served to spread Nazi ideas to a wider audience. These developments also underlined Hitler's central, unifying role and the need for the NSDAP to become a truly national party. Several right-wing *völkische* and racist groups were absorbed by the Nazis and party membership began to increase.

Economic revival and Nazi support

However, while Hitler had been in prison and the Nazi Party had almost disintegrated, the situation in Germany had begun to change for the better. Under Stresemann, who acted first as chancellor and then as foreign minister in the years 1923–29, the currency was stabilised by the introduction of a new currency, the *Rentenmark*. In 1924 the Dawes Plan was negotiated with the USA: it scaled down German reparation payments, made provision for important loans from the USA to regenerate the German economy and led to French troops leaving the Ruhr in 1925. It was also agreed that Allied troops would leave the demilitarised Rhineland in 1930, earlier than stated by the Treaty of Versailles.

By 1925, the German economy was beginning to pick up and extremist groups such as the Nazis on the right and the communists on the left were becoming increasingly marginalised. For example, the Nazis won only 14 seats in the December 1924 election and only 12 seats in May 1928. However, these figures do not reflect the full picture of Nazi strength in this period. Following their lack of success in establishing themselves in the major cities, Hitler began to concentrate on the rural areas. Though support for the Nazis was generally low, it was much stronger in such regions. In the agricultural districts of north and west Germany, for example, the Nazis sometimes polled as much as 10 per cent of the vote. They were also stronger in Protestant areas as Catholic voters tended to remain loyal to the ZP or the Bavarian People's Party (*Bayerische Volkspartei* or BVP). In such areas, they were able to pull support away from the DNVP and small right-wing groups, with support from landowners, peasant farmers and even agricultural labourers, who were particularly attracted by the Nazi promises of help and a return to an ideal rural folk community. Particularly important in helping to spread Nazi propaganda in the second half of the 1920s was the support of Alfred Hugenberg, the owner of a large chain of local and national newspapers and cinemas.

Nazi successes in such areas can also be explained by the fact that the Dawes Plan did not solve all of Germany's economic problems. It did contribute to a 17 per cent increase in German industrial production, which was a return to the level for 1913, despite the loss of land and resources imposed by the Treaty of Versailles. However, economic recovery was limited: farmers tended not to benefit from Stresemann's economic policies and unemployment remained at about 1 million. In addition, Germany's relative prosperity and its social welfare system were too dependent on foreign loans and investment. In 1928 alone, this amounted to over 5 billion marks. Furthermore, Germany's banking system was based on short-term loans to industry, which would not be repaid if they were to go bankrupt.

The collapse of Weimar Germany, 1929–33

By early 1929, it seemed as if Weimar Germany had overcome most of its political and economic problems and that, as a result, the Nazi Party had become redundant. In June, at a reparations conference in The Hague, Stresemann was able to secure a further reduction and restructuring of Germany's reparation payments. The Young Plan, which was negotiated with the USA, also included further loans for German industries. Then in October 1929 Gustav Stresemann died and the Wall Street Crash took place in the USA.

Depression and political paralysis

The crash of the US stock market signalled the end of US loans to Germany and the USA began demanding the repayment of those already received. This, combined with the onset of the Great Depression, rapidly brought an end to the relative prosperity Germany had experienced in the years 1924–29 and played a big part in the collapse of the Weimar Republic. Soon, many German industries began to decline and Germany was unable to afford to import the amount of raw materials and food it required. The number of bankruptcies increased significantly, as did unemployment, which was 1.4 million in 1928. This rose quickly to 2 million by the end of 1929; by 1930, the number of unemployed had risen to 3 million and several German banks had collapsed. In 1931 unemployment rose to 4 million and then to over 6 million in 1932. Millions more industrial workers were on short time and so also suffered a significant drop in income.

Agriculture also suffered as food prices plummeted, with small farmers particularly badly hit. Many small shopkeepers went out of business and the professional middle classes also suffered. More banks began to fold and industrial production soon dropped by over 50 per cent, while the unemployment rate rose to over 30 per cent.

As the economic crisis in Germany deepened, Hermann Müller's coalition government, composed of the SPD, ZP and DVP, found it increasingly difficult to agree on what measures to take. In March 1930 the coalition fell apart when the SPD refused to accept cuts in unemployment benefits. Its place was taken by a centre-right coalition headed by Heinrich Brüning of the ZP. However, he too failed to get his deflationary measures accepted by the *Reichstag* and President von Hindenburg began to resort to using presidential decrees under Article 48 of the Weimar constitution. This began the process of undermining normal parliamentary government in the Weimar Republic and played a big part in its final collapse. This system of government had never been very popular with large sections of German society, who were more familiar with the authoritarian rule of the kaiser than with democracy.

However, von Hindenburg's decrees were opposed by the *Reichstag* so, in an effort to increase his support, Brüning called an election in September 1930. The results were not what he had hoped for and he found that he still headed a minority coalition government. Though he was able to carry on as chancellor until May 1932, he was only able to govern by continued use of presidential decrees. In fact, from 1930 until its end in 1933, the Weimar Republic never again experienced a government with majority support in the *Reichstag*. Increasingly, parliamentary democracy was replaced by presidential rule by decree.

The role of von Hindenburg

Paul von Hindenburg, who was president from 1925 to 1934, was an important factor in the collapse of Weimar democracy. Ebert, the first president of Weimar Germany from 1918 to 1925, had used presidential decrees on only a few occasions. Von Hindenburg, however, was a militaristic, authoritarian man and had never liked democracy. Backed by the nationalists, the army, the landed aristocracy (the *Junker*) and certain industrialists (mainly those involved in iron and steel), von Hindenburg used decrees frequently, especially after 1929, even though Article 48 was only supposed to be used in times of real emergency. According to H. Boldt, 5 decrees were issued in 1930, 44 in 1931 and 60 in 1932. Von Hindenburg also increasingly used his power to appoint – and dismiss – chancellors: from March 1930 to January 1933, all Germany's chancellors were selected by him and they were all personal favourites. In addition, as shown by H. Ashby Turner, the group surrounding von Hindenburg, especially his son Oskar and his chief-of-staff Otto Meissner, played key roles in undermining Weimar democracy.

Brüning's deflationary policies restored international confidence in Germany's economy. The result of that was an agreement reached at the Lausanne conference in June 1932, by which Germany's reparations payments were cancelled. Despite this, many of Brüning's economic policies (especially cuts in government expenditure and increased taxation) initially worsened the impact of the depression. In 1932, Brüning helped von Hindenburg to be re-elected as president, but then he alienated the right by banning the SA and proposing that the estates of bankrupt *Junker* be taken over by the government and sold to landless peasants. So in May 1932 the Protestant von Hindenburg, advised by his son and a group of *Junker* and army officers (including General Schleicher), sacked the Catholic Brüning. Von Hindenburg was persuaded to appoint Franz von Papen, an aristocratic leader of the ZP, as the new chancellor.

Von Papen then formed a government composed of aristocratic landowners and industrialists (known as the 'cabinet of barons'), many of whom were admirers of Mussolini's authoritarian corporate state in Italy. He immediately declared a state of emergency and suspended the Prussian parliament, an SPD stronghold. As he had insufficient party support, he asked von Hindenburg to dissolve the *Reichstag*. New elections took place in July 1932 and, to secure Hitler's co-operation, von Papen lifted the ban on the Stormtroopers.

The growth of Nazi support

While the depression caused tremendous suffering for German people, it presented the Nazis with a real opportunity to break out of their weak and isolated position. By 1929, the Nazi Party had over 100,000 members and was increasing its support by targeting specific groups of people: peasant farmers, small shopkeepers, women, big business and the unemployed. The inconsistencies and contradictions within the party were successfully concealed by their concentration on local rather than national propaganda and by their focus on nationalist and racist ideas.

In the September 1930 election, the Nazis increased their number of seats from 12 to 107, winning almost 6 million votes (19 per cent of the vote). This made them the second largest party in the *Reichstag*. In the 1932 presidential elections, Hitler stood for the Nazis and gained 11 million votes (30 per cent) in the first round and 13 million votes (27 per cent) in the final ballot against von Hindenburg, who received 19 million votes. In this election campaign the Nazis had used propaganda effectively to raise Hitler's public profile and to portray the Nazi Party as a truly national force. Hitler used his charisma to sell his party's position to the German people. With increasing funds from leading industrialists, the Nazis were able to fight an even more extensive campaign in the July 1932 elections. This time, their number of seats increased to 230 (about 37 per cent of the vote), which made them the largest party in the *Reichstag*. It should be noted that under a 'first past the post' system, the Nazis would have been able to form their first government in July 1932.

However, this tremendous increase in support for the Nazis was also the result of their use of violence, which was stepped up in 1932. Despite their apparent abandonment of violence after the failed Munich beer hall *Putsch* in favour of democratic methods, SA violence had continued and was, in fact, much more extreme than the violence used by the Fascists in Italy in their rise to power.

The Nazis also benefited from the deep divisions and consequent lack of unity among the SPD and the KPD (the parties of the left), which, between them, polled more votes than the Nazis. The left had been quite strong – in 1919 they won 45.5 per cent of the votes – and although their combined share dropped to around 37 per cent in November 1932 they were still potentially a very powerful force. However, the SPD leaders distrusted the KPD and their call for a workers' revolution. As a result, they refused to discuss seriously a united front against the Nazis, which many ordinary members of both parties increasingly urged. Instead of combating the right, the leaders of the SPD were more concerned about the Communists: in 1932, for example, they allowed von Papen to take control of Prussia rather than call for a general strike which might have helped the KPD to gain recruits. In elections from 1930 to 1932, the more militant KPD certainly took votes away from the SPD, rising from 77 seats in 1930 to 100 in November 1932 as the SDP declined from 143 seats in 1930 to 121 in November 1932.

On the other hand, under instructions from Stalin, the leaders of the KPD followed the Comintern's 'third period' policy, which depicted the SPD (and all social democrats) as 'social fascists'. This clearly ruled out the possibility of any co-operation between the two parties. Communist policy during this 'third period' was that the depression would soon lead to a revolution that would sweep away both the SPD and the Nazis. In addition, many of the ordinary members of the KPD still bitterly hated the SPD for using the army and the *Freikorps* to suppress the Spartacist risings in 1919.

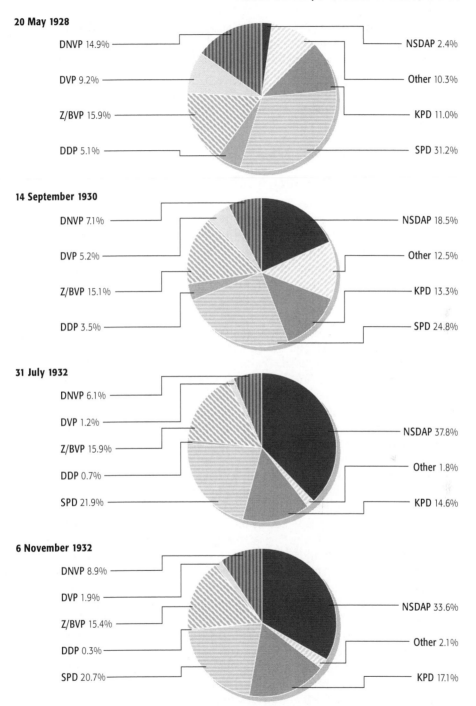

20 May 1928

DNVP 14.9%
DVP 9.2%
Z/BVP 15.9%
DDP 5.1%
NSDAP 2.4%
Other 10.3%
KPD 11.0%
SPD 31.2%

14 September 1930

DNVP 7.1%
DVP 5.2%
Z/BVP 15.1%
DDP 3.5%
NSDAP 18.5%
Other 12.5%
KPD 13.3%
SPD 24.8%

31 July 1932

DNVP 6.1%
DVP 1.2%
Z/BVP 15.9%
DDP 0.7%
SPD 21.9%
NSDAP 37.8%
Other 1.8%
KPD 14.6%

6 November 1932

DNVP 8.9%
DVP 1.9%
Z/BVP 15.4%
DDP 0.3%
SPD 20.7%
NSDAP 33.6%
Other 2.1%
KPD 17.1%

The Nazis' (NSDAP's) growing electoral breakthrough from 1928 to 1932 as percentages of seats gained in the *Reichstag*.

Hitler could also have been stopped by a centre-left coalition but, once again, these political groups in the period 1930–33 did not believe such co-operation was necessary. The centre included the right-wing liberal DVP and the left-wing liberal DDP but, although they remained committed to the Weimar Republic, they became increasingly powerless as their supporters in the middle classes switched their allegiance to the Nazis. There were also several conflicts between the SPD and the ZP. At the same time, parties such as the DNVP, which had been consistently hostile to the Weimar Republic, increasingly collaborated with the Nazis to weaken Weimar democracy.

The social base of Nazi support

Despite the significant increase in Nazi support in the years 1929–32, it is important to note that even as late as July 1932, this support varied widely. The hard-core Nazi supporters were from the lower 'old' sections of the *Mittelstand*: small shopkeepers, artisans and peasant farmers. Historians such as A. Bullock, K. D. Bracher and W. Kornhauser argue that by 1932 they were also winning votes from the upper layers of the *Mittelstand*: professionals (including doctors, teachers, civil servants and engineers) and from the 'new' middle classes, such as white-collar workers. Such *Mittelstand* groups tended to switch voting allegiances in the years 1930–32 – often away from the DDP and the DVP – and this goes a long way to explaining why the Nazi vote went up from 800,000 in 1928 to 13 million in 1932. These sections of German society believed that both the democratic and the authoritarian versions of Weimar government had failed to resolve their economic sufferings and to them the Nazis appeared to offer the only realistic alternative to the continued economic problems and the growing threat of communist revolution, even though the Nazis were violent and also spoke of revolution. The Nazis increasingly found supporters throughout the country, including farmers and landowners, Protestants and the self-employed, as well as those already mentioned. This widespread support resulted in the Nazis becoming a significant political force for the first time.

However, in the large cities the Nazis often only polled around 10 per cent – less than elsewhere – as many industrial workers continued to support the SPD or the KPD. Nonetheless, in the July 1932 elections the Nazis did receive about 25 per cent of the working-class vote, while some studies show that about 55 per cent of the SA and about 35 per cent of party members were from the working class. It is significant that those workers who supported the Nazis tended to come from the smaller towns and the villages.

Historians such as D. Mühlberger, T. Childers and R. F. Hamilton are still debating the actual extent of Nazi support among the traditional working class in the larger towns. In the past, it was thought that the Nazis received support from the working class as a whole, but local studies of results from particular electoral districts contradict this view. Such studies tend to show that most workers in trade unions, in large factories and in the bigger towns and cities continued to vote for the SPD or the KPD. Those workers who did vote for the Nazis, as Stachura and others have pointed out, tended not to belong to trade unions and mainly came from small firms and rural areas, and worked in handicraft and domestic industries.

The Nazi Party also failed to make significant gains among the unemployed. In the large industrial towns experiencing mass unemployment, the KPD often polled over 60 per cent of the vote. In places where the SPD lost votes, it was the Communists who benefited from this rather than the Nazis. In addition, most Catholic voters stayed loyal to the ZP or, in Bavaria, to the BVP.

Women were the other section of the population who came to support the Nazis in growing numbers in this period. This was mainly a result of Nazi propaganda about helping the family and a return to 'traditional values'. As with Nazi promises to other sections of society, there was clearly a contradiction between these promises of help and the fact that, in general, the NSDAP intended to force women out of the workplace.

Certain sections of young people, especially students, also came over to the Nazis in significant numbers during the early 1930s. These new voters were particularly attracted by the Nazis' apparently militant and dynamic attitudes to traditional institutions and by their simplistic solutions for solving the problem of unemployment.

Political intrigue and the elites, 1932–33

After July 1932 Hitler began to think seriously about becoming chancellor, but at this time the army and von Hindenburg were still supporting von Papen, so Hitler's chances seemed remote. This appeared to be confirmed beyond doubt after the November 1932 elections, which were called by von Papen to strengthen his position in the *Reichstag* after he was defeated in a vote of no confidence. This time, the Nazis' share of the vote dropped to around 33 per cent, with fewer than 12 million votes, and their representation in the *Reichstag* was reduced to 196 seats. This disappointing and unexpected result caused conflict within the Nazi Party, but Hitler was able to prevent any splits. By then, however, the collapse of Weimar democracy was accelerating, with the *Reichstag* meeting only 13 times in 1932, compared to 41 times in 1931 and 94 times in 1930.

By now the army had lost faith in von Papen as chancellor and in December 1932 army leaders persuaded von Hindenburg to replace him with Major-General Schleicher, who did have their confidence. Schleicher tried to split the Nazi Party by offering its left wing the chance to join a broad coalition which would include the SPD. This attempt failed as only Gregor Strasser was willing to make a deal – this led to his expulsion from the Nazi Party (see p. 154). Schleicher's willingness to make concessions to the trade unions began to worry the conservative elites in Germany. In fact, schemes for economic recovery via public works, implemented by Schleicher and, earlier, von Papen, would have been successful in time, given the fact that Germany no longer had to pay reparations. Indeed, these policies certainly helped Hitler reduce unemployment after 1933.

Von Papen began to approach important industrialists and landowners with a plan to remove Schleicher. He persuaded them that the Nazis had clearly passed their peak and that they could be tamed by the nationalists and conservatives in a new centre-right coalition under his leadership. Such a government was seen as increasingly necessary after the November elections, as the KPD vote – unlike that of the NSDAP – had continued to grow: the number of KPD seats went up from 89 to 100 in July.

The willingness of the conservative elites to trust Hitler was aided by several of Hitler's tactics after 1930. Like Mussolini, he was prepared to distance himself from the more militant sections of his party in order to get financial and political support from wealthy industrialists and landowners. For example, he had begun to hold discussions with traditional right-wing parties (especially the DNVP), army leaders, important industrialists (such as Fritz Thyssen and Emil Kirdorff, who were, respectively, steel and coal magnates), bankers and landowners. In October 1931 this strategy had resulted in the Harzburg Front being set up to oppose the Weimar Republic. Then, at a meeting held with leading industrialists in Düsseldorf in January 1932, Hitler had stressed his opposition to Weimar democracy and the threat of a communist revolution. He also assured them that he could and would control the more militant left wing of the NSDAP.

These elites were even more prepared to believe Hitler's promises by the end of 1932 when Gregor Strasser, the leader of the more militant section of the Nazis in north Germany, was removed from his positions within the party. He had openly opposed Hitler's increasingly close contacts with wealthy industrialists, landowners and conservative politicians, and the fact that these contacts were accompanied by less and less reference to the socialist points of the Nazi programme. The elites now came to believe that, if an emergency law were

President von Hindenburg with Hitler during the May Day celebrations in 1933, just one day before Hitler banned the trade unions. Why was von Hindenburg willing to appoint Hitler as chancellor in January 1933?

passed to bypass the *Reichstag* in favour of a government dominated by themselves, they could use the Nazis to bring about the destruction of the hated Weimar Republic on their own terms and leave the Nazis to end the threat posed by the increasing popularity of the communists.

At first, von Papen (playing a role similar to that played earlier by Giolitti in Italy) tried to persuade Hitler to accept the position of vice-chancellor in his cabinet. However, Hitler, as the leader of what was still the largest party in the *Reichstag*, refused and insisted on being made chancellor. Eventually, von Papen and his military, aristocratic and industrialist backers were able to persuade von Hindenburg (who detested Hitler on both a personal and a social level) to dismiss Schleicher. Thus, on 30 January 1933, Hitler was appointed chancellor of a coalition government, with von Papen as vice-chancellor. There were only two other Nazis in the cabinet. Ironically, this event took place after the worst effects of the depression were already over and Nazi support was declining. This was perhaps the clearest indication of how determined the traditional German elites were to destroy the democratic Weimar Republic.

The Nazi 'revolution', 1933–39

Along with other fascist parties, the Nazi Party claimed to be a revolutionary movement offering a 'third way' between the uncontrolled market of capitalism and the planned economy of socialism and communism. The Nazis promised they would create a 'new order' consisting of a classless national society, with all German speakers united under one leader. When Hitler came to power in 1933, therefore, many – including a large militant section of the NSDAP itself – expected to see the rapid implementation of a 'second revolution' as soon as his power had been established. However, Hitler (like Mussolini in Italy but unlike Lenin in Russia) became ruler of Germany by co-operating with the traditional ruling elites, not by overthrowing them. Thus, even though Hitler's power was reasonably secure after 1934, it is not surprising that for most of the period before the Second World War the Nazis' economic and social policies were cautious and conservative in order not to alienate the elites that had smoothed the way for Hitler's appointment as chancellor.

Economic policy

Hitler had little real interest in economic policy, except in so far as it would enable him to carry out his political, social and foreign policy objectives. Hence economic policy under the Third Reich, as pointed out by Bracher, tended to be inconsistent at best and, at times, contradictory and inefficient. Before 1933, the Nazi Party's economic policies (set out in their 25-point programme) had a populist and vaguely anti-capitalist element. The most important of these promised to limit big business monopolies, to help small shopkeepers by abolishing large department stores and to control finance capital in order to help small farmers and artisans. However, during the early 1930s (especially 1931–32) these were pushed to one side so as to win support from the German elites. In fact, the economic policies of Hitler and the Nazi leadership were even less radical than Mussolini's plans for a corporate state. However, the Nazis were prepared to intervene in the economy to ensure that Germany was strengthened in accordance with their plans for military conquest.

Main objectives

By 1933, there were three broad elements in the Nazis' plans for the economy: to restart the economy and solve unemployment via government expenditure on public work schemes (and also to increase their support), to establish German autarky (economic self-sufficiency and isolation from the international economic system) and to create a *Wehrwirtschaft* (war economy) so that Germany would be able to fight and win a 'total' war in the future. As early as February 1933, Hitler began talking of the need to create a 'military economy'. None of these aims, however, necessitated the ending of private ownership.

Schacht and his 'new plan'

The years 1933–36 have sometimes been referred to as a period of 'partial fascism' because during this time the Nazi state followed a policy of job creation to reduce unemployment, abolished trade unions and controlled wages and prices. Yet Nazi economic policy was not as consistent as the corporate policy followed by Mussolini in Italy. Significantly, the principles of private ownership and the capitalist market were respected by the Nazis in the first few years of the Third Reich, despite calls from the more militant sections of the NSDAP and the SA for action against big business. An early indication that Nazi economic policy would not be revolutionary was the role given to Hjalmar Schacht, a conservative banker and powerful financier with close ties to Germany's industrialists and bankers. Although not a Nazi, he acted as president of the *Reichsbank* from 1933 to 1939 and was minister of economics from 1934 to 1937. During this period, he played a role similar to that of de Stefani in Fascist Italy. His appointment as president of the *Reichsbank* had reassured the elites that the Nazis had no intention of implementing radical economic policies or of harming the interests of big business.

The biggest success of Nazi economic policy was reducing unemployment, which, in January 1933, had stood at over 6 million, an unemployment rate of over 30 per cent. More recent research has suggested that the unofficial unemployment figure was over 8 million, if the various labour service schemes and women are included. However, between 1933 and 1935, unemployment dropped to 1.7 million and continued to decline. This was largely the result of government spending on various public works schemes such as the building of *Autobahnen* (motorways), electrification, reforestation programmes and the construction of public buildings. Over 1 million young unemployed males were drafted and organised by the German Labour Front. Subsidies and tax concessions were also given to private companies to encourage them to employ more workers. As expenditure on armaments increased, more jobs in this sector became available. After 1935, conscription and the expansion of the armed forces also helped to bring down unemployment.

Some of the decrease in unemployment was, however, the result of earlier programmes set up by the last Weimar governments, which the Nazis simply extended. All these schemes were funded according to traditional conservative financial principles. As time went on, the Nazis' racial, gender and political prejudices led to the removal of certain groups (like the Jews, some married women and political prisoners in concentration camps) from the official unemployment statistics altogether.

The Nazis also benefited from the general improvement in the world economy that began in early 1933, just months after Hitler became chancellor. While many of the Nazis' own schemes were unco-ordinated, Schacht's policies had led to problems such as a tendency to inflation and, more seriously, a balance of payments deficit in foreign trade. To overcome these problems (which first appeared in the summer of 1934), Schacht was appointed minister for economics in June 1934 and was given wide powers to deal with the economy. In September 1934 he introduced a 'new plan' based on total government control of trade and currency exchange. It was designed to reduce imports linked to public consumption (such as cotton and wool) to ensure that imports for heavy industry in general and the armaments industry in particular were given priority. Schacht suspended all interest payments on Germany's foreign debts. He also signed a series of bilateral trade agreements to secure raw materials, increase exports and save foreign currency, mainly with countries in Latin America and, especially, the Balkans. These exchanges were often based on barter and any German purchases of raw materials had to be matched by the buying of German goods. Under Schacht the German economy soon began to show signs of recovery.

By the end of 1935 Germany had achieved a trade surplus, while industrial production was up by almost 50 per cent since 1933. However, these successes were limited and Schacht himself was aware that his measures were only short-term solutions. There was no significant increase in exports or efficiency and consumer production failed to expand. In particular, his policy of printing secret government bonds (known as 'mefo' bills) to conceal the true expenditure on armaments was inflationary. Also, despite the drive to self-sufficiency, Germany still needed to import raw materials for its rearmament programme. This was especially worrying as the cost of these products was increasing while Germany's reserves of gold and foreign currency were declining. In 1936 a new economic crisis arose over the state of the balance of payments, and Schacht argued that this problem could only be solved by reducing spending on rearmament in order to increase exports and Germany's reserves of foreign currency. These proposals ran counter to the Nazis' plans – from 1936 Hitler had insisted on a faster expansion of military strength – and were opposed by the armed forces.

The Four-Year Plan

In September 1936 Hitler responded to this crisis by placing Hermann Göring in charge of the Four-Year Plan, designed to make Germany's economy and military forces ready to fight a war in four years' time. The plan outlined the need to control all imports and exports, increase agricultural production, make Germany self-sufficient in all important raw materials (such as metals, oil, petrol, rubber and textiles) and retrain sections of workers in key industries. In theory, Göring's plan was to operate alongside Schacht's plan. In practice, Nazi control over industry increased and Schacht found his position and policies increasingly undermined as Göring encroached on the activities of his ministry.

In addition, his warnings about the looming balance of payments problem were ignored.

Eventually, in November 1937, Schacht resigned as minister of economics and his place was taken by Walther Funk. In practice, though, it was Göring who was deciding economic policy; this did not always suit the wishes of industrialists like the coal and steel magnates. The electro-chemicals industry (important for the drive for autarky and for weapons production), however, began to reap rich rewards. Göring's plan did represent a change in the degree of influence big business was able to exercise.

From 1936 Hitler and the Nazis were more able to give priority to their plans for military expansion. Massive amounts of state money were poured into research and development, and into armaments production (equivalent to about 50 per cent of all industrial investment in the German economy in the years 1936–40). This gave the Nazi regime a greater influence over some sectors of the economy. Later, the Nazis further interfered in the operation of a market economy when they used wage, price and dividend controls to curb inflation and insisted on firms expanding their enterprises. Some compulsory mergers were ordered to create monopoly firms which it was hoped would be more efficient. In fact, it was the large companies which benefited most from Nazi rule, especially those linked to military production such as motor transport, aircraft, machine tools and chemicals companies. In 1933, about 40 per cent of German production had been under monopoly control; by 1937, this had risen to over 70 per cent.

Profits certainly increased under the Nazis. In 1928 (a boom year), the average rate of profit had been 2 per cent of turnover; by 1938, it stood at 6.5 per cent. Those companies involved in rearmament did even better. Though increased state intervention after 1936 limited the influence of ordinary shareholders, it did not significantly weaken the power of the major directors. The Four-Year Plan also saw the establishment of several state factories, all of which were linked in some way to the rearmament programme: the Hermann Göring Steel Works, for example, soon became the Reich's largest firm. Despite these significant limitations on some aspects of a 'free' market economy, the Nazis never had any intention of abolishing private ownership.

Like Schacht's earlier policies and Mussolini's various 'battles' (see pp. 119–20), Göring's Four-Year Plan had mixed results. On the positive side, the plan resulted in big increases in the production of some key industries, such as aluminium. Many others also improved and this was done without significantly worsening Germany's reliance on the import of key raw materials. By the end of 1938, Germany's total industrial production had increased by just over 100 per cent since 1933. By this time, the official number of unemployed was down to 300,000. The continued decline of unemployment had much to do with the massive rearmament carried out under Göring's plan.

Despite their propaganda the Nazis were far from having carried out an 'economic miracle' and there were several crucial failures. First, their aim to be self-sufficient in raw materials (if necessary by the production of synthetic

Commodity	1936 output	1936 output as a % of 1940 plan target	1938 output	1938 output as a % of 1940 plan target	Plan target
Mineral oil*	1,790	12.9%	2,340	16.9%	13,830
Aluminium	98	35.9%	166	60.8%	273
Buna rubber	0.6	0.6%	5	4.2%	120
Nitrogen	770	74%	914	87.9%	1,040
Explosives	18	8.1%	45	20.2%	223
Steel	19,216	80.1%	22,656	94.4%	24,000
Iron ore	2,255	40.6%	3,360	60.5%	5,549
Brown coal	161,382	67.1%	194,985	81.1%	240,500
Hard coal	158,400	74.4%	186,186	87.4%	213,000

*including synthetic petrol

From J. Noakes and G. Pridham (eds), *Nazism, 1919-45, A documentary reader*, Exeter, 1984.

The relative achievements of the Four-Year Plan under the direction of Göring. Why was 1940 an important year in Nazi foreign policy?

alternatives) was not met. Though there was some improvement, it fell far short of the desired figures, especially for oil and rubber. For instance, the production of synthetic petrol only met 18 per cent of total needs; while 60 per cent of oil, 70 per cent of copper, 85 per cent of rubber and almost 100 per cent of aluminium requirements still had to be imported. In all, over 30 per cent of Germany's important raw materials and 20 per cent of its food still came from abroad. Rearmament also failed to reach its set targets. Thus by 1939, Germany was not in a position to fight any major long-lasting war, which was the purpose of Göring's plan.

Historians have debated the ultimate intention of the Four-Year Plan as well as the extent to which it can be seen as a success or failure. In the first couple of decades after the war, B. H. Klein and then A. Milward argued that fighting a total war was not the aim in the 1930s. Instead, the Nazis envisaged a series of short 'local' wars (*Blitzkriege*) in eastern Europe to win the raw materials Germany lacked, and Hitler's main aim was to keep the people content and supporting the Nazi Party. W. Sauer, on the other hand, argues that Hitler deliberately spent more on weapons and on keeping food prices low, thus creating a 'plunder economy' that would require a major war in the near future to keep the people well fed, without having to cut military spending (which rose from 1.9 billion RM in 1933 to 32.3 billion RM in 1938).

Some believe that the inconsistencies of the plan indicate that Hitler wanted to improve the overall growth of the economy and avoid any significant cuts in living standards in order to retain support. This is said to explain why military expenditure in 1938 was only 15 per cent of Germany's GNP. Others, such as R. J. Overy, argue that Hitler's ultimate aim was always world power, but that he did not see Germany as being ready until 1943. For this reason it is not surprising that the Four-Year Plan did not completely prepare Germany for total war in 1939.

The war economy

Some historians see the outbreak of war in 1939 as having much more to do with an attempt to solve a serious economic crisis than with the implementation of a predetermined war plan. For instance, the 'mefo' bills issued by Schacht were due for repayment in 1939; if the outbreak of war had not allowed Hitler to write them off, their repayment would have led to the collapse of the German economy. Also, as Schacht had feared, the cost of rearmament created huge problems for exports, gold reserves, foreign currency earnings and the supply of skilled labour to industries not linked to military products. Thus, with the German economy close to collapse in 1939, the temptation to plunder weaker states was strong. According to Göring, there were only two choices: abandon the rearmament programme or carry out several local 'lightning' wars in order to obtain the resources the German economy needed but could not afford to import if rearmament continued.

Göring stressed the importance of *Blitzkrieg*, as he knew that the German economy was not yet able to sustain any prolonged total war. Initially, despite Britain and France unexpectedly declaring war in 1939 following the invasion of Poland, successful military operations from 1939 to 1941 brought Germany the resources it needed. However, Britain managed to avoid defeat in 1940 while German troops began to face increasing setbacks in the USSR after 1941.

Once a full-scale European war broke out, Nazi economic policy (not surprisingly) underwent further changes. Despite the agricultural and industrial gains in 1940–41, the underlying weaknesses of the German economy remained. When Fritz Todt became minister of armaments in March 1940, he began a series of reforms that were continued and developed by his successor, Albert Speer, who took over in February 1942. They began to weaken the controls placed on German industry under the four-year plan. Instead, they set up a Central Planning Board (CPB) and established a new policy of 'industrial self-responsibility'. The CPB set up committees for each of the vital war industries. Although Speer controlled the entire German war economy, industrialists enjoyed a great deal of independence. From 1942 onwards, the production of weapons increased substantially and continued to rise until 1944, despite heavy Allied bombing of Germany's industrial cities.

By this time, with defeats in the Soviet Union and the Allied invasion of western Europe, the war economy began to collapse and there were serious shortages of raw materials and a lack of skilled labour. However, Hitler did not agree to the introduction of the central planning needed for total war until 1943. Nevertheless, industrialists continued to co-operate with the Nazis – especially those with contracts to supply the military – and continued to benefit from increased profits. Even with a situation of total war, however, the Nazis never established a command economy (as the Communists did in the USSR) and private ownership (even if owners did not have total control) remained virtually intact. Thus, Nazi economic policy failed to carry out any revolution in the ownership and power of Germany's economic elites.

The social impact of Nazism

Just as the Nazis' economic policies tended to consolidate the existing state of affairs, so too did their social interventions. Despite the revolutionary talk of a new classless society, in many respects the Third Reich remained very similar socially to what had preceded it.

Social revolution or social reaction?

There has been a historical debate as to whether the nature of Nazi rule should be seen as 'social revolution' or 'social reaction'. In the 1960s, for example, D. Schoenbaum argued that most German people did perceive the Nazis as having carried out the *Volksgemeinschaft* aim of a classless people's national community, with Germans working together for the good of Germany. Others have argued that the unintended destruction of Germany as a consequence of the Second World War laid the basis for the disappearance of the old *Junker* class and thus the creation of a modern class system in Germany, albeit not until after 1945. In the main, however, most historians have seen the Nazis' rule as essentially reinforcing the traditional class and gender patterns of power and wealth that had existed in pre-1933 Germany and, in some respects, since the nineteenth century.

If there was anything that was revolutionary about Nazism, it was its extreme racist pursuit of the extermination of Jewish people. Thus many argue that the Nazis' social policy and impact were much more reactionary than revolutionary. In order to assess the social impact of Nazism it will be necessary to examine the fortunes of the different social classes, the degree of implementation of the policy of *Volksgemeinschaft* and the fate of certain sections of German society such as young people, women and Jewish people.

The social classes

In the period 1933–39 many Germans accepted the Nazis' claims to have carried out an economic miracle following the depression, especially as regards the reduction of unemployment. From 1933 to 1938 wages began to improve and food consumption increased by about 15 per cent, while the purchase of clothing and household goods also increased, by 25 per cent and 50 per cent respectively. This played a big part in the German people's toleration – and support – of the Nazi regime. There were significant variations in the material benefits received by the different social classes in the Third Reich. For example, although the national income in 1938 was 20 per cent higher than it had been in the boom year of 1928, the total wages' bill declined as a proportion of the national income (from 57 per cent of GNP in 1932 to 52 per cent in 1939). This shows that there was a clear redistribution of wealth away from the lower classes to the higher classes. Furthermore, average German consumers were less well off than those in Britain, let alone those in the USA. The real benefits of the economic recovery after 1933 tended to be felt by the wealthy elites rather than the social groups to which the Nazis had promised so much in the years 1925–33.

The *Mittelstand*

The *Mittelstand* were an important element of the middle classes of Germany. They included the 'old' middle class of small retailers, self-employed craftsmen, peasant farmers and pensioners and the 'new' middle class of white-collar, non-manual employees. These groups tended to compare the Weimar Republic unfavourably with the German imperial period and turned to the Nazis in increasing numbers after the depression set in.

This group became the backbone of Nazi support in elections in the 1930s and they expected to benefit significantly following the Nazi victory in 1933. However, Nazi promises to help small businesses were, in the main, not carried out. The Law for the Protection of the Retail Trade, passed in 1933, did place some general restrictions on the further expansion of the large department stores, imposed special taxes on them and attempted to place limitations on certain services, such as baking, catering, hairdressing and shoe repairs taking place in department stores. The department stores were not closed down, however, and, in fact, the five main chains experienced a 10 per cent growth in the years 1936–39. In 1937 the Nazis placed restrictions on the setting-up of new small businesses by issuing a decree which stated that all new businesses should have capital amounting to at least \$200,000. They also forced existing businesses with capital less than \$40,000 to close. This affected about one-fifth of all small businesses. The reason for this move was clearly linked to the Nazis' reliance on big business for their rearmament programme as well as to the general economic trends of the 1930s. As a result, *Mittelstand* businesses found themselves increasingly squeezed out of the German economy by the continued growth of big business, which increased its share of ownership of wealth from about 40 per cent in 1933 to 70 per cent by 1937.

The artisans were another section of the *Mittelstand* that had expected help from the new Nazi government. In 1933, the Law for the Provisional Construction of German Craft Trades re-created a guild system and stated that anyone planning to set up a craft business had to possess a master's qualification in a registered trade and this certainly did benefit existing craftsmen and artisans. Qualified tradesmen also benefited indirectly from increased government expenditure on public buildings and the subsidies given to homeowners to install toilets and bathrooms. Despite this, the number of self-employed and independent artisans continued to decline: by 1939, the total number of artisans was 1.5 million compared to 1.65 million in 1933.

Farmers and peasants

The Nazis were strongest in the rural areas as the farming community had been attracted by Nazi promises to give help and by the general Nazi emphasis on 'blood and soil', which depicted small peasant farmers as the embodiment of all that was good about the German *Volk*. Yet even here the impact of Nazi policies was somewhat mixed and, overall, the main beneficiaries after 1933 from, for example, the rapid increase in land values were the owners of the larger estates and commercial farms, who retained their large landholdings despite earlier Nazi promises to redistribute land to smaller farms. Nonetheless, smaller farmers did gain in some ways. A significant number of them had their farm debts written off and a 20 per cent increase in food prices (resulting from the government controlling imports and setting prices) benefited farmers in the years 1933–37.

The effects of the Reich Entailed (hereditary) Farm Law of 1933, which applied to medium-sized farms (7.5 to 125 hectares), was mixed. Small landowners were given security of tenure as long as they were able to prove Aryan blood ancestry back to 1800. This effectively took land from the Jews, which was then redistributed. However, farmers resented the clause in the law which prevented the selling, mortgaging and especially the splitting of such farms as it created problems for raising cash for improvements and for families wishing to provide for second and subsequent children.

Agricultural labourers tended to experience even more problems. Initially, their wages increased more rapidly than those of industrial workers because of the general improvement in food prices. By the late 1930s it had become apparent that there was still a significant discrepancy in agricultural and industrial wages, with most labourers continuing to suffer from low wages and poverty. As a result, the drift from low-wage rural areas to higher-wage urban centres continued, with a migration rate of about 2.5 per cent each year (compared to about 1.5 per cent a year in the period before 1933). This led to a serious labour shortage in farming areas which undermined Nazi attempts to increase food production.

The industrial working class

Industrial workers – by far the biggest group of this section of German society – did not really expect to benefit from Nazi rule. In fact, the majority of industrial workers before 1933 had not supported the NSDAP. Despite this, many saw their material situation improve in the period 1933–39 as a result of the reduction in unemployment. By 1938, most families were able to rely on a regular wage. They also benefited from controls on rents and the recreational opportunities provided by the Strength through Joy (Kraft durch Freude or KDF) scheme set up by the Nazi regime, which encouraged employers to offer extra benefits such as sports facilities, cultural activities and cheap holidays. These mainly benefited white-collar and the better-off skilled manual workers. Even these initiatives were not totally positive, as both the KDF and the Beauty of Labour (Schönheit der Arbeit or SDA) schemes, which were supposed to help ensure that living standards did not fall too low because of the priority given to rearmament, gave employers added opportunities to exploit their workers and led to increased control of workers' leisure time.

This sector of the population was most affected by the banning of the trade unions in May 1933. In 1934 the Nazis set up the German Labour Front (Deutsche Arbeitsfront or DAF), led by Robert Ley, in their place. Once industrial workers had lost all their independent bargaining rights, they had no way of obtaining the pay increases they desired or of resisting any decline in their working conditions. According to Nazi propaganda, the DAF would create a social and productive 'community'. The DAF was supposed to be an independent body that would act as a neutral arbiter in any disagreement between employers and employees over wages, hours of work or working conditions, but this is not what happened in practice. This was not surprising as, when the DAF was set up, all contracts that had been negotiated with trade unions were cancelled; in addition, employers were called 'leaders' (or 'masters') with workers referred to as 'followers'. National and regional wage rates were abolished and were replaced by individual piece-rates and the 'performance principle', by which workers could earn a higher rate by attaining certain targets and which mainly benefited the young, the healthy and the skilled.

At the same time, the pre-1933 Nazi organisation for factory workers – the Nazi Factory Cell Organisation (NSBO) – was purged of its militant leaders (such as Strasser) and placed under the authority of the DAF. The DAF tended to prevent workers from asking for increased wages; instead it set wage levels that were acceptable to employers. As a result, despite the great drop in unemployment, it was not until 1938 that industrial workers returned to the level of real wages that they had enjoyed before the onset of the depression. In the period 1933–39 wages of both skilled and unskilled workers actually declined, by 1 per cent and 3 per cent respectively, despite the fact that the working week was longer after 1933.

In 1933, the average working week was 43 hours; this increased to 47 hours by 1938 and to 48 hours by 1939. Overall, there was an increase in the working week in the period 1932–39 of more than 10 per cent. One result of the longer hours of work was a rise in the number of fatal accidents, from 217 in 1932 to 525 in 1936. The decline in real wages was also partly due to increased levels of income tax, KDF payments and health insurance contributions, which rose to 35 per cent of wages in total.

Workers were also the losers in the Volkswagen 'scheme' which began in 1938. By 1936, car ownership in Germany was only 500,000, compared to 1 million in Britain and 23 million in the USA. Workers paid 5 marks a week into a fund that would eventually buy them a car. However, this was essentially a myth, as the chassis built for these cars were later converted to military vehicles and the few that were built went to SS officers and others in the Nazi elite – no ordinary German worker ever got one. The workers' savings were diverted to spending on weapons. In addition, workers found that the Nazi government restricted their freedom to move to other jobs: the workbook each person had to carry could be retained by the employer and without the workbook no one could be legally employed. Employers could also blacklist a worker. However, those who worked in industries related to the rearmament programme did much better than those employed in consumer-related industries.

An indication of how little German industrial workers benefited under the Nazi regime is the fact that the largest part of their wages still had to be spent on food: in 1938, they spent 45 per cent of their wages on food, compared to 41 per cent in Britain. According to R. Overy, consumption of important food items in Germany declined in the years 1927–37: meat consumption, for example, dropped by 18 per cent. Beef consumption in Nazi Germany was 33 per cent below the US figure, while potato consumption was 50 per cent higher than in Britain. On these and many other counts, the average German worker was worse off than he had been in the period before 1929.

	1927	1937	% change
Rye bread (kg)	262.9	316.1	+ 20.2
Wheat bread (kg)	55.2	30.8	- 44.2
Meat and meat products (kg)	133.7	109.2	- 18.3
Bacon (kg)	9.5	8.5	- 10.5
Milk (ltr)	427.8	376.2	- 14.2
Cheese (kg)	13.0	14.5	+ 11.5
Eggs (number)	404	237	- 41.3
Fish (kg)	21.8	20.4	- 6.4
Vegetables (kg)	117.2	109.6	- 6.5
Potatoes (kg)	499.5	519.8	+ 4.1
Sugar (kg)	47.2	45.0	- 4.7
Tropical fruit (kg)	9.7	6.1	- 37.1
Beer (ltr)	76.5	31.6	- 58.7

Source: R. J. Overy, *The Nazi economic recovery 1932-1938*, 2nd edn, Cambridge, 1996.

Food consumption figures among German working-class families in the period 1927–37. What do these figures tell us about the relative prosperity of the working class under Nazism?

Volksgemeinschaft

The Nazis' claim that they were carrying out a 'social revolution' was based mainly on their stated intention to create a new kind of society: a *Volksgemeinschaft* that would transcend the old class and religious divisions and unite all Germans behind the leader. It is important to bear in mind that the Nazis' concepts of race were central to all of these policies. In fact, as we have seen in the previous section, there is little evidence of any objective social revolution taking place. There were no significant alterations in the distribution of wealth, property, income or power between the different social classes in Germany. Private industry was not taken into state ownership and over 15 per cent of farmland remained in the hands of fewer than 17,000 *Junker* families (about 0.5 per cent of all German families). There was thus clearly no fundamental redistribution of property ownership in the years after 1933. The confiscation and redistribution of property that did take place was from Jewish people and, after 1939, from foreign nationals. Most of this went straight into the hands of leading Nazis such as Himmler and Göring or into the hands of lesser party bureaucrats or businessmen, rather than ordinary Germans.

The one area where Nazism did bring about a reasonably significant change was in the degree of social mobility that became available to ordinary people. The rapid expansion of various Nazi bureaucracies after 1933 created a huge number of new white-collar jobs which had to be filled. These were so numerous that they could not all be filled by recruits from the upper and middle classes and thus new opportunities were created for those from the lower social groups. After 1938, individuals from the traditional elites like the *Junker* and upper middle classes were removed from the foreign ministry and the armed forces, which again provided opportunities for those lower down the social scale. This tendency increased after the July Bomb Plot in 1944 (see p. 209), when over 5,000 senior officials were dismissed, including some from the old *Junker* aristocratic families. Nevertheless, as D. Geary points out, the more privileged sections of society still tended to hold many of the most influential positions as business leaders, senior bureaucrats and diplomats. Also, it would seem that most of the social mobility was short-range rather than long-range.

Although the traditional elites managed to maintain their dominant position in the higher echelons of the army – in 1939, 11 out of the 18 field marshals were from *Junker* backgrounds, while the remaining 7 were from the upper middle classes – at the rank of general the proportion of aristocrats was only 25 per cent by 1936, compared to just over 60 per cent in 1920. On the whole, the elites successfully resisted Nazi penetration of the officer corps, at least until the later stages of the war. Although there was more support for the Nazis from the junior officers, most of the army's higher-ranking officers tended to be traditional, conservative German nationalists. In fact, Hitler later blamed the defeat of the Third Reich on his failure to carry through a social revolution in the higher ranks of the army.

If the Nazis failed to effect any significant objective changes to Germany's economic and social structures, there is evidence to suggest they were more successful in transforming the beliefs and values of many Germans. The NSDAP had always claimed to be more than a political party and its *Volksgemeinschaft* policy was clearly different from both the liberal individualistic values of Weimar democracy and the class-based politics of socialism and communism. Once in power, Nazi propaganda attempted to encourage and enforce new social, gender, racial and religious attitudes and principles throughout the Third Reich.

Young people

For the Nazis, the long-term future of their new *Volksgemeinschaft* lay with the young and so they adopted several different approaches in their efforts to control the minds and thoughts of young people. As early as 1933 Hitler had said, ' "Your child belongs to us already" . . . In a short time they will know nothing else but this new community.' Increasingly education was given over to imparting Nazi views and the values of the 'new order' and the 'new man' they intended to create, to ensure that the Third Reich would continue for at least 1,000 years. In 1934, Hitler's government took the responsibility for education away from the *Länder* (local provincial government) and created instead a centrally controlled system under the auspices of the ministry of education and science, led by Bernhardt Rust. The Nazis also established several new elite schools for boys which were designed to produce students who would be 'fit' for political leadership in the new people's community the Nazis were planning to create. The Adolf Hitler schools and the national political educational institutions for secondary school students, and the *Ordensburgen* for college students, all concentrated on physical education and paramilitary activities as well as political education.

Apart from these, the Nazis made few other changes to the organisational structure of state education. What they did change were the curriculum and personnel. The school curriculum was altered to allow more time for physical education (15 per cent of the timetable) and greater emphasis was placed on German, history and biology. Other academic subjects such as maths and the sciences were given less and less time. In German and history lessons, much time was spent on nationalism, militarism, the different roles of men and women and the greatness of Hitler and the NSDAP; in biology, 'race science' was taught in order to indoctrinate children with the Nazis' racist ideas. In all subjects and in the specially written new textbooks, Jewish people were singled out as being traitors to Germany – even maths books had exercises which involved, for example, calculating how many Jews in Warsaw could be killed with a German bomb.

To ensure that children were effectively indoctrinated, the Nazis also purged the teaching professions of any politically unreliable or racially 'unsuitable' members. Others were sent on special courses to 'recondition' them to the new principles they would have to teach. The Nazi Teachers' League (*Nationalsozial-istischer Lehrerbund* or NSLB) was also given increased influence and by 1937 97 per cent of all teachers belonged to it. All this undermined the status of teachers and resulted in a shortage. To overcome this problem, the Nazis simply reduced the qualifications needed to become a teacher.

The universities (which had produced many world-class academics before 1933) were also 'Nazified'. The Nazis were especially keen to control the universities in an attempt to limit the impact of liberal and left-of-centre intellectuals who supported ideas such as democracy, civil rights and freedom. The Nazi regime took over the appointment of university rectors and removed power from the senate committees as well as the independence of the Association of University Lecturers. This purge of the universities was much more extensive than the one carried out by Mussolini in Italy: in all, over 3,000 lecturers and professors were sacked for political or racial reasons; in some universities such as Berlin and Frankfurt, about 30 per cent of staff lost their jobs. Their banning of 'Jewish physics' actually worked against them later on as scientists such as Einstein and Frank fled abroad, which gave the Allies a crucial lead in the development of the atomic bomb. However, most university staff stayed, despite the decline in academic standards and knowledge, and even taught a new university subject: racial sciences. Under the Nazis, the number of students applying for university places dropped from over 125,000 in 1933 to under 60,000 by 1938. Those who did go to university had to do four months' labour service in an SA camp and three hours of sport each week as part of their degree.

The Nazi's main way of creating the new *Volksgemeinschaft* generation was through the various Hitler Youth organisations for boys and girls between the ages of 10 and 18. Like Mussolini, Hitler hoped these organisations would successfully indoctrinate the future generations with Nazi ideology. Activities were geared towards general political and racial indoctrination and physical fitness as well as the roles expected of the different genders in the Third Reich: boys undertook paramilitary training while girls were prepared for their future role as housewives and mothers. All the children had to wear uniforms and swear allegiance to the Führer. Despite the emphasis on sport, the number of children suffering from childhood diseases actually doubled under the Nazis, while the amount of juvenile crime in 1939 was three times the level it had been in 1933.

Before 1933, only about 100,000 young people belonged to the various Hitler Youth groups (this was only about 1 per cent of those young Germans who belonged to a youth group). Not surprisingly, by 1938, Nazi figures give a total membership of over 9 million – about 90 per cent of all young people. However, such figures do not necessarily indicate genuine support, as membership of the Hitler Youth (as with membership of the NSDAP) gave members access to various privileges and preferential treatment. In addition, membership was made compulsory in 1939. Despite the propaganda films, recent research suggests that many German young people were not won over by the Nazis and that many tried to avoid membership, partly because they disliked the strict rules and regimentation. Some children did not join as their parents could not afford the cost of the uniforms, the monthly subscriptions and the summer camps. The Hitler Youth, under von Schirach, did little to weaken class differences, break up traditional friendship loyalties based on schools and neighbourhoods or undermine Germany's traditional social structures.

The overall impact of Nazi policies for youth was also limited by the frequent conflicts and overlapping responsibilities of Rust and von Schirach, who often clashed with each other as well as Wilhelm Frick, the minister of the interior, who also wanted to be in control of education and the indoctrination of the young. Also, the emphasis on physical education and the anti-academic attitudes of the Nazis contributed to an overall decline in academic standards. Many teachers were not happy about the way in which the Hitler Youth movement detracted from schoolwork. Ironically, army leaders later commented on this drop in academic skills and thus the abilities of army conscripts.

Women

Before the Nazis came to power in 1933, the position of women in German society had been changing significantly. From 1900 to 1933, the number of women in employment had increased by over 30 per cent, significantly more than the actual increase in the number of females over the same period. At the same time, the average family decreased in size: in 1900, over 2 million children were born; in 1933, this dropped to under 1 million. This was a trend in all industrial countries in the early twentieth century and was the result of a combination of several factors: the realisation that fewer children could mean a higher standard of living, the greater availability of contraception and the desire for better education and employment opportunities for women. These trends, which were a significant departure from the militaristic, conservative and masculine values of Imperial Germany, were amplified by Germany's involvement in the First World War. During the war, it had been necessary to mobilise large numbers of women into the factories to take the place of men at the front, while the economic problems in the early 1920s had made it necessary for many women to continue in employment after the war. The dreadful slaughter of the war had led to a surplus of nearly 2 million women of marriageable age and a large number of women whose disabled husbands were unable to work. Changes in industrial production technology led to an increased demand for unskilled workers, while the amount of non-manual employment also increased. These developments tended to favour the employment of women, especially as they were paid less than men.

Nazi ideology was utterly opposed to social and economic equality for women and therefore to the early feminist movement which existed in Weimar Germany. The public statements made by the Nazis stressed that men and women had different roles to play, not because women were inferior, but because 'Nature' had allotted the genders two quite different and separate functions. According to the Nazis, it was their task to return people in their new people's community to their 'proper' positions. This was encapsulated in the three Ks slogan: 'Children, kitchen and church' (*Kinder, Küche, Kirche*). The family was seen as the centre of the new people's community ('the germ cell of the nation'). The Nazi belief in a woman's place being in the home was put into practice in their own party structures: as early as 1921, a regulation banned women from holding any senior party position and there was not one female NSDAP deputy in the *Reichstag*. Although the Nazis allowed women to retain the right to vote, women were no longer allowed to be political representatives at either the local or the national level and were barred from becoming judges.

The new Nazi government soon turned its attention to increasing Germany's population. This was to be achieved by several policies aimed specifically at women that were intended to drive them out of the workplace and back into the home. Between 1933 and 1936, married women were excluded from employment in medicine, the law and the higher ranks of the civil service. Legislation was introduced to reduce drastically the number of female teachers and university students. These policies tended to affect mainly middle-class women, but working-class women were also pushed out of employment by a variety of measures. In June 1933, interest-free loans of 600 RM (the equivalent of four months' wages) were given to all young women who gave up work in order to get married. Employers and labour exchanges were instructed to favour men rather than women. Once these policies were set up, the Nazis set about trying to increase Germany's birth rate, which had dropped in the period 1914–32. Laws against abortion were enforced, birth-control clinics were closed and contraception was increasingly restricted, while maternity benefits and family allowances were increased to 10 RM per month for the third and fourth child and an extra 20 RM per month for each subsequent child by 1938. Newlyweds were offered loans of 1,000 RM, at only 3 per cent interest. Under this scheme, 25 per cent of the original loan was declared to be an outright gift for each of the couple's first four children, thereby encouraging women to have children. Women were also encouraged to have large families by being awarded the Honour Cross of the German Mother: for four children they were given a bronze medal; for six, a silver; and for eight, it was gold. All of this was accompanied by extensive propaganda, which included the slogan 'I have donated a child to the Führer.'

To help spread their views on the role of women, the Nazis set up three women's organisations, even though women were specifically excluded from politics in general. These were the National Socialist Womanhood (*National-sozialistische Frauenschaft* or NSF), the German Women's Enterprise (*Deutsches Frauenwerk* or DFW) and the Reich's Mother Service (RMS). The NSDAP leadership saw the NSF and the DFW as tools to spread the official party views; NSF campaigners who later pushed for a greater role for women within the party were quickly removed from positions of influence. The NSF claimed almost 3 million members and promoted the family and the importance of race; the DFW claimed almost 6 million members and advocated the importance of attending cookery classes; while the RMS promoted child care.

The practical results of these Nazi policies were mixed. Although the percentage of women in paid employment in the period 1932–37 declined from 37 per cent to 31 per cent, the actual numbers increased from about 5 million to 6 million. From 1937 to 1939, both the percentage and the numbers increased, from 31 per cent to 33 per cent and from 6 million to just over 7 million. In addition, about 4 million more women were working for their husband's farm or business. After 1935 this was partly the result of the introduction of conscription and the drive for rearmament, which had led to a labour shortage, and partly the result of a general increase in economic activity. Employers were also putting pressure on the government as they resented having to lose unskilled women workers who could be paid lower wages than men. Women who were well qualified, however, never regained the position and status they had had in the Weimar Republic.

The Nazis' attempts to promote restricted and traditional roles in their new *Volksgemeinschaft* were undermined by a combination of economic realities and the contradictory aspects of their own policies. They were eventually forced to drop their marriage loan scheme, for example. These contradictions were seen especially clearly once the Second World War had broken out: Nazi ideology meant that the government was extremely reluctant to mobilise the population fully for total war, as this would mean conscripting large numbers of women into the factories. When Speer finally suggested this in 1943, many leading Nazis (including Hitler) opposed his idea. Although an increasing number of women did enter the labour market after 1939, the official Nazi attitude to the role of women never changed. Their slowness to carry out a full industrial mobilisation of women, compared to countries such as the USSR and Britain, weakened Nazi Germany's ability to fight a total war. Even the attempts to increase the birth rate were not a total success: although there was a clear increase from a low point in 1933 up to a new high in 1939, the birth rate then began to decline once more. Furthermore, historians are not agreed on whether the increase can be ascribed to Nazi policies alone, as other factors (such as a trend to marry earlier and greater confidence once the depression was over) must be taken into consideration.

Jewish people

Membership of the Nazis' *Volksgemeinschaft* was open to all 'good' Aryans (all those who were not 'asocials' such as homosexuals, tramps or gypsies, or did not suffer from hereditary physical disabilities or mental problems) who accepted Hitler's leadership and the Nazi regime. Right from the start, however, one group of Germans was specifically and clearly excluded – those citizens who were Jewish. In many respects, anti-Semitism was the central policy of the Nazis' *Volksgemeinschaft*, and thus received an exceptional amount of attention and resources. Essentially, Hitler and the Nazis believed in the superiority of the Aryan race, who, they believed, were the 'master race' (*Herrenvolk*) and the 'founders of culture'. Jewish people and, among others, the Slavic peoples were seen as the 'destroyers of culture'. In all, there were fewer than 500,000 Jewish people in Germany (about 1 per cent of the population) but, because of earlier restrictions placed on Jewish activities (some dating back to the Middle Ages), they were often concentrated in certain professions. Jews made up 16 per cent of lawyers, 10 per cent of doctors and 5 per cent of writers and editors. Often this resulted in Jewish people being among the more affluent members of society, thus making them easy targets of envy and, later, worse. In addition, because of their distinctive customs, some members of the Jewish community in Germany were highly visible.

Anti-Semitism had existed, to varying degrees, in most European countries for centuries. In late nineteenth-century Germany there was a resurgence of an extremely nationalistic version of anti-Semitic racism. As some socialist leaders were also Jewish, Bismarck, for example, deliberately stirred up anti-Semitism in an attempt to slow the growth of socialism in Germany. As early as 1900, the *Reichstag* contained several small specifically anti-Semitic parties and their racist views seemed to be becoming increasingly respectable. Similar developments were taking place in Austria, Hitler's country of origin. Historians have explained this development in Germany by referring to the impact of industrialisation and the nationalistic fervour associated with the process of unification which resulted in less tolerance of those seen as 'aliens'. This process was given some semblance of intellectual support by a few academic writers who attempted to link their anti-Semitism to various versions of Social Darwinism. Anti-Semitism declined slightly in the years before the First World War as Jewish people in Germany began to receive civil rights and, during the war, some Jews were even promoted to officer rank. After 1918, however, anti-Semitism began to increase again.

It was against this background that Hitler developed his extreme version of anti-Semitism and his bitter hatred – obvious throughout *Mein Kampf* – found a ready response among many members of the Nazi Party. Following Germany's defeat, the Treaty of Versailles, the early economic problems of Weimar Germany and then the depression, there were Germans who were looking for a scapegoat for their problems.

Hitler's action against the Jewish community can be divided into three clear stages. To begin with, between 1933 and 1938, the Nazis moved cautiously and mainly restricted themselves to a legislative attack on Jews. Some historians continue to debate whether, at this stage, expulsion or the extermination of all Jewish people was Hitler and the Nazis' ultimate aim. The Nazis' first move came in April 1933 when Hitler announced an official boycott of all Jewish shops and professional services. This was not widely supported and was quickly dropped because of both domestic and international opposition and its ineffectiveness. It was almost immediately followed by the Law for the Restoration of the Professional Civil Service, which removed all Jewish people from government posts and officially classified Jews as non-Aryans. Further laws in 1934 banned them from other professions, such as hospital doctors and judges, and from the media. In all, the Nazis passed some 400 racial laws. During this period, violence towards Jewish people was unco-ordinated and was unofficially carried out by the SA and SS. Hitler and the Nazis were unable to give full vent to their hatred, however. Von Hindenburg, for one, insisted that Jewish civil servants who had either fought or lost a relative in the war should retain their jobs. Frick tried to limit the impact of these measures and there is evidence that some Nazis were embarrassed at the extreme racism of those like Julius Streicher and his newspaper, *Der Stürmer*. Nonetheless, the Nuremberg race laws were passed in September 1935: the Reich citizenship act deprived all of Germany's Jewish people of all their civil rights, and the Law for the Protection of German Blood and German Honour banned sexual relations or marriage between Jews and German citizens. There is some evidence that these laws were, at least in part, the result of pressure from the lower levels of the Nazi Party. There appear to have been four different drafts of the race laws, with Hitler going for the least extreme. In 1937, further measures, known as 'Aryanisation', were taken to remove Jewish people from the professions and from business. Some towns declared their wish to be 'Jew free' (*judenfrei*) or 'Jew pure' (*judenrein*). Propaganda depicting Jewish people as the 'polluters' of the Aryan race was stepped up and Jewish children were increasingly humiliated in front of their classmates in schools. Such propaganda resulted in a growing number of Germans discriminating against Jewish people in housing and employment, banning them from public places and even refusing to serve them in shops and restaurants. Much of this, however, was the result of local Nazi activists acting on their own initiative.

However, the Nazi campaign intensified and became more violent in the second phase, which lasted from 1938 to 1941. In 1938 over 15,000 Polish Jews living in Germany were expelled and in July Jewish people were banned from all commerce. All Jews had to have compulsory 'Jewish' forenames such as Israel or Sarah, register all their wealth or property and carry identity cards and internal passports. Then in November a Nazi-led pogrom of Jewish people, known as *Kristallnacht*, was carried out, ostensibly in response to the assassination in Paris of a German diplomat by a Jew who was protesting against the treatment of Jews in Germany. It resulted in the destruction of thousands of Jewish homes, shops and synagogues, and the deaths of over 100 Jews; a further 25,000 were sent to concentration camps. These actions were started by Goebbels and supported by Hitler. Later in November, all Jewish pupils in state schools were expelled and in December all Jewish businesses were closed and sold off and all Jews in skilled jobs were sacked.

Not surprisingly, by 1938 almost 150,000 Jewish people had decided to emigrate to escape this growing persecution; the remaining 300,000 stayed on in the hope that the persecution might eventually lessen. When all Jewish valuables were confiscated in April 1939, the possibility of emigration became much more difficult as they could no longer buy or bribe their way out, while no other country was prepared to accept a significant number of impoverished Jews. Thus by 1939 Jewish people had been 'eliminated' from the economic, political, social, cultural and legal life of Germany.

After the outbreak of the Second World War in 1939, Nazi treatment of Jewish people worsened – as early as January 1939, Hitler had threatened that the outbreak of war in Europe would result in the 'annihilation of the Jewish race'. The Nazis' first move was to impose a curfew; then, in 1940, they began the first deportations of Jewish people to ghettos that had been established in Poland. By then, the Nazi conquests of Poland, France, the Netherlands and Belgium had placed another 3.5 million Jews under Nazi rule.

In the third phase of the Nazis' Jewish policy, which lasted from 1941 to 1945, the situation became even more serious. After the Nazi invasion of the Soviet Union in June 1941, Hitler himself called for a 'war of extermination' to be waged against communists and Jews. With a much larger Jewish population at their mercy, systematic mass murder of Jewish people began. Special SS Action Squads (*Einsatzgruppen*) and the armed Order Police (*Ordnungspolizei*) went into the USSR to round up and exterminate all Jews – with varying degrees of assistance from regular German army units of the *Wehrmacht* – in a systematic programme of mass murder. In September, all Jews living in Nazi-occupied Europe were compelled to wear the yellow Star of David to enable easy identification. Then on 20 January 1942 at the Wannsee conference in Berlin, party and government officials decided on the 'final solution' as the way to deal with the 'Jewish problem': all Jewish people living under Nazi control in Europe were to be exterminated. By the spring, several extermination camps had been built in Poland and in the summer of 1943 the mass transportation of Jewish people began. The result was the murder of almost 6 million Jewish people. Others deemed by the Nazis to be 'outsiders' also suffered: over 300,000 people were forcibly sterilised under the 1933 Law for the Prevention of Hereditary Disease because they had a hereditary disease, suffered from mental problems

A German soldier shoots a Jewish mother and her child as they attempt to run away across a field. Why were such methods later replaced by the use of death camps?

such as schizophrenia or were communists. Later some 70,000 people suffering from mental or physical disabilities were gassed, over 10,000 tramps and beggars were sent to concentration camps and more than 500,000 Roma and Sinti (gypsies) also perished in the death camps.

The main historical debate concerning this mass murder is between 'intentionalists' and 'structuralists'. The former argue that, because of Hitler's extreme and long-standing hatred of Jews and his overall power, the Holocaust was the natural conclusion of all earlier Nazi policies against Jewish people. The fact that Nazi policy was at first more moderate and did not become really extreme until after 1939 is explained by the fact that the Nazis did not have complete power until 1934 or even later, so they were unable to move to extermination straight away. Some, such as Burleigh and Wippermann, argue that the massive resources devoted to the 'final solution' during the war shows that it was a core Nazi policy. By 1944, hundreds of thousands of police, guards and members of the SS and the Gestapo were involved in the mass extermination, rather than being used to fight the Red Army. Thus, they argue that this mass murder happened because Hitler and other leading Nazis had wanted it all along. The lack of any written evidence to show that Hitler actually ordered the 'final solution' is explained by the deliberately vague method of making decisions which Hitler set up after 1933.

On the other hand, structuralists such as Mommsen argue that there was no long-term plan or intention to exterminate Jewish people. They point instead to the confused nature of Nazi government and the competition between various Nazi leaders that led to improvised and sometimes contradictory policies. This was compounded by the Nazi occupation of large areas of eastern Europe and the USSR with their larger Jewish populations and by the general chaos of war, especially in eastern Europe. They see the Holocaust as an unplanned response to the situation and circumstances in which the Nazis found themselves after 1939. They point, for example, to the plan to expel forcibly all Jewish people to the African island of Madagascar (the 'Madagascar option'), which was considered – even by fanatic anti-Semites like Himmler – right up until the late 1930s. However, intentionalists point out that leading Nazis expected this plan to result in the death of most Jews because of the poor conditions and disease there.

The churches

The Nazis' failure to create a new culture is also shown by the fact that they were unable to destroy the influence and ideas of the Christian religion and of the different churches. In the new secular *Volksgemeinschaft* the Nazis planned that Christianity would die away. Initially, the Catholic and Protestant churches were willing to co-operate with the new Nazi regime, as Hitler's statements about restoring 'traditional values' and 'strengthening' the family seemed to be an improvement on the open secularism of the Weimar Republic. A speech Hitler made in March 1933, in which he assured Germans that Christianity was the foundation of 'the moral and ethical life of our people', seemed to point to future good relations between the churches and the Nazi government. It soon emerged, however, that these promises were intended to allay fears while Hitler consolidated his regime.

In July 1933, the 28 regional Protestant churches (*Landeskirchen*) were merged to form one centralised Reich Church under the leadership of Reich Bishop Müller. In 1935 the Reich Church was placed under the control of a minister of church affairs. More in line with Nazi views, however, was the establishment of the German Christians (DC), a pro-Nazi group which attempted to spread Nazi racial beliefs and the worship of the Führer in the Reich Church.

Relations with the Catholic Church also promised to be smooth. The Catholic ZP supported Hitler's Enabling Act in March 1933 and Catholics in general approved of the Nazis' actions against ungodly communism. In July 1933 a concordat was signed between the Catholic Church and the government: in return for the Catholic Church withdrawing totally from politics, the state promised not to interfere with their freedom to worship or their schools. As with the Protestants, however, the Nazis soon set up various organisations (such as the Cross and Eagle League and the Working Group of Catholic Germans) to infiltrate Nazi ideas into the Catholic Church. At the same time, the Nazi government held 'immorality' trials in which monks and nuns were deliberately discredited in order to weaken the influence of the Catholic clergy. These developments led the pope to criticise government actions in 1937, and in subsequent years the rift widened.

Some leading Nazis set up the German Faith Movement, which tried to establish pagan ceremonies and openly attacked the entire Christian religion. Despite these various measures, the Nazis made few inroads into the religious beliefs of most Germans. I. Kershaw has shown that there was no significant decline in church membership between 1933 and 1939 and there is evidence of an increase during the war. The clergy were also able to maintain considerable influence over their congregations. It is clear, therefore, that the Nazis failed to break down religious beliefs or allegiances.

Propaganda and the 'Hitler myth'

An important element in the Nazis' attempt to spread the values and ideas of their *Volksgemeinschaft* was the general propaganda machine run by Joseph Goebbels. He was appointed as Reich minister of popular enlightenment and propaganda in March 1933. He worked closely with Hitler to strengthen Nazi control through the various forms of the mass media and spread Nazi propaganda to create a strong ideological commitment to the regime and unite all Germans behind their Führer. The intention was to 'Nazify' German culture by condemning and banning modernism and any works produced by Jewish artists or other 'outsiders'.

The mass media

The two most important forms for propaganda were the radio and the press. Both were skilfully manipulated by the Nazis – mainly under the direction of Goebbels – in their rise to power. The radio was the main form of home entertainment and so the Nazis were especially keen to control this method of mass communication. One of Goebbels' first acts as minister was to set up the Reich Radio Company in order to centralise all broadcasting in Germany (before 1933 it had been supervised by the *Länder*). He then sacked about 13 per cent of the staff on political or racial grounds and replaced them with those who were in tune with Nazi ideology.

As fewer than 25 per cent of German households (about 4.5 million) had a radio by 1933, the Nazi government quickly set about mass producing cheap radio sets. By 1939, over 70 per cent of German households (about 16 million) possessed one of these 'people's receivers' (*Volksempfänger*), one of the highest percentages in the world. In order to reach those people who did not have a radio at home, Goebbels had radios and loudspeakers put in all the main public spaces, such as town squares, streets, restaurants and cafés, and factories and offices. The Nazis also appointed 'radio wardens', whose task it was to ensure that people listened to all the important speeches and announcements.

Nazi control of the press was not as easy to achieve. Nevertheless they were able to establish a more extensive control of the media than Mussolini had done in Italy. In 1933, there were more than 4,500 daily newspapers in Germany; this included national newspapers as well as many strong regional papers in the different *Länder*. Most were privately owned and many identified strongly with particular political parties or religious denominations. Clearly they could frustrate Nazi plans to create an ideologically united people's community. It was no surprise that the Nazis, under Goebbels, quickly began to take steps to bring them under Nazi control. The first move came when the government banned all the SPD and KPD newspapers. Then the NSDAP's own publishing house bought up as many of the remaining newspapers as possible. By 1939 the Nazis owned over 60 per cent of all newspapers.

In 1938 the various news agencies were merged in order to establish one central agency, the DNB, which was under government control. This step allowed Goebbels to vet and officially approve the news and pictures which appeared in all newspapers. Goebbels also established a press department, which set up the practice of giving daily press conferences in his ministry's offices in order to guide editorial policy and comment. Finally, the introduction of the Editors' Law in October 1933 stated that all newspaper articles were the responsibility of editors, whose function was to ensure that their newspapers' content met with the approval of Goebbels' ministry. Any editor failing to do so would have to suffer the consequences. All journalists and editors also had to swear an oath of loyalty and allegiance. The Nazis thus established a system of censorship at one remove, which ensured nothing would be published that might conflict with the ideals of the Nazis' *Volksgemeinschaft*. By 1944, over 80 per cent of all newspapers totally supported the Nazis in contrast to the 2.5 per cent that had supported them in 1933. All of them, though, were supportive of the Nazis' aims. By then the total number of newspapers had fallen to under 1,000 and there was only one national newspaper: the Nazi Party's *Völkischer Beobachter*, the circulation of which rose from 116,000 in 1932 to almost 1.2 million by 1941.

The control of culture

These ideals were also pushed in the cinema, literature, music and art, which also came under Goebbels' jurisdiction. To ensure Nazi control, Goebbels established a Reich chamber of culture in 1933. Its role was to co-ordinate the development and dissemination of the new Nazi culture. The organisation had seven sub-chambers to deal with different aspects of culture. To begin with, all 'subversive' or 'degenerate' art was destroyed: in May 1933 the 'burning of the books' took place in Berlin when thousands of books which contained liberal, left-wing, pacifist or Jewish elements, taken from libraries and bookshops, were burned by Nazi activists. The Nazis banned over 20,000 titles. It was decreed that literature and art had to serve the Nazi state and promote the values that would bind Germans together in the new people's community. These values were based on anti-Semitism and Aryan superiority, nationalism and militarism, 'blood and soil', the rejection of Christian values and the cult of the Führer. To spread these ideas as widely as possible, the Nazis built many new theatres and libraries (the number of state-run libraries increased from 6,000 in 1933 to 25,000 in 1940). They also put on an increasing number of cultural events that attracted many people. On Hitler's insistence architects were forced to abandon the 'degenerate' modernism that had made Weimar Germany famous and revert instead to the grand classical styles (also favoured in Fascist Italy). In addition, Goebbels organised mass rallies (especially the annual Nuremberg rallies) and various public celebrations (such as Hitler's birthday) to widen support for Hitler, the Third Reich and their *Volksgemeinschaft*.

The results of all this propaganda were mixed. Although sales of books increased under the Nazis, most were second-rate novels featuring the backgrounds favoured by the Nazis (either war or the rural 'good life'). Over 2,000 important Germans from the art world left Germany and most of what was produced under the Nazis was, at best, mediocre. The plays tolerated by the Nazis tended to be musicals and those that extolled the merits of Nazi politics. These proved to be so unpopular that the Nazis were forced to increase the number of acceptable classical plays that were produced.

The exception to this unpopular and mediocre artistic production was the German cinema, which had already established a good international reputation in the 1920s. Goebbels realised the importance of this new form of mass entertainment and was able – at least most of the time – to reconcile film directors to producing work that was, in broad terms, compatible with the Nazis' political objectives. Although all film scripts had to be approved by the relevant body, Goebbels tried to ensure the films did not seem to be obvious pro-Nazi propaganda. The cinemas were used to show newsreels which carried important announcements, as well as films of Hitler's speeches and party rallies made by the propaganda ministry. These were specifically designed to promote Hitler's image as a demi-god and to show his mass support.

A. Steinweis has argued that many artists, musicians and architects actually welcomed the cultural chambers set up by the Nazis, as they helped give them a higher status and improved conditions – for some. Overall, however, the Nazis failed to create and impose a new cultural identity in the minds of the *Volk*, although it is possible that if the Nazis had been in power for many more years they might have had more success. Some historians, such as D. Schoenbaum, however, argue that the Nazis did succeed in changing the values and beliefs of German people in their 12 years of power. An example is the Nazis' success in persuading many Germans that class was less important under their government, which was a vital part of their propaganda about the *Volksgemein-schaft* they were creating. As D. Geary points out, given the fear and terror and the lack of any overt alternatives, it is extremely difficult to distinguish what was genuine support for Nazi aims and values from what was merely passive acquiescence.

The Hitler 'myth'

Goebbels also worked hard to establish the 'Hitler myth', which portrayed Hitler as the all-knowing, all-caring, hardworking and all-powerful Führer whose task was to unite all Germans in their new people's community. According to this, any errors or mistakes were the fault of others in the government or the NSDAP, and Hitler was thus seen as 'above' the party and its regime (although this was less true when Germany began to experience Allied bombing). Generally, though, Hitler was portrayed as a 'man of the people' – unlike the aristocratic Göring or the corrupt officials of the Nazi regime – who symbolised a national unity and harmony which had been lacking in Germany since the collapse of imperial Germany and the creation of the Weimar Republic. This was especially true of the period 1936–42 when there was relative economic success and a series of diplomatic and military victories. The 'myth' also depicted Hitler as the representative of law and order and as someone who was less extreme than the Nazi thugs who committed many acts of violence and brutality on the ground. It also allowed Hitler to remain untarnished, even in periods when the Nazi regime was less popular.

Foreign policy and war

There has been much debate among historians about the aims of Nazi foreign policy, especially about whether Hitler always intended to launch a world or, merely, a major war. Certainly, many point to the fact that in *Mein Kampf* Hitler spoke of the need to create a greater Germany which could go on to win *Lebensraum* (living space) in the east. Furthermore, Hitler's hatred of communism, and the general Nazi ideas about struggle and war, seemed to point to the inevitability of, at the very least, a major conflict with the Soviet Union. While most historians agree that it was Hitler who was the creator of and the driving force behind the international ambitions and actions of Nazi Germany, there are those who argue that it was other forces, such as the dynamism of the Nazi movement itself or internal economic and political factors, that shaped the unfolding of foreign policy.

The 'revisionist' phase, 1933–36

Continuity

To begin with, despite the rhetoric of *Mein Kampf* and Nazi election propaganda, German foreign policy did not undergo any dramatic changes when Hitler became chancellor in 1933. From 1923–28, Gustav Stresemann had followed a policy of gradually and peacefully persuading the Allies to revise parts of the Treaty of Versailles. This was based on the belief that a cautious and moderate approach would lead to concessions regarding the terms of the treaty which most Germans saw as a diktat or slave treaty. This approach resulted in Germany signing the Locarno Treaty and the Kellogg–Briand Pact and being allowed to join the League of Nations. After Stresemann's death in 1929, Weimar politicians continued with this approach, although there were signs after 1931 of a more unilateral attempt to revise the treaty.

This continued to be the German policy in the early years of Nazi rule (although Hitler did accelerate the pace) for a number of reasons: the German economy was still suffering from the depression, Hitler's political position was not yet secure and Germany's armed forces were too weak. On becoming chancellor, Hitler allowed the previous foreign minister, the conservative Nationalist Constantin von Neurath, to carry on, partly because this would reassure Germany's neighbours that there would be no dramatic changes to foreign policy, but chiefly because Hitler's main aim at this time was to establish control of Germany itself. Thus Hitler tried to maintain good relations with

Britain and Italy, while trying to isolate France and weaken its influence. As early as 3 February 1933, however, Hitler told German army officers of his intention to expand Germany's military strength to make it the most powerful force in Europe by 1938; after that, Germany would seek *Lebensraum* in the east, especially at the expense of the Soviet Union.

By 1933, the European and international situation was still largely shaped by the effects of the Wall Street Crash in 1929 and the subsequent depression. This had led to the Japanese invasion of Manchuria in 1931 and the public exposure of the League of Nations' inability to take an effective stand against aggression. With the USA still not a member of the League, Britain and France were its leading powers. Britain was concerned about its empire in Asia and was reluctant to see the League have sufficient power to act as the policeman of the world. By 1933, the impact of the depression in France had led to a growing political instability which weakened the ability of French governments to pursue a consistently vigorous foreign policy. For the first few years of his regime Hitler was thus able to take advantage of this situation, despite Germany's relative weaknesses.

First steps

When Hitler came to power, Germany was participating in the World Disarmament Conference, which had begun in 1932. In 1933, Germany proposed that either all nations should disarm to the level imposed on Germany by the Treaty of Versailles or Germany should be allowed to rearm to France's level. When France refused to accept this (even though Britain supported the idea of both states having an army of 200,000), Hitler immediately withdrew Germany from the conference in October 1933 and then from the League. France had thus been made to appear unreasonable, and Hitler won sympathy from some British politicians. France was further isolated and weakened by Hitler's January 1934 decision to sign a 10-year non-aggression pact with Poland, despite the fact that all Weimar governments had objected to the loss of Upper Silesia, Danzig and the Polish Corridor. Poland now believed that agreement could be reached with Germany, thus undermining the earlier defensive system of alliances France had made with Poland and some other eastern European states. These treaties had been designed to put pressure on Germany's eastern frontier and so deter a future invasion of France. Although this move angered many officials in the German foreign ministry and Nazi activists, in the international arena Hitler again appeared to be a reasonable statesman even though France's position had been undermined. Despite growing sympathy in Britain for Germany's desire to revise parts of the Treaty of Versailles, Hitler's support for the 1934 attempt by the Austrian Nazis to stage a coup (which resulted in the murder of the Austrian prime minister) alienated both Britain and Italy. Italy was so concerned that Mussolini placed 40,000 troops on Italy's borders with Austria to deter a possible German invasion.

Hitler further alienated Britain and Italy in March 1935 when he announced that, contrary to the military restrictions of Versailles, Germany again had an airforce (*Luftwaffe*) and that, as he no longer felt bound by the military restrictions of Versailles, he was introducing conscription in order to build up the German army to 550,000 men (the limit imposed on Germany in 1919 had been 100,000). In fact, the army had already been expanding: by mid-1934, it was 240,000 strong. Hitler was encouraged to make these unilateral moves by the return of the Saarland (important for coal and iron) in January 1935, which had voted to return to German control after 15 years of administration by the League of Nations. The consequence of these announcements dismayed Hitler: Britain, France and Italy met at Stresa in Italy and decided to form the Stresa Front to resist any further moves by Germany to overturn the treaty without further negotiation.

However, the Stresa Front's unity did not last long and Hitler was soon able to continue. In June 1935 Britain, unhappy at France's hardline stance over Germany and its pact with the USSR, signed a naval agreement with Germany which allowed the German navy to expand beyond the limits set in 1919, provided it was never more than 35 per cent of the size of Britain's. Britain had not discussed this agreement with France or Italy, thus undermining the Stresa Front. Hitler was further helped when Mussolini invaded Abyssinia in October 1935. Britain and France eventually (though half-heartedly) opposed the invasion, although France in particular was concerned not to alienate Mussolini. Hitler offered his support to his fellow fascist and Italy soon left the Stresa Front and moved closer to Nazi Germany, signing the Rome–Berlin Axis in October 1936.

Following this fresh evidence of the League's weakness in the face of aggression by a powerful country, Hitler decided to press on with his unilateral revision of the Treaty of Versailles. In March 1936 he sent German troops into the Rhineland, a demilitarised zone since 1919, thereby also breaching the Treaty of Locarno. Hitler seemed to ignore the fact that the German army was still not strong enough to fight Britain or France. Both the foreign ministry and the German high command opposed this risky gamble. Hitler was finally persuaded to allow German troops to retreat at the first sign of opposition from the Allies. Even though only 22,000 German troops were sent in, Hitler calculated that there would be no resistance and was proved correct. Britain persuaded France to take no action. This success weakened Hitler's critics and strengthened his resolve to take a more aggressive stance in the immediate future. In November 1936 Hitler signed the Anti-Comintern Pact with Japan.

The Four-Year Plan

Despite Hitler's success over the reoccupation of the Rhineland, Germany still faced certain political and economic problems which had to be overcome before any serious war could be fought. In particular, the traditional elites in the foreign ministry and the army wanted to continue pursuing diplomacy as a way of creating a stronger Germany, while the economic crisis of 1936 underlined the fact that Germany was not yet able to fight any sustained war. One response to this economic crisis was the Four-Year Plan, which, under the direction of

Göring, was designed to get Germany ready, economically and militarily, to fight a war. It also led to increased economic penetration of the Balkans by Nazi Germany. There was conflicting advice about the diplomatic course to follow: several leading Nazis wanted to reach a closer understanding with Britain, while von Ribbentrop wanted Germany to join forces with Italy and Japan. Although Hitler preferred the British option (mainly to achieve the destruction of the Soviet Union), the fact that there were few signs that Britain wanted a close relationship with Germany led him to sign the Rome–Berlin Axis with Fascist Italy in November 1936. Prior to that, these fascist states had been co-operating since July 1936 in giving military assistance to the Nationalists in the Spanish Civil War. The members of the League of Nations had adopted a policy of non-intervention in the civil war, which was never enforced. By the end of 1936, Nazi Germany had succeeded in tearing up most of the Treaty of Versailles relating to Germany and its western borders without suffering any military consequences. As a result, Hitler now felt able to turn his attentions to his long-term plans to win *Lebensraum* in the east.

The Hossbach Memorandum, 1937

Before 1937 Hitler had been able to achieve his territorial ambitions without going to war. However, by November 1937 Germany appeared to be in a stronger position and Hitler began to despair of ever achieving an Anglo-German alliance. Rearmament was well under way, the economic crisis of 1936 was mainly over and Göring's Four-Year Plan seemed to be producing results. In addition, in 1937 Italy joined the Anti-Comintern Pact, which Germany had signed with Japan in 1936. This meant that both Britain and France were now uncertain about the fate of their Asian colonies and felt a growing unease about the situation in Europe.

On 5 November 1937 Hitler called a meeting with Foreign Minister von Neurath, War Minister Blomberg and the three commanders-in-chief of the armed forces. Historians are divided about the significance of this meeting and the record of what was apparently said at it. Colonel Hossbach, Hitler's adjutant, took no notes during the meeting and made a summary of its main points the following day. These notes have become known as the Hossbach Memorandum. According to Hossbach, Hitler told those present to get Germany ready for conquests in the east and stressed that this campaign should be completed by 1943–45 while Germany was still militarily superior to Britain. Hitler apparently also spoke of plans to seize Austria and Czechoslovakia, even if this provoked war with Britain and France. Historians like A. J. P. Taylor have questioned the reliability of this document and whether 1937 was a conscious turning point in Hitler's foreign policy. Some historians have seen what Hitler said at this meeting more as his way of justifying his rearmament programme to doubting conservatives than as a definite plan. Hitler was further encouraged when Lord Halifax arrived from Britain in November 1937 to say that Neville Chamberlain's government would support legitimate revisions of Germany's borders with Austria and Czechoslovakia, provided this was done peacefully.

The pre-war crises, 1938–39

Regardless of the debates surrounding the Hossbach Memorandum, Hitler's foreign policy became more adventurous in the years 1938–39. Hitler first made several personnel changes to ensure greater personal control of the foreign ministry and the army. In January 1938, exploiting the opportunity presented by sex scandals, he dismissed the moderate war minister, von Blomberg, who had married a former prostitute, and von Fritsch, the commander-in-chief of the army, who was falsely accused by the SS of being a homosexual. Hitler took over the post of minister for war and declared himself to be the supreme commander of all the armed forces. He also created a new personal high command (*Oberkommando der Wehrmacht* or OKW) for the armed forces under the command of General Keitel, a known supporter of Nazi plans. Göring was made a field marshal and other leading positions were also filled by convinced Nazis. Later von Ribbentrop, another leading Nazi, replaced von Neurath as foreign minister.

Anschluss with Austria

With his personal power secured, Hitler's next important territorial step was taken in Austria. Hitler first attempted to achieve union (*Anschluss*) with Austria, which was specifically forbidden by the Treaty of Versailles, in 1934. Hitler used the Austrian Nazi Party to create a crisis in Austria and, following an invitation by the Nazi members of the coalition government to restore order, he sent German troops into Austria in March 1938. With no opposition from either Britain or France, Hitler was able to carry out a successful *Anschluss* with Austria without a shot being fired.

Czechoslovakia, 1938–39

With Britain following a policy of appeasement, Hitler turned his attentions to the 3.5 million German-speakers living in the Sudeten border region of Czechoslovakia. These former citizens of the Austrian empire, stirred up by the pro-Nazi Sudeten German Party, provided Hitler with another excuse for military action. Convinced that Britain and France would not risk a war over Czechoslovakia, Hitler seems to have intended its complete destruction. However, the crisis built up to such an extent that by September 1938 the prospect of war seemed a reality, especially as Czechoslovakia had had a defence treaty with France since 1924. In addition, France and the USSR had both signed an undertaking to protect Czech independence in May 1935.

The Czechs had an efficient, though small, army and seemed prepared to resist. Hitler's military advisers warned that Germany was not yet ready for a European war. In the end, Britain, France, Germany and Italy (neither Czechoslovakia nor the Soviet Union was present) agreed at the Munich Conference in September 1938 that the Czech government should hand over the Sudetenland to Nazi Germany. In return, Hitler promised that this would be his last territorial demand. With no offer of help, despite the treaties, the Czech government was forced to comply. Later in the month, Poland and then Hungary seized land from Czechoslovakia.

Once again, Nazi Germany had increased its population and added significantly to its agricultural and industrial resources without having had to resort to fighting. In addition, with its former border defences in German hands, Czechoslovakia's ability to resist future aggression was severely reduced. Within three weeks of occupying the Sudetenland, Hitler ordered his armies to get ready to invade the rest of Czechoslovakia.

Poland

By the end of 1938, Hitler was convinced that Britain would not oppose his plan to obtain *Lebensraum* in the east by invading the USSR. He correctly calculated that Britain was more concerned about communism than the ambitions of Nazi Germany in the east. At the same time, Stalin came to believe that his attempts to build an anti-Nazi alliance with Britain and France were doomed to failure. For very different reasons, both Germany and the Soviet Union began to consider the possibility of reaching a temporary understanding. While European diplomacy was still undecided, Hitler ordered the invasion of the rest of Czechoslovakia in March 1939 and received no opposition from Britain or France.

However, in February, Britain had moved closer to France and had signed a military alliance. When Britain and France announced that they had signed a pact with Poland, guaranteeing its independence, Hitler's plans to move against Poland without facing opposition seemed to be somewhat undermined. In order to counter this, Hitler decided to strengthen his military alliance with Fascist Italy and, in May 1939, Hitler and Mussolini signed the Pact of Steel. More importantly, Hitler also decided to pursue negotiations with the USSR, so that there would be no ally for Britain and France in the east.

It was not until July/August that Britain began, half-heartedly, to consider a pact with the USSR against Nazi aggression. In July 1939 trade talks between Germany and the Soviet Union began and, in August, a 10-year non-aggression pact (containing a secret clause for the joint dismemberment of Poland) was signed between these two states.

On 1 September 1939, confident that Britain and France would not honour their pledges, Nazi Germany invaded Poland. To Hitler's surprise, the commitments were honoured and on 3 September Britain and France declared war on Germany, after Hitler had refused to comply with an ultimatum ordering him to withdraw German troops from Poland. Significantly, this came at a time when the Four-Year Plan and the rearmament programme had not yet reached the desired levels of economic and military preparedness.

The Nazi state at war, 1939–45

For the first eight months, the war presented Hitler with no immediate problems as what became known as the 'phoney war' existed on Germany's western borders. German forces in the east were able to secure 'their' share of Poland after only three weeks of devastating *Blitzkrieg* (lightning war).

Early successes, 1939–41

After this easy victory and having failed to persuade Britain and France to make peace, Hitler turned his attentions to the west. His plan was to invade France and so leave Britain with no choice but to agree to further German expansion into eastern Europe and to accept German hegemony in continental Europe. After overcoming the reluctance of some of his military commanders, Hitler launched a new *Blitzkrieg* against several western European states in April and May 1940. Within three months, Norway, the Netherlands and Belgium had been invaded and occupied, and France was also defeated and then partially occupied.

Despite his inability to defeat Britain in the autumn of 1940, Hitler turned his attention to invading the Soviet Union (see pp. 77–78). The German attack (code-named Operation Barbarossa) was originally intended to begin in the spring of 1941, but was delayed until June 1941 as Germany had to divert troops to North Africa, Greece and the Balkans in order to assist the Italian armies facing serious problems in those theatres of war.

Despite these delays and diversions, the initial *Blitzkrieg* against the USSR seemed destined to be as successful as the earlier campaigns. Up till then, the German people had benefited from the tremendous amount of goods and raw materials that had been taken from the newly conquered territories. Hitler was also reluctant to cut living standards to help pay for the war (the social welfare programmes, for example, continued unchanged) or to mobilise women for industrial work (as this might make family life more difficult and conflict with Nazi ideology on gender roles).

Defeat, 1941–45

By the winter of 1941, however, the German army began to suffer from determined Soviet resistance and the effects of a bitter winter, neither of which it was really prepared for. Hitler compounded his problems in December 1941 by declaring war on the USA, which, since the Japanese attack on Pearl Harbor, was now at war with his ally in Asia. From then on, despite achieving some successes now and again, the period 1941–45 was one of growing military defeat for the Nazi war machine.

The winter of 1942–43 was clearly a turning point. The main reason for this was Hitler's fanatical insistence on defeating the USSR, which meant that the bulk of Germany's military might was concentrated on the eastern front even after it had become clear that the situation was hopeless. Also important was Hitler's interference with purely military matters, his growing differences with army commanders and the fact that Germany was not able to fight a prolonged total war on so many fronts at once.

Göring's Four-Year Plan was designed for fighting a limited war using *Blitzkrieg* methods. Evidence suggests that the leading Nazis did not expect Germany's economy and military to be really ready for war until 1943–45. Although some 60 per cent of all German investment from 1936 to 1940 was on war-related items, this percentage dropped to about 40 per cent of GNP after 1940 and did not rise to over 50 per cent until 1942. In contrast Britain had been spending over 50 per cent of its GNP on war-related items since 1940. The German economy was not put on a total war footing until 1943, when Speer, the new minister for armaments, was given wide powers to organise raw materials and mass production. At the same time, the new minister for labour began to make more use of German women as well as conscripted foreign workers and Soviet slave labour. Although Nazi Germany's production of weapons was boosted throughout the period 1943–44 from an index of 100 in January 1942 to 322 by July 1944 – despite the effects of Allied bombing – it never matched the capacities of the USSR, the USA and Britain. This situation – which was not helped by the conflicting demands of local *Gauleiter* and the huge semi-independent economic empire run by the SS – was ultimately responsible for the defeat of the Third Reich in May 1945. Before then, with the Soviet Union's Red Army already in the suburbs of Berlin, Hitler committed suicide on 30 April.

The historical debate

One of the assumptions behind the Nuremberg trials that followed the end of the Second World War was that Hitler had deliberately planned such a war, even before he came to power. This was based on a study of his book *Mein Kampf*. There was certainly the belief that after 1933 he followed some masterplan which he pursued consistently up to and beyond the start of the war. Initially, most historians shared this view, pointing to how Hitler began attempts to drive wedges between Poland and France, and between Italy and its Stresa Front partners, Britain and France, as early as 1934. H. Trevor-Roper, for instance, argued that Hitler had systematically followed a foreign policy which, step by step, was designed to achieve his long-term aims. The examination of specific crises tended to confirm this view: during the Czech crisis, for instance, Hitler had set a date for the invasion (1 October) as early as May 1938. Similarly, once the whole of Czechoslovakia had been invaded and Memel taken from Lithuania, Hitler then set 1 September 1939 as the date for the invasion of Poland – even before he had secured the Non-Aggression Pact with the Soviet Union.

This orthodox view, known as the intentionalist school, was first strongly criticised by the historian A. J. P. Taylor in *The origins of the Second World War*, published in 1961. His claims that Hitler had not followed a pre-determined masterplan for war, and his questioning of the reliability of the Hossbach Memorandum as historical evidence, provoked heated historical debate. Taylor argued that Hitler's foreign policy was essentially improvised and based on simply making the most of opportunities when they arose. The furious historical arguments which this opportunist (or structuralist) position unleashed led him to issue a foreword to a second edition of *Origins* in 1963, entitled 'Second thoughts', in part to reject claims that his book somehow 'vindicated Hitler'. He stressed that simply directing 'his generals to prepare for war' did not mean that Hitler was actively intending to start a war. He pointed out that from 1935 British and French governments also directed their generals to prepare for a possible war. His argument was that such plans 'were precautions, not "blueprints for aggression"'. He also stressed how Hitler's desire to overturn the Treaty of Versailles and also to restore German greatness was an aim 'shared by all German politicians, by the Social Democrats who ended the war in 1918 as much as by Stresemann'. Taylor claimed that German rearmament after 1936 was not as great as Hitler claimed, to the extent that by 1939 Germany's armed forces were not strong enough to sustain a world, or even a European, war.

Since then the debate has continued, with historians divided into two camps:

The orthodox-intentionalists

A. Bullock (1971) continued to argue that there was a firm connection between *Mein Kampf* and Hitler's later direction of foreign policy to obtain *Lebensraum* in the east, though he did concede that opportunism was important as regards short-term tactics. Other historians, such as A. Hillgruber (1965) and K. Hildebrand (1973), have argued that Hitler was clearly following a carefully staged plan (*Stufenplan*) which was intended to go beyond the conquest of Europe and culminate in a war against the USA for world domination. G. Weinberg (1980) and M. Hauner (1981) have stressed Hitler's personal direction of foreign policy, in spite of the existence of competing factions and groups within the Third Reich. The intentionalists argue among themselves over whether Hitler ultimately intended to defeat the USA and so achieve world domination (the globalists) or whether he was merely aiming for European hegemony (the continentalists).

The revisionist-structuralists

This school of thought rejects the idea of Hitler being in firm control of foreign affairs or of having a clear or consistent long-term plan. K. D. Bracher (1973) argues that Hitler's foreign policy was essentially a spontaneous response to internal problems and external opportunities. M. Broszat (1970) also believes that Hitler's foreign policy was linked to domestic considerations. T. Mason (1977 and 1981) stresses how foreign policy and war preparation were limited by the economic problems of the 1930s and how Hitler's foreign policy was more confused than planned, and was often an escape from the economic problems he could not (or would not) solve. T. Mason, in particular, sees war in 1939 as a deliberate ploy on Hitler's part to escape the economic difficulties that resulted from the Nazis' unco-ordinated economic and military policies which took Germany near to collapse. Thus Hitler needed short *Blitzkrieg* wars to avoid the impending crisis.

Continuity or discontinuity?

Historians are also divided over whether German foreign policy after 1933 was merely a more aggressive continuation of previous policies of expansion or whether it was a distinctive break arising from Hitler's personal priorities. Most historians – G. Eley (1980) and F. Fischer (1986) among others – stress the continuity in general principles, even though the addition of anti-Semitism and the policy of extermination of ethnic minorities stemmed from Hitler's personal prejudices and his Austrian (rather than German) roots. Others argue that after

Stresemann died German foreign policy moved from peaceful collaboration to a more unilateral stance. An example is when Germany first attempted *Anschluss* with Austria in March 1931, when Brüning tried to create a customs union with Austria – this scheme was quickly blocked by the Allies. Rearmament, too, was first begun by von Papen in July 1932, when he authorised secret increases in the army and weapons produced, in breach of the Treaty of Versailles. There was also a considerable degree of continuity as regards military and diplomatic personnel from the Weimar period until Hitler's reorganisation in 1938.

The Nazi 'revolution'

8.1 The role of the Nazi Party, 1934

Furthermore, the Führer stressed that those people who maintained that the revolution was not finished were fools; they did this only with the intention of getting particular jobs for themselves. The Führer described what difficulty he had in filling all the posts with the right people and went on to say that we had people in the movement whose conception of revolution was a permanent state of chaos . . . The Party must bring about the stability on which Germany's future depended. It must secure this stability.

Source: F. McDonough, *Hitler and Nazi Germany*, Cambridge, 1999, p. 40

8.2 Index of wages, 1928–38 (1936 = 100)

1928	125
1933	88
1934	94
1936	100
1938	106

Source: S. Lee, *Hitler and Nazi Germany*, London, 1998, p. 75

8.3 Nazi wages policy: a historian's view

The regime, as Siegel has argued, pegged real wages at depression rates, and turned a blind eye to employers who undercut the official levels. Many of the re-employed worked on work-creation schemes, or in some form of labour service, where there was little cash pay at all. Average earnings were actually lower in 1933 and 1934 than in the last depression year, 1932. Changes in productivity were used to boost profits and investments rather than raise wage rates. Expressed as either wage-rates or earnings, the real value of incomes peaked in 1929–30 and declined thereafter. Real earnings only regained the 1929 level in 1941 under pressure of wartime labour scarcity.

Source: R. J. Overy, *The Nazi economic recovery 1932–1938*, 2nd edn, Cambridge, 1996, p. 31

8.4 Classes in the Nazi state: a speech by Hitler, 1 May 1937

We in Germany have really broken with a world of prejudices. I leave myself out of account. I, too, am a child of the people; I do not trace my line from any castle; I come from the workshop. Neither was I a general: I was simply a soldier, as were millions of others . . . By my side stand Germans from all walks of life who today are amongst the leaders of the nation: men who once were workers on the land are now governing German states in the name of the Reich . . . It is true that men who came from the bourgeoisie and former aristocrats have their place in this Movement. But to us it matters nothing whence they come if only they can work to the profit of our people. That is the decisive test. We have not broken down classes in order to set new ones in their place: we have broken down classes to make way for the German people as a whole.

Source: N. Baynes (ed.), *Hitler's speeches 1922–39*, vol. 2, Oxford, 1942, pp. 620–21

8.5 The impact of Nazi economic policy

The small businessmen are in a state of gloom and despondency. These people, to whom the present system to a large extent owes its rise, are the most disappointed of all. The shortages of goods restrict their turnover, but they cannot respond by putting up their prices because the price decrees prevent them from doing so . . . one can say of many of them that inwardly they have long since turned away from the system and would welcome its fall.

Source: Extract from a secret SPD report on the situation in central Germany, July 1939, in J. Laver, *Nazi Germany 1933–1945*, London, 1991, p. 21

8.6 Women and the Nazi state

The slogan 'Emancipation of Women' was invented by Jewish intellectuals and its content was formed by the same spirit. In the really good times of German life the German woman had no need to emancipate herself . . .

If the man's world is said to be the State, his struggle, his readiness to devote his powers to the service of the community, then it may perhaps be said that the woman's is a smaller world. For her world is her husband, her family, her children, and her home . . .

We do not consider it correct for the woman to interfere in the world of man, in his main sphere. We consider it natural if these two worlds remain distinct . . .

Source: Extract from Hitler's 'Address to Women', Nuremberg party rally, 8 September 1934, in J. Laver, *Nazi Germany 1933–1945*, London, 1991, pp. 63–64

Document case-study questions

1 Explain, *briefly*, who the 'fools' referred to in document 8.1 were and what happened to them in 1934.

2 How does the evidence of document 8.2 support the view given in document 8.3 about wages under the Nazis?

3 Assess the reliability of document 8.4 about Nazi claims to have created a 'classless' *Volksgemeinschaft* as historical evidence.

4 How useful is document 8.5 as historical evidence of the feelings of sections of the *Mittelstand* towards Nazi economic policy?

5 What can you learn from document 8.6 about the role played by women in the Nazi state?

6 How far do these six documents, and any other evidence known to you, support the view that Hitler's claims to have carried through a Nazi 'revolution' were false?

Consolidating and maintaining the Nazi dictatorship, 1933–39

When Hitler became chancellor in January 1933, his position was far from secure. Von Hindenburg had only agreed to Hitler becoming chancellor because von Papen assured him that he could limit Hitler's powers: von Papen had said that within a couple of months 'we will have pushed Hitler so far into a corner that he'll squeak'. Furthermore, as events in the years 1930–33 show, chancellors were dependent on the support of the president and it was clear that von Hindenburg detested Hitler. Yet within weeks of Hitler's appointment the Nazi Party had taken control of Germany and had already begun to establish a Nazi dictatorship.

Creating the Nazi dictatorship

In the main, Hitler and the Nazis were able to create their dictatorship, and so destroy the hated Weimar Republic, by using legal methods to which the NSDAP had been committed – theoretically – since 1925.

First steps

As Hitler's Nazi–Nationalist coalition was still without a majority in the *Reichstag*, his first move – within 24 hours of becoming chancellor – was to call an election for March 1933. Hitler expected this to result in a Nazi majority in the *Reichstag* or at least increase the number of Nazi seats and thus strengthen his position; either way, he intended this to be Germany's last election.

The campaign itself was far from democratic. Hitler obtained presidential decrees that enabled him to ban the main opposition parties' political meetings and newspapers. At the same time Göring, who was also minister of the interior in Prussia (the largest *Land* in Germany), was given sweeping powers when Hitler dissolved the provincial parliament there. Already in control of 60 per cent of Germany's police, Göring immediately drafted an extra 50,000 (most of whom were members of the SA and SS) into an auxiliary force to assist the Prussian police. He then ordered them to take action against the SPD and the KPD: meetings were broken up and about 70 people died as a result of the Nazi violence. Hitler used this violence to his advantage in the election campaign by claiming that it – like the economic devastation of the depression and the humiliating Treaty of Versailles – was the result of Weimar democracy.

A donation of over 3 million Rentenmarks from big business leaders enabled the Nazis to wage an extremely effective propaganda campaign. With such funds, and Goebbels' skilful use of the Nazi monopoly of the state media (especially the radio), the Nazis felt confident that they would win many more seats in the election.

The *Reichstag* fire

The Nazis' election chances were further improved when the *Reichstag* building was set on fire on 27 February. Although a young Dutch communist, Marinus van der Lubbe, was arrested on the scene and later executed, it is still far from clear whether he or the Nazis themselves were responsible for this act.

Hitler made good use of the incident to move Germany closer to dictatorship by portraying the fire as a signal for the start of a communist revolution. On 28 February, he instructed Minister of the Interior Frick to draft a Decree for the Protection of the People and State, which was approved and signed by von Hindenburg. This decree outlawed the KPD and gave the government the power to suspend most of the civil and political liberties established by the Weimar constitution. As a result, thousands of the Nazis' political opponents (especially Communists and Socialists) were arrested at will, their newspapers were shut down and SA violence and intimidation were stepped up. It also provided for the suspension of *Länder* governments, thus strengthening central government.

Despite all this, the Nazis were only able to push their share of the vote up to 43.9 per cent from the 33.1 per cent they had gained in November 1932. In many working-class and Catholic areas, in fact, the Nazis were heavily outvoted. Not surprisingly, the overall votes of the KPD declined, but the SPD did extremely well to hold its own. Support for the DVP and other middle-class parties also declined.

The Nazis then simply seized control of several *Länder* governments where their opponents were in power, sometimes without official approval and usually accompanied by extreme violence. In fact, the chaos resulting from the activities of some local Nazi parties was so great that the minister of the interior was forced to intervene.

The Enabling Act, March 1933

Although the Nazis still did not have an absolute majority in the *Reichstag*, their 288 seats did enhance their position. By negotiating with the 52 deputies of the DNVP for their support, the Nazis were able to claim a majority. Yet even this was not enough to overturn the Weimar constitution, as a two-thirds majority was needed to make any changes. Nonetheless, Hitler requested full emergency powers for four years in order to deal with the 'communist threat.' This would allow him to make laws without the approval of the *Reichstag*. To achieve this, two methods were used. Hitler first needed to obtain support from other centre-right parties in order to allay conservative fears about the growing pressure from some of the more militant lower sections of the NSDAP. On 21 March, Goebbels organised the opening ceremony of the new *Reichstag* in the Potsdam garrison church. At the ceremony, at which many important conservatives were present (including von Hindenburg, army generals and the son of the deposed kaiser), Hitler claimed that the Nazis were in tune with the values of Imperial Germany.

This 'Day of Potsdam' was followed, two days later, by the first session of the *Reichstag*. Hitler executed the second part of his plan when he excluded all communist deputies, while large numbers of the SA and the SS crowded into the room and behaved in a threatening way. Hitler then persuaded the ZP to support his demands for emergency powers by promising to respect the rights of the Catholic Church and Christian principles in general. In this way, with only SPD deputies voting against him, Hitler obtained the necessary two-thirds majority to have this legislation, known as the Enabling Act, passed.

Gleichschaltung

Hitler thus undermined the democracy of the Weimar constitution in what has been described as a 'legal revolution'. Hitler and the Nazis then turned their attention to how to use their power to establish a one-party totalitarian dictatorship under the personal leadership of Hitler. The main method they used is usually referred to as *Gleichschaltung* (meaning 'bringing into line' or 'co-ordination'). This was an attempt to co-ordinate as many aspects of German political, social and cultural life as possible with Nazi ideology and values. Although in some respects this was achieved by using the rank-and-file of the Nazi movement in a 'revolution from below', it was much more a 'revolution from above' as the process was directed and controlled by the Nazi leadership. At first the prime targets were other political parties, the *Länder* and the trade unions, all of which stood in the way of the Third Reich the Nazis were determined to construct.

The *Länder*

The first steps in creating the Nazi dictatorship were directed at the system of local government in the *Länder*. Even under the Second Reich, the provinces had had a considerable degree of political autonomy and the Weimar constitution had perpetuated this as a way of preventing the central government from becoming too strong. Since February/March and the passing of the Law for the Protection of the People and State, Nazis in the provinces had been intimidating their opponents (this included the use of torture and murder in several areas) and undermining the *Länder* governments.

In an attempt to control this, and not alienate conservatives, who were uneasy about the increase in SA violence, Hitler took steps in April 1933 to formalise Nazi control of local government. Nazi-dominated *Länder* governments were given powers to make laws without having to obtain the approval of the provincial parliaments (*Landtage*). Hitler also appointed 10 Nazi officials, known as Reich governors (*Reichstatthalter*), who were often the local NSDAP *Gauleiter*. These governors were given wide powers to govern and to carry out the Führer's decisions on policy.

The administrative situation in the provinces was confused by Hitler's decision to retain the regional minister-presidents (*Ministerpräsidenten*), responsible for local administration, because their responsibilities overlapped with those of the Reich governors. In January 1934 the Law for the Reconstruction of the Reich abolished all the *Landtage*, and all federal governments, including the minister-presidents and the Reich governors, were placed under the central control of the ministry of the interior. Despite these measures, some local Nazi parties continued to take matters into their own hands, leading Frick to order all Nazi activists to stop committing 'excesses' in October 1933. In the cities, the post of lord mayor was retained, but in January 1935 a new post of delegate of the NSDAP in the municipality, with the power to dismiss mayors and councillors, was created, to which Nazi officials were appointed.

The trade unions

The trade unions in Germany had a large membership and a considerable amount of latent power. Most trade union members had strong loyalties to the Catholic Church or to the SPD and KPD and were therefore hostile to the Nazi Party. However, their power and membership had been eroded by the effects of mass unemployment.

Trade union leaders consciously did not use the potential power they retained in the early days of Hitler's government as many believed that it would soon fall and thus it was wiser not to provoke any possible retaliations. Some even believed a moderate policy might make it possible to continue to operate under a Nazi government. This seemed plausible when the Nazis declared that 1 May (International Workers' Day) would be a national holiday. However, on 2 May 1933 SA and SS members occupied trade union buildings and most leaders and the more militant activists were arrested. Trade unions were then abolished, their funds confiscated and all workers were ordered to join the Nazi German Labour Front (*Deutsche Arbeitsfront* or DAF). It was intended that this organisation would impose Nazi control over the workers and it had no power to negotiate freely on wages or working conditions.

Big business

German industry and business, in theory at least, were also 'co-ordinated'. In June 1933, the various employers' associations merged to form the Estate of German Industry; then in January 1934 the whole of German business was reorganised on functional and territorial lines, with the Reich economic chamber in overall control. In practice, however, businessmen, industrialists and their directors retained control of their companies' affairs and were able to resist the appointment of Nazis to key positions.

The political parties

As the Nazi Party wished to establish a dictatorship, they soon turned their attention to eliminating all other political parties. This was achieved through a series of staggered acts. The Communist Party had already been banned in February after the *Reichstag* fire. On 22 June 1933 the SPD was also abolished. In the following weeks, the combination of pressure and opportunism led the remaining political parties either to announce their merger with the NSDAP or simply to wind themselves up voluntarily.

On 14 July Hitler imposed the Law against the Formation of New Parties which formally declared Germany to be a one-party state and the Nazis to be the only legal party. Anyone discovered engaging in non-Nazi political activity faced a three-year prison sentence. Thus, within six months of being appointed chancellor, Hitler had turned Germany into a one-party dictatorship. Another election took place in November 1933, but, with only the Nazi Party allowed to contest it, all the seats in the Reichstag were won by the NSDAP.

The people

In order to 'co-ordinate' the ordinary German people, the Nazis used their party structures to control and report on them. The block leaders (*Blockleiter*), over 400,000 strong, were particularly useful: although they were on the lowest rung of NSDAP officialdom, they were in charge of one block of flats or group of houses and spied on their neighbours and reported any critics to their superiors.

The Night of the Long Knives, June 1934

Although by June 1934 the process of *Gleichschaltung* had gone a long way towards establishing a Nazi dictatorship, Hitler's position was not yet fully consolidated. The German army had not been 'co-ordinated' and remained a force with the power to oppose and even overthrow him. At the same time, Hitler's position as well as that of other leading Nazis within the party was being increasingly threatened by the more militant populist sections of the rank-and-file of the party who now wanted Hitler to carry out a 'second revolution' based on the socialist sections of the party's programme. In particular, Ernst Röhm, who was one of Hitler's earliest colleagues and the leader of the 2.5-million strong SA, was demanding that the regular army be merged with the SA to form a new People's Army under his command. Nazis such as Röhm had been worried for some time by Hitler's growing contacts with the conservatives and industrial leaders and had been further dismayed by Hitler's speech to the *Reichstatthalter* on 6 July 1933 in which he said that the Nazi 'revolution' was at an end.

Such threats to the German establishment elites, especially Röhm's call for the formation of a people's militia, were not going to be tolerated by the aristocratic commanders of the army, who clearly despised the SA 'upstarts'. Hitler did not wish to upset the army commanders, not least because their support and military expertise were essential if his foreign policy objectives were to be met. In fact, as early as April 1934, the army generals had met with Hitler on the battleship *Deutschland*, although there is no written record of any deal regarding support for Hitler's bid to become president.

Hitler was concerned that the activities of Röhm and his followers, if not checked, might provoke the *Reichswehr* (army) into taking action against the new Nazi regime as a whole. It was also clear by June 1934 that von Hindenburg did not have very long to live. At the same time, Hitler (who had never genuinely supported the 'left-wing' populist elements of the party's programme) was determined to establish total control of the NSDAP. Other leading Nazis, like Himmler and Göring, saw Röhm as a real rival to their influence within the party. He was potentially the most powerful of the Nazi chiefs as the SA was strong enough to carry through a 'second revolution' with or without official approval. There is evidence that Hitler was encouraged in his decision to move against Röhm and the SA by Nazis like Himmler, Göring and Hess as well as by von Papen, who warned him that failure to act soon might result in conservative opposition to his government. So on 30 June 1934, on Hitler's orders, the SS (with weapons and transport provided by the army) arrested and shot many of the leaders of the SA, including Röhm. In all, over 400 people were murdered over the next few days, including Gregor Strasser, the former leading Nazi who had been part of the party's militant populist wing that wanted action against the bigger capitalist firms. Some leading monarchists were also murdered as Hitler was concerned that the conservative elites might try to persuade von Hindenburg to replace his regime with the monarchical option.

This ruthless action effectively removed the possibility of a Nazi 'second revolution' from below. It was also popular with the army and, on 1 July, War Minister von Blomberg gave Hitler a public vote of thanks for his swift action. When von Hindenburg finally died on 1 August, the army supported Hitler's takeover of the post of president and its merger with the role of chancellor, which had been introduced by the Law concerning the Head of State of the German Reich. Hitler now called himself Führer and Reich chancellor. On 2 August the army swore an oath of personal loyalty to the new Führer and 'supreme commander of the armed forces'. At the Nazi Party rally in Nuremberg in September 1934, Hitler announced that there would be no other revolution in Germany for the next thousand years.

The Nazi state

The various political methods of achieving *Gleichschaltung* and the ruthless extermination of opponents within the NSDAP were not the only ways in which Hitler ensured the domination of the NSDAP and his own position of power.

The 'legal revolution'

As well as transforming the German political system which they inherited from the Weimar Republic, the Nazis also took steps to ensure the judicial system would be in keeping with their objectives. The entire judicial system was brought under government control by appointing as judges only those who were considered loyal and insisting that all would-be judges be trained in the 'ideological foundations' of Nazism. It was also stated that the theory of the legal system should be based on what was in the best interests of the 'national community', as determined by the Führer and the Nazi Party. The liberal basis of law which had characterised Weimar democracy was deliberately rejected. This has been described by I. Kershaw as the 'subjugation of legality'. In fact, many of the existing judiciary were national-conservatives who had never liked the liberal principles introduced by the Weimar constitution and they were often prepared to accept the 'will of the Führer'.

A parallel Nazi legal system was also created. Special courts (which had no juries) were set up in March 1933 to administer Nazi 'justice' more swiftly. Decisions about punishments were left to each court. In April 1934 a People's Court (*Volksgerichtshof*) was established in each area to deal with 'treason'. It had five judges (though only two needed to be lawyers) and a jury made up of NSDAP officials and there was no right of appeal.

All lawyers had to become members of the Nazi Lawyers' Association and the role of defence lawyers was greatly reduced. The Nazification of the entire judicial and legal system is well illustrated by the refusal of the authorities to investigate the attacks on Jewish people and properties during *Kristallnacht* in November 1938. However, it was not until 1941 that a Nazi, Thierack, was given the post of Reich minister of justice; before that the post had been held by the non-Nazi Gurtner until his death in that year. However, Gurtner had few problems reconciling himself to the Nazi concept of legality. He accepted the *Reichstag* Fire Decree (the *Lex van der Lubbe*), which, in defiance of liberal legality, retrospectively imposed the death penalty for arson and officially sanctioned the murders that took place on the Night of the Long Knives by ruling that Hitler had 'anticipated' treason.

From 1941, Germany's entire legal system came increasingly under the control of the SS. One result of the Nazification of the legal system was the increase in the number of offences carrying the death penalty: up from 3 in 1932 to 46 by 1945. In addition, it was common for prisoners to be sent to concentration camps as soon as they had completed their sentences. This led to a drop in the crime rate for several offences and was very popular with the suburban middle classes, who looked on it as a return to traditional values of law and order, and who were happy to see the streets cleared of tramps, beggars and gypsies.

Institutional terror

Another way in which Hitler maintained the Nazi dictatorship was the creation of a police – or terror – state. The cornerstone of the Nazi terror state was the SS, which had first been created in 1925 as a special bodyguard for Hitler and as a balance to the SA. In 1929, leadership of the SS had passed to Heinrich Himmler. He presided over its rapid growth and in 1931 formed a special Security Service (*Sicherheitdienst* or SD) to act as the Nazi Party's own internal police. Under his direction, the SS had grown by 1933 to over 50,000 fanatics who were deeply devoted to Hitler and the Nazi cause. During 1933 Himmler was given control of all the political police in the *Länder*. In 1934 he took over the Secret State Police (*Geheime Staatspolizei* or Gestapo), which had been set up by Göring in Prussia the previous year, and delegated the day-to-day administration of the SD and the Gestapo to his deputy, Reinhard Heydrich. Significantly, Hitler used the SS to wipe out the SA leadership in June 1934. In 1936 all police powers and organisations were united under the control of Himmler, who was made chief of the German police and *Reichsführer*. By 1939, the Gestapo and the SD had complete power to arrest, torture and execute all 'enemies of the state'.

From then on, this SS–SD–Gestapo–police empire became an increasingly powerful force and power bloc in Nazi Germany, extending its influence into all areas of German life, including the economy and even the army. Its three main sections were the *Leibstandarte*, which acted as Hitler's personal bodyguard; the *Waffen SS*, which formed military vanguard divisions to fight alongside the regular army – by 1944 it had 35 divisions; and the Death's Head Units (*Totenkopfverbände*), which ran the concentration and, later, the extermination camps. According to D. Schoenbaum, the SS ultimately came to control everything, including foreign policy.

Concentration (or detention) camps were set up almost as soon as Hitler became chancellor. The first one was at Dachau whose inmates were the communists arrested after the *Reichstag* fire in February 1933. As Hitler moved to extend his control of Germany, other prisoners soon followed, including members of the SPD, trade unionists, Jewish people, Roma and Sinti, members of religious sects who refused military service and 'anti-socials' such as beggars and homosexuals, as well as ordinary criminals. After 1934 control of these concentration camps was transferred from the SA to the SS. In all, between 1933 and 1945, over 3 million Germans were held in prisons or concentration camps for political offences. With the Gestapo's total power to arrest and detain, and the *Blockleiter* reporting to the police anyone who showed signs of not fully supporting Hitler, most of Germany was soon living in a state of constant fear. This was made worse by the fact that, as was shown by official documents after the fall of the Nazi regime in 1945, thousands of ordinary Germans were actively willing to denounce neighbours and work colleagues, and even family members, to the authorities.

Power in Nazi Germany

The traditional image of the Nazi state is that it was an extreme right-wing, one-party, totalitarian dictatorship, under the control of Hitler, who was able to make his will supreme. Certainly, the Nazis made sure that they did not face any opposition or restrictions from a parliament, other political parties, a free press or an independent trade union movement. However, there remains the question of opposition from the remaining influential elites, power blocs and informal pressure groups. Until at least 1938 Hitler did not believe it wise to antagonise groups such as the *Junker* landowners, big business, the army or the civil service. Since the 1960s, historians have differed over the question of exactly how power was distributed and used in the Nazi state and, especially, the extent to which Hitler can be seen as the dominating force in the Third Reich he created.

Institutional chaos?

Historians are generally agreed that the nature of the Nazi state and its decision-making processes was highly complex. Many have seen the different organisations of Nazi Germany as semi-independent empires, acting in competition with each other. According to J. Noakes, the system of government during the Third Reich was a 'labyrinthine structure of overlapping competencies, institutional confusion and a chaos of personal rivalries'. This was partly due to the fact that from 1931 to 1932 Hitler had turned the Nazi Party into a propaganda- and election-winning machine. As a result, by 1933 it did not possess the organisational structures it needed to run a modern industrial state.

The confusion spoken of by Noakes also resulted from the frequent overlap of responsibility between parallel and often competing state and party institutions and agencies. For instance, although Schacht was minister of economics from 1934 to 1937, with tremendous economic influence, after 1936 he was often in conflict with the growing economic empire built up by Göring and his office of the four-year plan. Göring himself, though charged with getting Germany ready for war, was often involved (especially after the failure of his *Luftwaffe* to defeat Britain in the Battle of Britain in 1940) in clashes with Todt, the minister for armaments until 1942. Goebbels had also built up the propaganda ministry into a hugely powerful institution, while von Schirach (in charge of the Hitler Youth) also had a great degree of autonomy and often clashed with the ministry of education.

The most powerful of these Nazi empires, though, was the SS, which was ruled by *Reichsführer* Himmler, who was answerable only to Hitler. From 1933, he gained more and more control over all security and police matters and, once the war began, the security role of the SS increased as the Third Reich conquered more and more territory. By 1945, the Gestapo itself had over 40,000 members. As the German army raced across eastern Europe, it was the Death's Head Units and the *Waffen SS* which were given the task of exterminating Jewish people and creating the 'new order'. Himmler and the SS used prisoners of war, slave labour from the countries in Nazi-occupied Europe and the inmates of the death camps to work in their many industrial complexes that were to be part of this 'new order'. In all, the SS had over 150 industries, which produced a wide range of items, including armaments. Between this and the plentiful opportunities to plunder the victims of Nazi policies, many SS members became extremely wealthy as well as powerful. In 1944 the SS also took over military intelligence. By 1945 the SS had become a virtually independent empire within the Nazi state, more so than any other Nazi institution, and Himmler's power was second only to Hitler's.

Thus decision-making in Nazi Germany can be seen as a complex process, involving different Nazi 'warlords' and elites and their conflicting organisational power bases. Many of these were often as concerned to further their own financial interests as they were to push for particular policies.

At the same time, it is clear that the Nazi state was not monolithic. Some pre-1933 German institutions continued to exist and exert different degrees of influence and even independence. Although the more militant sections of the NSDAP wanted to smash the hold of the traditional elites and create an entirely new state administration, the rest of the Nazis (including Hitler) realised that these elites were not only well entrenched but were also experienced and efficient. As a result, the Nazis tended either to attach themselves to these established administrative organs and simply supervise them or to create new offices that worked parallel to them. Especially in the early years of the Nazi regime, various historians say that this resulted in the Third Reich becoming a 'dual state' (although this situation continued to exist in one or two areas right through until the last years of the war).

Personnel changes were not imposed immediately either: three key ministries (war, foreign affairs and economics) remained headed by representatives of the traditional elites until the late 1930s. It was not until February 1938 that every ministry was headed by a top Nazi. The German civil service, for example, though quickly purged of Jewish employees in 1933, remained staffed largely by traditional conservatives and nationalists even though Rudolf Hess, the deputy Führer, was given the power in 1935 to vet the appointment and promotion of civil servants. It was not until 1939 that membership of the Nazi Party was made a compulsory qualification for all new recruits. Although foreign office staff also remained fairly constant, at least up to 1938, the Nazis did create several shadow bureaus which often duplicated its work.

Part of this confusion in the first few years after 1933 resulted from the Nazis' need to avoid alienating the traditional elites and thus to appease many different interest groups. Confusion also arose because Hitler himself was never really clear what the relationship between the party and the state should be. For example, in December 1933 the Law to Ensure the Unity of Party and State talked vaguely about the party being 'inseparably linked with the state', yet in February 1934 Hitler told the party that its tasks were to concentrate on conducting propaganda and carrying out government decisions. Then in September 1934 he told the party congress that it was the party, not the state, that was in command.

Party control over the state was enhanced by Martin Bormann, who was allowed to create two new structures: the department for internal party affairs, whose function it was to discipline party members, and the department for affairs of state, which was intended to establish the party's supremacy. After 1941 Bormann was able to increase the power of these two bodies – and his own personal position when he became Hitler's secretary in 1943. Although after 1943 the independence of the traditional power blocs was increasingly limited under his direction, it was never totally destroyed. One reason for this failure to establish complete party dominance over the administrative bodies and personnel of the state was the fact that the party itself was full of rival groups and power bases.

The power of the churches, which had a long tradition of independence from the German state, was also left largely intact, despite various Nazi attempts to weaken it. The army was another organisation that was able to avoid Nazi infiltration and control for most of the existence of the Third Reich. Between 1933 and 1938 Hitler left the army alone, and kept its commanders happy with his rearmament programme and the crushing of the SA leadership. In 1938, however, Hitler removed some of the army's top commanders, including 16 generals, made himself the supreme commander and, as the war progressed, began to interfere more and more in the military decision-making process. Despite this, the majority of the traditional and aristocratic officers remained in post and, after 1943, several of them began to plot Hitler's overthrow and even his death. It was not until after the failed July Bomb Plot in 1944 (see p. 209) that the Nazi Party, via the SS, was able to achieve real control over the German army.

As a result of all this institutional overlap and rivalry, the Nazi Third Reich is sometimes said to be the clearest example of a chaotic state. From the late 1930s onwards the institutional dualism (the 'dual state') was gradually resolved, in the favour of the various Nazi bodies, as both Nazi leaders and activists extended party control over all aspects of the German state and society. Nonetheless, these ongoing conflicts greatly reduced the potential efficiency of the Third Reich.

Hitler as Führer

Not surprisingly, the debate about the nature and distribution of power in the Nazi state revolves, to a great extent, around Hitler's supremacy and style of rule. According to F. Neumann, the towering figure of Hitler, the charismatic Führer, dominated the four power blocs in Nazi Germany: the party, the army, the bureaucracy and big business. However, historians are now divided over whether Hitler was a strong or weak dictator. In theory, at least, Hitler was at the apex of a rigid pyramid of authority and, as a result, had unlimited political and state power. This 'Führer-power' (*Führergewalt*) enabled him to make the final decision on all issues and be confident that all his orders would be carried out. The importance of the personal oath of loyalty to Hitler and the *Führerprinzip* (leadership principle), which prevailed at all levels of the party and the state, ensured that he remained in overall control. The *Führerprinzip* had its roots in the myth of the superman and was central both to Nazi ideology and to Hitler's ultimate authority. Hitler's power, therefore, was based not on his official position as chancellor and head of state but on being the Führer of the German *Volk*.

The practice, however, might have been rather different. Despite the massive propaganda surrounding the Hitler myth and the cult of the Führer, Hitler does not seem to have been a very efficient leader or administrator. He disliked meetings and administrative paperwork, frequently did not even begin work until midday, then hurriedly got through the paperwork so that he could have lunch and then relax in the afternoon and evening. Where there were policy differences within the Nazi leadership, Hitler would sometimes wait until he had an idea of which group had most support before making a decision, in case he harmed his reputation by siding with a weaker faction. This is far removed from the propaganda portrait of Hitler as the dynamic and charismatic leader of the party and the nation. He seemed content to keep the 'Führer's will' deliberately vague, which often led to conflicting policies and variations in the way they were implemented. He was also not a very well man and, during the war, often took cocktails of medicines and drugs in order to function at all.

However, there has never been any dispute about his ultimate authority. His deliberately vague policy statements, which led to confusion and competition among the leading Nazis, allowed him to play off one group against another and thus enhance his own position. This confusion and uncertainty surrounding the powers and responsibilities of the different organisations can be seen as putting into practice the Nazis' belief in aspects of Social Darwinian theory: that the fittest or most ruthless should be allowed to predominate through struggle.

Hitler's dislike of meetings meant that he did not call many cabinet meetings (the number was continually reduced: from 72 in 1933, to 6 in 1936, 1 in 1938, and none thereafter). This ensured that he was able to deal with each minister on an individual basis and meant that other leading Nazis could not join forces to impose any collective policies on him. Neither the cabinet nor the *Reichstag* had any significant role in legislation; this was the responsibility of the Reich chancellery, which was under Hitler's direct control. Usually any draft law was circulated to all ministries by the office of the Reich chancellery; approval was dependent on whether the appropriate bodies had been consulted. However, this process was frequently undermined by Hitler, who often made law by issuing 'Führer edicts' or 'Führer directives' after discussions with the relevant minister, without informing the other ministers of his government. The confusion was increased after 1941, when a rival party chancellery was set up under Martin Bormann. Bormann used his position to build up his own power. By 1942, the leadership of the Nazi Party was divided between Goebbels, Göring and Speer, who felt increasingly excluded, and a group headed by Bormann, which included Lammers and Keitel, and was known as the 'committee of three' (Goebbels referred to them as 'this evil trio'). While some historians have argued that by 1945 Bormann was second only to Hitler as regards political power, others (such as P. Longerich) have thought this to be an exaggeration, arguing that Bormann was never able to dominate the powerful Nazi 'barons' such as Himmler, Goebbels, Göring and Speer.

The situation was made even more confusing by Hitler's tendency to by-pass government machinery by setting up rival institutions and specialist bureaus. It has been calculated that by 1945 there were 42 separate bodies in the Third Reich with the power to implement policy. Because of the *Führerprinzip*, a *Gauleiter* who had access to Hitler could have more power than a Reich minister, thus further undermining ministerial influence over the decision-making process. According to D. Welch, there existed a 'tripartite structure' consisting of government departments, party organisations and ad hoc bodies. Although the resulting confusion was brought to Hitler's attention (Frick, for instance, tried to rationalise this 'administrative chaos'), he refused to sanction any proposals to make the machinery of government more efficient. Some historians believe this administrative confusion and inefficiency contributed to the final collapse of the Nazi dictatorship.

Though he played little part in the development of economic or social policy, Hitler made sure that he played a much more decisive role in those areas which interested him most of all: foreign policy, war and race. Historians of the intentionalist school (such as A. Bullock, K. Hildebrand and K. D. Bracher) tend to stress that, although there were administrative confusion and rivalry between the different power blocs in Nazi Germany, all important steps were only taken with Hitler's approval and on his authority. The historian S. Haffner refers to this as 'controlled chaos'. The structuralists (such as M. Broszat and H. Mommsen), on the other hand, see Hitler as lazy and 'weak' and argue that his failure to give clear and consistent directions resulted in a chaotic administrative system where the real power was exercised by a variety of different institutions and individuals, including Hitler himself. This chaotic government structure – seen by many intentionalists as a deliberate attempt by Hitler to 'divide and rule' and so enhance his own power – is said by structuralists to have resulted in Hitler's role mainly being one of simply approving policies which originated from, and were pushed by, the various power blocs centred around Himmler, Göring and Goebbels. This institutional chaos has been described by Mommsen as a 'polycratic' form of government.

It is sometimes said that Hitler's importance was restricted to being the driving force behind core Nazi beliefs (such as anti-communism and anti-Semitism) and being an effective propagandist for them. Instead of Nazi Germany being a disciplined and well-organised totalitarian regime, the reality was that, while no one challenged Hitler's ultimate authority, it was the competing Nazi chiefs who pushed forward their own institutional interests, often in conflict with other sections of the Nazi Party and the state.

Support for Hitler and the Nazis

Assessing the popularity of Hitler and the Nazis is difficult as there were no free elections after March 1933 and no opinion polls either. It is also difficult to attempt to distinguish between active and passive support, both of which existed. For many Germans – at least in the years before the war started to go badly for Germany – Hitler (and possibly Nazism) filled a gap which had existed ever since the collapse of Imperial Germany and the birth of the Weimar Republic. Nazi propaganda portrayed Hitler as a *Volkskaiser* able to unite the people in a new *Volksgemeinschaft*. His attacks on the Versailles settlement, the politics of Weimar Germany and the communist threat undoubtedly appealed to a large cross-section of the German people. The whole Nazi ritual – of mass display of flags and banners bearing the Nazi swastika, the public display of Hitler's photograph, the rallies and the various Nazi public holidays – restored a sense of ceremony and belonging (even for the majority of Germans, who did not join the party) not seen since the days of Imperial Germany. Support for Hitler and the Nazi Party can also be seen in the fact that party membership increased by almost 200 per cent in the period 1933–34 and rose to nearly 5 million by 1939 (according to official party figures). While some of this was undoubtedly due to people jumping on the bandwagon as a way of obtaining the best jobs, it also reflected popular opinion.

Once Hitler had become chancellor, Nazi control of the media and Goebbels' skilful use of propaganda ensured the creation of a powerful Hitler cult. This enabled him to develop a huge personal popularity and to maintain it, even when other Nazi leaders or the party itself became less popular. Even his ruthless murder of the SA leaders in June 1934 was convincingly presented to the public as a moderate Hitler preventing the thugs and hotheads of the party from threatening the security of the state. Many Germans saw him as a hero for taking such firm action. Significantly, many of the most criminal and violent of the Nazis' activities – such as the mass extermination of Jewish people – were carried out in secret or outside Germany.

The popularity of Hitler and Nazism also rested on their ability to achieve results (the drop in unemployment between 1933 and 1935 and the relative prosperity of the period 1936 to 1938). Even though the economic recovery after 1933 was due as much to previous German governments and to a general upturn in the international economy, Hitler benefited from it. The underlying weaknesses that resulted from conflicting Nazi policies (e.g. the economic crisis and the shortages of 1935–36) did not receive public exposure and the impact of these problems was postponed by the extra resources gained as a result of German conquests in the years 1938–41.

The successes of Hitler's foreign policy also led to considerable support from the majority of Germans, as his actions were seen as putting right the many injustices imposed on Germany after 1918. Such general support for Hitler is confirmed by the secret reports sent to the SPD leadership in exile. The support for some aspects of Nazism, however, was not so widespread: the core policy of anti-Semitism did not at first evoke mass support and the first official boycott of Jewish shops in 1933 was stopped in part because so many ordinary Germans ignored it or even complained about it. Yet by the time of the 'final solution', Goebbels had been able to increase the acceptance of Nazi values sufficiently for many thousands of Germans to act as Hitler's 'willing executioners'. Such was the effectiveness of Goebbels' propaganda that, even when Germany began to suffer a series of major defeats and the war began to adversely affect the German people, support for Hitler and the belief in the Hitler myth remained high.

Opposition to the Nazis

Despite the Nazis' extensive political control and their widespread use of terror and fear, they were opposed by Germans throughout the existence of the Third Reich. In the last fully free elections in Weimar Germany in November 1932, the Nazis won only about 30 per cent of the vote, and it is unlikely that former supporters of the KPD, SPD or ZP would have genuinely supported the actions and policies of the Nazis. However, most historians point out that there was a great deal of support for the Nazi regime and stress that opposition was very much a minority activity – I. Kershaw refers to it as 'resistance without the people'. While individual protests, such as listening to foreign radio broadcasts, reading banned books or even hiding Jewish people or 'politicals', did take place, despite the risks, such unorganised opposition made little impact on the Nazi state. Not all resistance, however, took place on an individual basis.

Political parties

Although all political parties were abolished by the Nazis in July 1933, some parties did try to continue their activities and oppose the Nazis, despite repression by the Gestapo. The KPD carried out what was probably the most determined opposition; it was certainly the largest opposition group and suffered the greatest losses. Of the 300,000 members the KPD had in 1933, half were imprisoned by the Nazis and over 30,000 were executed or simply murdered. The KPD set up secret underground units or cells to produce and distribute anti-Nazi literature, mostly to industrial workers. They also wrote anti-Nazi graffiti, stuck up posters and tried to organise industrial sabotage and even illegal strikes. Many of their activities were organised by leaders who had been able to flee from Germany and by the Communist International in Moscow. Such activities were increased after 1941 when Nazi Germany attacked the Soviet Union. One communist group which played an important role in resistance during the war was the Red Orchestra (*Rote Kapelle*). This group established contacts in the military and economic organisations of Nazi Germany and then passed information about German war plans on to Moscow. They also wrote and distributed anti-Nazi literature. However, they were betrayed to the Gestapo in 1942 and their leaders were tortured and then executed.

The SPD also set up a new leadership in exile – the SOPADE, first in Prague and then in Paris. They soon developed a secret underground movement in Germany, where members gathered information about public attitudes to the Nazis and smuggled in banned literature, which was distributed where possible. Supporters of the SPD also stuck up anti-Nazi posters and later carried out acts of industrial sabotage. The New Beginning (*Neu Beginnen*), a more radical group of the SPD, frustrated by the continued lack of co-operation between the KPD and the SPD, tried unsuccessfully to establish a broad left coalition of resistance.

Young people

There was also significant resistance to the Nazis among the youth of Germany for both political and cultural reasons. At the University of Munich in 1943 the White Rose Movement produced leaflets opposing Nazism and the war, which they distributed to students in all the other universities in south Germany. An indication of their success was when the *Gauleiter* of Bavaria and his SA escort were thrown out of a meeting by university students, who then held a protest demonstration in Munich. This was the first serious public protest against the Nazis since 1933 and, not surprisingly, the Gestapo acted swiftly. Sophie and Hans Scholl, the leaders, were eventually arrested, beaten up and then sentenced by a People's Court to be executed. They were later beheaded.

This photo, taken in 1942, shows Hans and Sophie Scholl and Christoph Probst, the main leaders of the White Rose Movement.

Other young people resisted the Nazis in different ways. Although membership of the various Hitler Youth organisations was made compulsory in 1936, many young Germans refused to join them. In all, about 2 million youngsters avoided membership, many of whom began to develop youth sub-cultures that were in direct opposition to the values of the Hitler Youth and of the Nazis in general. Working-class teenagers in the Rhineland were the most organised of such groups, forming what became known as the Edelweiss Pirates (*Edelweisspiraten*), named after the edelweiss badge they wore on their distinctive checked shirts. These 14–17-year-olds formed gangs which sang pre-1933 songs, beat up Hitler Youth patrols and covered walls with anti-Nazi slogans and graffiti. We can gain an idea of the extent of this opposition from the fact that, on one day alone in December 1942, the Gestapo broke up 28 such gangs and arrested over 700 members, many of whom were hanged in public. Despite this, such groups continued to exist and many of them later joined forces with army deserters to attack the Nazi regime towards the end of the war. Other working-class groups which resisted Nazi propaganda and brainwashing included the Navahos and the Raving Dudes. These groups sang American hit tunes, smashed up shops and wrote anti-Nazi slogans in public spaces.

There were also several middle-class youth groups which tried to resist Nazi culture. The most important of these were those known as the Swing Movement and the Jazz Movement. They took their names from types of music the Nazis defined as 'degenerate'. The Gestapo frequently raided the clubs where these young people came together to wear English- and American-style clothes and to listen to illegal records.

The churches

The Nazis also faced opposition from some religious groups and individuals. The Christian churches were the only non-state organisations in Germany to retain most of their pre-1933 autonomy, even though there was a clear incompatibility between Nazi and Christian values. Nazi attempts to Nazify the Protestant churches (see p. 176) were not popular with all Protestants. When the Nazification process was intensified, Pastor Martin Niemöller set up the dissident Confessional Church. The Gestapo soon cracked down on this opposition: in 1937, Niemöller was imprisoned and, later, about 800 other members of the Confessional Church were sent to concentration camps. Continued resistance led Hitler to drop the German Christians and his attempts to directly control the Protestant religion, in return for their promises not to oppose the Nazi regime.

Hitler also faced opposition from the Catholic Church which, in July 1933, had signed a concordat with the Nazi government (see p. 176). When the Nazis began to infiltrate the Catholic Church in order to spread Nazi propaganda, to ban Catholic newspapers and to restrict the activities of Catholic schools and youth groups, the Catholic leadership protested. Though they eventually lost this battle, they were able to insist on the continued use of the crucifix. Though hundreds of Catholic priests ended up in concentration camps, the Catholic hierarchy in general tried to avoid any direct conflict with the Nazi government.

The elites

There were also elements of resistance to be found among sections of the traditional German elites, such as civil servants, the diplomatic staff and the army, although most of this did not emerge in a serious way until the closing stages of the war. Some were involved in the Kreisau Circle, an informal grouping of aristocratic and influential people who met to discuss their dislike of Hitler, but they never thought of overthrowing him. More determined resistance, however, came from staff in the foreign office, for example, which was never completely 'co-ordinated'. Several diplomats maintained contacts with opponents of the Nazis in the army, as well as with British and US officials in neutral countries. The most important of these were Adam von Trott zu Solz and Ulrich von Hassell. There were also opponents of the Nazis in the *Abwehr* (the military intelligence unit) who were linked to those in the foreign office and the army. They also established links with Allied officials and even compiled a secret dossier on Nazi war crimes. The most important figures of this resistance were Admiral Canaris and Colonel Hansen.

The most significant elite opposition to the Nazis, however, was found in the army. The army had been able to avoid Nazification and retained a large degree of autonomy throughout the Nazi period. Army opposition to Hitler emerged as early as 1938, when Colonel Beck (chief of the army general staff, 1935–38) became so concerned about the growing crisis over Czechoslovakia that he plotted to overthrow the Nazi government. The other main plotter was Carl Goerdeler, the lord mayor of Leipzig; hence those involved in this resistance are known as the Beck–Goerdeler group. Beck's first moves involved informing the

British government of Hitler's real intentions, but this plot came to nothing as Beck received no encouragement from the British prime minister Neville Chamberlain. After the signing of the Munich Agreement, Beck resigned from his post in disgust, but continued to develop contacts with others in the army and elsewhere who wanted to remove Hitler. Goerdeler, who had resigned as lord mayor in 1937, worked closely with Beck to build up a network of like-minded people in the foreign office, the intelligence services and the Berlin police. However, although the Beck–Goerdeler group wanted to remove Hitler, they did not want to return Germany to democratic rule. Their aims were for a return to an authoritarian regime such as had existed under the kaiser before 1918 and for a strong, expansionist Germany that would dominate central Europe. Many of these, and later, army plotters tended to move against Hitler only because they thought his extreme nationalism and his willingness to take huge risks in foreign policy might lead to the destruction of Germany.

Attempts by army officers to overthrow Hitler became more serious after 1943, by which time the defeats suffered on the eastern front indicated that Germany might lose the war. By then, the leading army resisters were Field Marshal von Witzleben, Major-General von Tresckow and Colonel von Stauffenberg. These plotters were closely linked to the Beck–Goerdeler group, though von Stauffenberg supported the idea of Germany becoming a social democracy once Hitler had been removed. During 1943, plans against Hitler tended to focus around his assassination rather than simply removing him from power – there were six unsuccessful attempts in all on his life. An indication of the rising opposition to Hitler in the army is that, in 1943, the plotters were able to persuade Field Marshal Rommel to join them. By 1944, Germany's defeat seemed imminent and the plotters increased their activities, which included making contact with British and US diplomats. One suggestion was a separate peace which would leave Germany free to continue the war against the Soviet Union. Though this was rejected, von Stauffenberg continued with plans to assassinate Hitler. On 20 July 1944, he planted a bomb which, although it exploded, only injured Hitler slightly. While the conspirators hesitated, the SS struck and arrested and tortured several suspects. Von Stauffenberg was executed immediately, but Beck, Rommel and von Tresckow avoided a similar fate by committing suicide. During a massive crackdown, over 5,000 conspirators and oppositionists were executed. Many of them came from important aristocratic families: members of the debating Kreisau Circle were among these victims. Afterwards, NSDAP political officers were appointed to indoctrinate the army, while the Nazi salute was made compulsory for the army – up until then, the army had been the only section of German society exempted from this legal requirement. When Himmler was appointed commander-in-chief of the home army in August 1944, this SS control ended what independence the army still retained.

Comparisons and contrasts

Now that the three dictatorships have been examined, we will return to the three questions raised at the start of the first chapter. First, to what extent were the ideologies and regimes associated with Lenin and Stalin similar and thus both part of communism? Second, to what extent were the movements of Mussolini and Hitler the same and how far were their fascist states similar? Finally, there is the much more controversial question of the degree of similarity between the communist and fascist ideologies, movements and states, with the related issue of whether the Soviet, Fascist and Nazi states were authoritarian or totalitarian dictatorships. Although these questions will be addressed in turn for ease of understanding, it is important to realise that in many ways they are interrelated.

Leninism and Stalinism

The historical debate essentially falls into two schools: one which argues that these two ideologies and regimes were fundamentally different, and the other which perceives more similarities than differences between the two and so sees Stalinism as the logical outcome of Leninism. These schools of thought are sometimes referred to, respectively, as propounding the discontinuity theory and the continuity theory.

Discontinuity theorists argue that Leninism was a much more varied ideology than was allowed by Cold War politics and considerations. They point out that, although Lenin talked about the leading role to be played by his vanguard party in *What is to be done?* (1902), in *State and revolution* (1916) he put forward a strong argument for state bodies to be kept to a minimum and called for the 'withering away' of the workers' state as soon as possible after the revolution. This is seen as diametrically opposed to Stalin's extremely statist approach. This, these theorists argue, is because Marxism itself contained both libertarian and authoritarian elements. According to H. Arendt, Lenin's Russia was a 'revolutionary' dictatorship as opposed to the totalitarian one established by Stalin in 1929 and completed in the 1930s. Those who support this view point out that Lenin remained committed to a revolutionary form of democracy and that any aberrations were made for pragmatic reasons and were seen by Lenin as temporary distortions of revolutionary ideals (especially the introduction of the ban on factions and opposition parties in 1921). Such historians also believe the abandonment of war communism and its replacement by the NEP along with the ending of the 'Red terror' and the curtailment of the Cheka's powers after the civil war are evidence of Lenin's aversion to creating a fully fledged dictatorship. They point out that the NEP, in particular, was an essentially moderate compromise policy very different in kind and nature from Stalin's brutal introduction of collectivisation and industrialisation in the late 1920s and the 1930s.

Others argue that in the last years of his life Lenin's actions indicate that he had no intention of establishing a totalitarian dictatorship and that, on the contrary, as soon as he became aware of the drift to bureaucracy and dictatorship, he tried to remove Stalin from his powerful position as general secretary of the Communist Party. They point to the Postscript to his Testament in which he recommended that the party replace Stalin with someone else and to the significance of Lenin's attempts in 1922–23 to persuade Trotsky to join him in a campaign to reduce bureaucracy and to restore inner-party democracy. At first, Lenin believed the problem of bureaucracy stemmed from the administrative 'bourgeois specialists' on which the new workers' republic had to rely, a view he continued to hold until November 1922. However, between December 1922 and January 1923, Lenin's views changed dramatically and he began to seek support from Trotsky against Stalin and his associates over such issues as the state monopoly of foreign trade and especially over the nationalities policy in Georgia. According to Trotsky, Lenin asked him in December 1922 to join him in a joint bloc against bureaucracy and Stalin's conduct as head of the Orgburo (there is no independent documentary evidence to support this claim). According to M. Lewin, Stalin's methods and his cult of personality were 'wholly different' from Lenin's rule and were only achieved by a 'thorough perversion of Bolshevik ideology'.

The opposite view is presented by, among others, G. Leggett, who emphasises the similarities and the continuity between Lenin's and Stalin's politics and methods of rule. According to Leggett, any differences between the two regimes are differences of degree only. Lenin's Russia is thus seen as only slightly less totalitarian than Stalin's, and Stalin's regime is seen as the next logical step in Lenin's legacy. According to R. Pipes, the Leninist organisational principle of democratic centralism led inevitably to Stalinist dictatorship. In contrast to these arguments, discontinuity theorists believe that democratic centralism under Lenin was not just a theory but shaped actual practice. They also point out that the Bolsheviks initially operated in a multi-party system and that the party itself was made up of different groups and factions, and that it was only under Stalin that the party became monolithic.

However, as the continuity theorists point out, Lenin himself introduced measures against multi-party politics during and immediately after the civil war, terror was used during the civil war, purges of party members took place before 1924 and the number of labour camps increased from 80 in 1919 to 315 by 1923. Discontinuity theorists, though, argue that Leninist terror and Stalinist terror differed both quantitatively and qualitatively: at the end of the civil war, defeated opponents were allowed to go into exile, Lenin never attempted to have his party colleagues killed, while the numbers of people who were affected never approached the massive scale that they did under Stalin. Continuity theorists point out that Lenin appointed Stalin to the crucial role of general secretary in

1922, but discontinuity theorists argue that, at the time, this was not an important post and that as soon as Lenin came to realise that Stalin was abusing his position he tried to get him removed from power. Some also point out that Trotskyism or Bukharinism were, at least before 1928–29, more likely successors to Leninism than Stalinism.

Fascism and Nazism

The several features that these movements had in common have led many historians to argue that there is a generic fascism to which Italian Fascists and German Nazis, and other parties, belonged. The similarities include: the call for national regeneration or rebirth; the emergence of an all-powerful leader based on the *Führerprinzip*; an authoritarian, repressive and coercive state based on terror or the fear of terror; ultranationalism and an aggressive foreign policy; as well as a fanatical hatred of liberalism and left-wing movements. Other shared features include the love of uniforms, parades and paramilitary groups; emotion and violence being seen as positive; and concerted efforts to use modern technology and methods of mass communication to spread their message and to indoctrinate different sections of the nation.

As well as the above features – and in spite of their wholehearted acceptance of some aspects of modernism – there was a general conservative and even reactionary attitude to others on the part of both Fascists and Nazis. For instance, the rural ideal was held up to be superior to urbanisation, which tended to be denigrated as creating centres of decadence, socialism and communism. Both Fascist and Nazi ideology were strongly opposed to the modern trend of female emancipation and equality. In both Fascist Italy and Nazi Germany, attempts were made to force women out of paid employment and into what was seen as their 'natural' role as housewives and mothers. Other important features they shared were the fact that they achieved power with the approval, if not collusion, of their respective country's economic and political elites, and that once in power their earlier promises to limit the wealth and power of the large capitalist firms were quickly abandoned. These two regimes were also determined to make their respective economies self-sufficient (autarky) and saw territorial expansion and conquest as one way of achieving this, whether it was the *spazio vitale* of Italian Fascism or Hitler's *Lebensraum*.

However, there were also differences between the two regimes, most notably on the issues of racism and the establishment of the 'terror state'. At first, Mussolini dismissed Hitler and the Nazi Party's obsession with anti-Semitism and their 'race science' as nonsense. Nothing in Mussolini's early writings makes race a central issue, in the way Hitler did in *Mein Kampf*. Although Mussolini later introduced racial laws in Italy in 1938 under Hitler's influence, they attracted little popular support. In fact, by the end of the 1930s, the Italian Fascist Party had recruited a large number of Jewish people into its ranks. However, both Mussolini and Hitler – and their respective movements – were rooted in Social Darwinism and its beliefs in the forceful struggle for the 'survival of the fittest'.

The other main difference between the two regimes is that Mussolini never achieved the degree of independent political power established by Hitler in Germany. One consequence of this is that the extent of state terror in Fascist Italy was considerably less than it was in Nazi Germany. Non-fascist institutions, such as the monarchy and the Roman Catholic Church, retained some independence in Italy, and the level of cultural and artistic control was also less comprehensive there than it was in Germany. Thus the historical debate continues over whether or not it is possible to identify a generic fascism or whether these differences make such a task impossible.

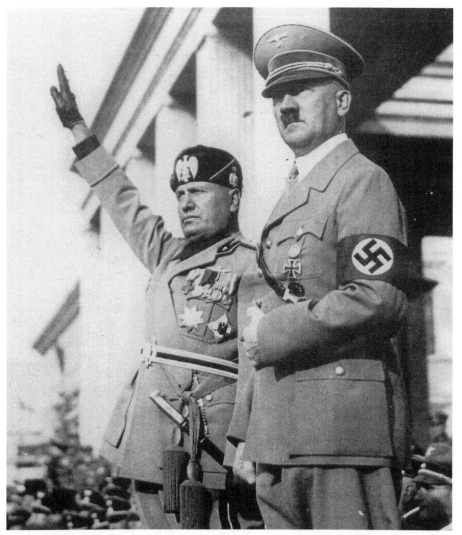

This photo shows Hitler and Mussolini reviewing troops in Munich in 1937. Were there more similarities than differences between these two types of fascism?

Fascism and communism

Several historians (initially writing during the Cold War) have attempted to establish certain similarities between these two ideologies and movements, while others (mainly Marxist) have argued that they are diametrically opposed. Marxists see fascism as an extreme defence of capitalism, while communism is defined as being totally opposed to capitalism. As has been seen, those who argue that they are similar do so mainly on the basis that all three regimes were totalitarian dictatorships. Such comparisons focus on the ideologies and the nature of the states that were established by these political movements. According to R. Pipes, for instance, all three regimes were united not only by similar political philosophies and practices, but also by a 'common psychology' based on hatred and violence. When comparing these movements and regimes, however, it is also important to distinguish between the outward forms of political structures and methods of rule on the one hand, and between principles and actual policies on the other.

Similarities

One common factor between these two ideologies is that both were extremely hostile to liberal parliamentary democracy and its bourgeois values, and both movements destroyed it and replaced it with markedly different political systems based on one-party rule. In their early days both political movements were revolutionary in that, unlike the traditional established political parties, they relied on mass mobilisations around an ideal, utopian ideology rather than elections to achieve power, and promised a partial or even total overthrow of existing political and economic structures. However, although transformations were promised by both ideologies, fascism often did not live up to its promises.

This issue is complicated by the fact that Mussolini once described himself as the 'Italian Lenin' and was, in his early political career, a militant socialist. He also later congratulated Stalin during the Great Purge for having 'converted' to Fascism. According to D. Mack Smith, Mussolini's final years in the Salò Republic provide evidence of him returning to his earlier socialist beliefs. Whether or not this is the case, it is certainly true to say that the Salò Republic was an attempt to revive the 'socialist' elements of the early days of Fascism. Another shared aspect was the way in which ideology was frequently adapted and even abandoned for pragmatic reasons.

The regimes of Stalin, Mussolini and Hitler also shared the concept of the charismatic 'superman' leader, around whom a cult of personality was developed to the extent that almost all public places contained an image of the leader. However, the way in which this leadership myth was ended after Stalin's death seems to suggest that it was not as crucial to the survival of the Soviet regime as it was for the two fascist dictatorships. It has also been argued that Stalin's regime was every bit as nationalistic as Mussolini's or Hitler's, with the policy of 'socialism in one country' marking the victory of nationalism over the internationalism which had been central to Soviet foreign policy under Lenin.

This development was strengthened by the USSR's experience of the Second World War, during which Stalin deliberately played on national sentiments, and even the Tsarist past and religion, to mobilise the people to resist the German invaders. Some historians have seen the first signs of this during the civil war when foreign intervention turned many Russians round to supporting the Communists on the basis of nationalism. After the Second World War, those who argue that the three regimes were similar, rather than different, political phenomena point to the vast empire that Stalin created in eastern Europe during the late 1940s which, to a greater or lesser extent, remained intact for over 40 years.

All three regimes also placed a great emphasis on censorship and official propaganda to ensure compliance among the people. They also all made a particular effort to indoctrinate the young through education and by the creation of special youth movements and groups.

When attempting to portray the two ideologies and movements as essentially similar, several historians have concentrated on the issue of totalitarianism and especially the use of coercion and terror. All three regimes relied heavily on the use of secret police forces to eradicate and prevent any opposition. All three regimes also resorted to the use of terror: Germany used concentration and extermination camps, while the USSR relied on the construction of Gulags. In Fascist Italy the number of deaths resulting from terror was relatively low: according to Friedrich and Brzezinski, this was because Italian Fascism was 'less total, less frightful, and hence less "mature"' when compared to the other two regimes. There has been much discussion among historians about the respective 'victims' count' or 'atrocity toll' for Hitler's Germany and Stalin's Soviet Union, which has been complicated by attempts to distinguish between 'intentional' and 'unintentional' deaths. As S. J. Lee points out, there was nothing in the Soviet Union like the structures for deliberate extermination of people which existed under the Nazis; and the deaths which occurred in Stalin's Gulag system were more the result of 'neglect and overwork' than deliberate mass murder. As has been mentioned earlier, if the total number of deaths resulting from deliberate terror, famine and war are added together, then there appears to be little difference between Hitler's regime and Stalin's. In the recent past, some historians attempted to underline the similarities between these two regimes by claiming that the racial genocide of the Nazis was essentially a reaction to a 'class genocide' carried out by the Bolsheviks. Nevertheless, as I. Kershaw and M. Lewin have pointed out, Hitler's earliest writings – before the 1917 Revolution in Russia – were deeply entrenched in extreme anti-Semitism, and that anti-Bolshevism only came later as another way of creating and using hatred of the Jews. It is also important to bear in mind that not all historians accept the view that the deaths resulting from the famine brought about by forced collectivisation in the Soviet Union stemmed from a deliberate policy decision, and even the numbers who were killed during the Great Terror are still a matter of historical debate.

Differences

However, there are also several significant differences between communism and fascism, in terms of both theory and practice. In fact, from 1918 to 1945, the Soviet dictatorship was unique in that the 15 others that existed during these years (including those of Mussolini and Hitler) were all from the far right. On the ideological front, communism differs from fascism in that it has a systematic doctrine with clear origins, while fascism does not have anything like the coherent and disciplined ideological structures of Marxism–Leninism. Apart from the writings of various, often unconnected, nineteenth-century thinkers, fascism's main 'theories' are to be found in Mussolini's article in the *Encyclopedia Italiana* and Hitler's rambling *Mein Kampf*. Both fascist leaders tended to base their ideology on recycled ideas pulled from a range of disparate sources. In addition, fascism was clearly based on an overt anti-intellectualism, anti-positivism and a rejection of reason, whereas communism maintained its commitment to reason, positivism and the theoretical development of Marx's ideas.

Communism was also grounded, in theory, on internationalism, borne out by the setting up of the Communist (Third) International in 1919. Even under Stalin, who was, to a large degree, a communist who put the interests of his country first, the Soviet Union remained committed – on paper, at least – to the international working-class movement and world revolution. This continued to be official Soviet policy after Stalin's death in 1953. By way of contrast, fascism rejected internationalism and instead glorified the nation and its destiny and called for national rebirth and regeneration or 'palingenesis'. This is what has led R. Griffin to define fascism's 'mythic core' as being – in varying forms – 'a palingenetic form of popular ultra-nationalism'.

In theoretical terms, the two ideologies also had a fundamentally different attitude to the state: according to Marxist theory, the state should 'wither away' as soon as the workers had taken power and would be an extremely minimal state once communism had been achieved. Fascism, on the other hand, had at its core the idea that the state should be everything and the individual nothing: this was the 'holistic national third way' referred to by R. Eatwell. However, it is important to remember that, in practice, the Soviet state grew in power, especially under Stalin. Fascism was also based on the positive role and importance of elites as opposed to the masses (taken from the writings of G. Mosca and V. Pareto). In theory, communism was against this belief but, in practice, elites soon began to emerge among senior party officials and state administrators. They came to enjoy significant material privileges, although they never had the right to private ownership of economic assets, which remained the property of the state. In fact, this had been one of Lenin's concerns in the last years of his life, though it is possible to see his ideas on a small vanguard party of revolutionaries as being similar in some respects to the fascist idea of a 'superman' leader and a leadership elite.

In terms of policy goals, communism is clearly committed to the overthrow of capitalism, and the construction of socialism and then communism. While early fascist programmes did talk of a 'third way' and contain some anti-capitalist policies, they never expressed any promises to destroy capitalism and replace it with socialism and then the 'classless' communist ideal. Although fascism tended to stress the national community and the state over the individual, this was not the same as destroying all class barriers in order to create a classless society, which was the ultimate goal of communism. Instead, fascism tended simply to suppress class conflict, theoretically in the interests of the nation. In practice, however, the interests of the upper sections of society received priority, while those of the working and lower middle classes suffered. Essentially, therefore, communist ideology was consciously based on class and class struggle, whereas fascism was based on the nation or the race.

At the same time, there were clear theoretical differences between these two ideologies over the emancipation and role of women. Under Lenin and the early Bolshevik regime, steps were taken almost immediately to implement policies designed to liberate women and ensure equality between the genders, based on what had always been an important aspect of Marxism. Early reforms included contraceptive advice, making abortions freely available and giving women the right to obtain a divorce. In contrast, fascist ideology in both Italy and Germany was based on distinct and separate male and female roles, with women encouraged, and later forced, to return to the traditional female roles of housewife and mother. It is important to remember, though, that under Stalin many of the reforms and advances made under Lenin were restricted, such as limiting the number of abortions and instead encouraging women to produce more babies. During the Second World War, Stalin's Russia made a much greater effort to mobilise women fully for war work from the very start of the invasion, something which the Nazis, for instance, were much slower to implement as it was a clear departure from their core beliefs.

As regards results and outcomes, the most obvious differences relate to how these leaders came to power and what the eventual outcomes were. Despite the myth of the March on Rome and Hitler's unsuccessful beer hall *Putsch* and the use of paramilitary violence in the streets, both fascist movements under consideration came to power legally and enjoyed, to varying degrees, the tacit approval (if not always the direct support) of the elites of their respective countries. In contrast, the establishment of the communist regime in Russia required a genuine revolution against the existing elites and, after seizing power in defiance of these elites, a brutal civil war in order to hold on to power.

This difference between coming to power either by invitation or through a bitterly contested class struggle is deepened by an examination of the outcomes. In both Italy and Germany, the main economic elites remained the owners of their businesses even if, at times, their overall control was restricted by state direction (though this is more true of Nazi Germany than of Fascist Italy). The two fascist regimes – especially the more powerful Nazi regime – swept away far fewer of the existing structures and institutions than did the communist regimes of Lenin and Stalin. In particular, the more militant sections of the two fascist parties, who called for a 'second revolution' against the largest capitalist firms (as promised in early programmes and manifestos), were either politically sidelined or, in the case of Nazi Germany, physically eliminated by the party leadership.

In total contrast, the Bolshevik Revolution of 1917 was followed almost immediately by the dispossession of the entire industrial capitalist class. In the countryside large landowners (whether the Tsar, the aristocrats or the Church) had the vast bulk of their estates confiscated and passed over to the peasants, who replaced them as the new private owners. In a 'second revolution' under Stalin's policy of forced collectivisation the vast majority of the land owned by the peasants was nationalised and turned into collective state farms. In other words, all the main economic elites experienced the confiscation of all their major assets. This was something entirely absent in the two fascist states, where the economic elites not only retained their property but also actually experienced a very significant increase in profits. Furthermore, under Stalin and his successors, a massive industrialisation programme vastly increased the amount of state property; at the same time, the Soviet state made sure that there would be no re-emergence of capitalism in the USSR. This attitude towards private property remained in existence throughout the 74 years from 1917 to the collapse of the Soviet Union in 1991.

It was also the case that after 1945, as Stalin increased Soviet control over the countries of eastern Europe, a similar far-reaching 'revolution' was imposed, which also resulted in the dispossession of the pre-war economic elites in these countries. The Nazi invasions of Europe were simply accompanied by the transfer of property and assets either to German capitalists or to senior Nazi officials. It was not until the collapse of the communist regimes in eastern Europe and the Soviet Union itself in the period 1989–91 that state property was sold off to private owners.

Hitler and Stalin

In many respects, recent historical research and writing have tended to focus on comparing the specific regimes of Hitler and Stalin, rather than fascism and communism as a whole. This has been possible because the end of the Cold War has reduced, though not entirely removed, political controversy from the idea of comparing Nazism and Stalinism and from the use of the term 'totalitarian'. Rather than looking for detailed examples of 'sameness', the search has moved on to trying to establish what has been referred to as the 'common ground' approach. This is based upon recognising qualitative and fundamental differences between the two ideologies, alongside an examination of how such different countries developed similar regimes during the same historical period. As I. Kershaw and M. Lewin point out, neither of these regimes survived long after the end of the Second World War. Hitler's Third Reich perished on Germany's defeat, while some of the fundamental aspects of Stalinism (notably the terror and the all-powerful leader) were dismantled by Stalin's successors in the years immediately following his death in 1953.

Problems with totalitarianism and fascism

Now that the three dictatorships have been examined, and many of the main historical arguments have been explored, it will be useful to consider some of the ongoing historical arguments which concern the main concepts and definitions used in relation to this period.

Totalitarianism

As we have already seen, this concept (which came to be used in the context of the Cold War) has always been problematic. Some historians define totalitarianism as a system in which the dictator was able to impose his will on party, state and society, which themselves were strictly disciplined. It was generally agreed that the label applied particularly to Stalin's Soviet Union, but also to Hitler's Germany. A growing number of historians have begun to question the associated picture of society passively responding to the state. Instead, they argue that society at times also interacted with the state. Even R. Conquest now concedes that Stalin was not always able to impose his will on the people.

In order to distinguish totalitarian regimes from general authoritarian dictatorships (which tend to be conservative and traditional and attempt to force all sections of society to be politically and organisationally passive), historians and political scientists have stressed that totalitarian dictatorships have more radical programmes and attempt to mobilise the masses. They stress that it is important to bear in mind that the degree and purpose of mobilisation vary considerably according to the ideology of the political movement being examined. Attempts have been made to synthesise the varying definitions of totalitarianism in order to produce one that is generally accepted. One such example identifies four common characteristics:

- a distinctive ideology, which is applied to all areas of human society and activity;
- a political system which dispenses with multi-party politics and is under the control of a single party and, especially, of a single leader around whom there is a cult of personality;
- the subjugation of the individual to the needs of the state and the creation of consent through a twin-track approach which combines indoctrination (in education, the arts, the media and through popular policies) with coercion and terror;
- attempts to impose complete control over the economy.

Using such definitions, it is argued that the Leninist state was not a totalitarian state, though Stalin's regime was. The fascist dictatorships were imperfect totalitarian states which swept away far fewer of the existing institutions and made fewer attempts to establish a centralised and planned economy than did the communists in the Soviet Union.

Despite such attempts, though, historians are still essentially divided into two broad schools of thought on how to describe the main European dictatorships during the inter-war period. For Stalin's Soviet Union, there is the pluralist (or social) group and the totalitarian group and, as M. McCauley has pointed out, these two schools mirror the two main theories about the nature of Hitler and the Nazi state (the structuralists and the intentionalists). For Stalinism, the pluralist group argue that the Soviet state acted as a referee for different competing interest groups such as managers and technical experts. S. Fitzpatrick sees Stalinist society as more dynamic than allowed by the totalitarians, with different hierarchies and opposing interests. She identifies 'revolution from below' as well as 'revolution from above'. As regards Nazi Germany, the structuralists see a semi-chaotic polycratic power structure, while the intentionalists see Hitler as the strong leader, always able to impose his policy agenda on society.

These problems over definitions have led historians like R. Tucker to develop an approach which tries to combine both elements; for the Soviet Union, this is known as the 'reconstruction–consolidation (or 'reccon') approach. This tries to give due importance to the role of the state, but also looks at social resistance to official policy. Thus the concept of totalitarianism is seen by many historians as no longer being of any great value in understanding the nature of these dictatorships.

Related to the totalitarian argument is the view that both ideologies should be seen as examples of social and economic modernisation of relatively backward or war-damaged economies via the use of 'developmental dictatorships'. As a result, it is argued that a large degree of similarity or convergence is not surprising. Certainly, both the communist regime in the Soviet Union and the Nazi regime in Germany brought about a significant degree of increased social mobility in comparison to the situation before they took power. However, several modernisation theorists point out that communism and fascism were alternative models, while H. A. Turner rejects the view that fascism was a modernisation movement arguing instead that the emphasis on the rural ideal was, in fact, a retreat from modernisation.

Fascism

There is also continued unease about attempts to develop a generally applicable definition of fascism. Attempts to base fascism on a common ideology – generic fascism – are often criticised on the basis of fascism being more a collection of 'half-baked cliches and prejudices' (R. Pearce) than a coherent and identifiable political ideology. While the elements of the strong leader and an aggressive nationalism are usually present, aspects such as the corporate state or anti-Semitism are not. Thus the proponents of generic fascism themselves point out that this is not an all-inclusive definition or even the only label which can be used; their concern is to establish a 'fascist minimum'.

E. Nolte made the first important attempt to do this in the 1960s when he identified three common aspects of fascist states: negatives (anti-Marxism, anti-liberalism and anti-conservatism), style (the strong leader and a militarised party) and a general goal (totalitarianism). This approach was taken up by S. Payne, who focused on negations, ideology and programme, and style and organisation.

Critics of generic fascism argue that each of the authoritarian dictatorships to which historians have applied the label 'fascist' was separate and unique. They point out that some were monarchical or military dictatorships and that many were not based on new 'anti-positivist' ideology but on traditional religious (Catholic) values. Even those historians who see the concept of generic fascism as a useful means of classification are nonetheless concerned that such a label overemphasises common factors when differences are often more apparent. This is especially true of the question of anti-Semitism: Mussolini thought Hitler and the Nazis' 'scientific' racism was sheer nonsense. Proponents of generic fascism simply omit anti-Semitism from the list of the fascist 'ideological minimum'.

These problems have led others to shift the focus away from ideology to methods of political rule. This historical approach concentrates on the mass rallies, militaristic trappings and the leadership cult as being common methods used to indoctrinate the masses. Also important in the creation of a totalitarian state are the methods of coercion used, especially the use of terror. This often leads into definitions of fascism which see it as a mainly opportunistic method of seizing political power. The focus on methods of rule, however, leads back to the other contentious issue of totalitarianism, given the use of terror in Stalin's Soviet Union. This immediately raises the question of whether fascism was a genuine philosophy of modernisation which attempted to find a 'third way' between capitalism and communism or whether it was an extremely reactionary terrorist movement (despite its often 'modern' forms) which sought, in alliance with – and often in the pay of – big capitalists, to prevent a socialist revolution. According to R. Pearce, it might therefore be best to attempt to define fascism using a check list which incorporates ideology, style and methods of rule, and its policy outcomes. R. Eatwell has attempted to deal with the whole concept of the 'fascist minimum' by identifying a list which (although it might overlap with other regimes and even, at times, with other ideologies) contains four elements that together form the core of fascist beliefs. These elements are:

- nationalism, whether cultural or biological (i.e. based on race);
- holism, where the community is more important than the individual, who should be devoted to the leader;
- radicalism, with some element – usually in its early phases – of opposition to the establishment, alongside rebirth;
- the 'third way' which, in theory, offers an alternative between individualistic capitalism and the class basis of communist politics.

The historical debate about how to define fascism continues, along with the question of identifying fascist support.

Comparative themes

Now that we have examined the three dictatorships, it will be useful to attempt to compare and contrast them using five different aspects of this type of rule. A more detailed comparison will be achieved by referring back to the relevant chapters in this book.

Leaders

All three regimes depended on the leadership of a single dominant leader. Stalin, in theory, was subject to the collective leadership of the Communist Party (via its congresses and the Central Committee) and was supposed to use the communist ideology of Marx as adapted by Lenin. In practice, though, Stalin increased his personal power, which far exceeded the power wielded by Lenin. Stalin was also able to make significant alterations to and departures from orthodox Marxism by inventing and imposing his version of Marxism–Leninism.

In Nazi Germany, in theory, Hitler had total power as Führer and faced no constraints. He has been described by M. Broszat as having more power than any monarch ever had. He claimed that he was the 'saviour' of the people and the embodiment of the 'will of the people'. In practice, though, Hitler was not always in full control of the party or the state machine. Mussolini had even less control than Hitler as he was officially the appointee of the king, and the army and state officials swore loyalty to the king, not to Mussolini.

Nature of the parties

As we have seen, communism is the most coherent ideology and is based on a systematic doctrine and philosophy originating from the ideas of Marx and Engels, redefined and adapted (or even perverted) by Lenin and Stalin. It is based on economic theory (economic determinism), a philosophy of historical development (historical materialism) and a belief in progress to a classless communist society. Fascism, on the other hand, is much looser and incoherent and, at times, contradictory.

In the Soviet Union, the party came to dominate the state (both the legislative and the executive branches) and exercised control through its Central Committee with its Secretariat, Orgburo and Control Commission. In Nazi Germany, most of the old state structures remained in place with some minor alterations, such as combining the posts of chancellor and president to create the position of Führer. There was a similar adaptation of existing structures in Fascist Italy, where Mussolini's party had even less control as the king retained the power to appoint and dismiss the government.

As regards the party base, in the Soviet Union the role of the vanguard was emphasised both before and immediately after the November Revolution, but genuine mass involvement and control became increasingly limited when the centralism aspect of democratic centralism was emphasised. In his purges in the 1930s, Stalin eliminated most of the party's independence – however, his appointees within the party had more control over state organs than was the case in the fascist states, where the traditional governing elites retained more power. In Nazi Germany, the mass base of the party was also active at the start of its rise to power, but became increasingly dominated by the leader (especially after the Night of the Long Knives in 1934). However, some historians point out that the party rank-and-file probably retained more autonomy than was enjoyed by those in Stalin's Soviet Union. As regards party penetration of state structures, though, this was never as significant as it was in the Soviet Union.

Social and economic impact

All three dictatorships tried to create a 'new man' who would be in tune with the new ideology and state being constructed. Most historians see this aspect as having gone further in the Soviet Union. This was mainly achieved through the state's almost total monopoly of mass communications and education, which allowed mass indoctrination. Another social aspect which should be compared is the degree to which the regimes carried through a social revolution. This was most extensive in the Soviet Union, with the change from an agrarian to an industrial economy, and the opportunities for social mobility this (and the expansion of the party and state machines) presented to millions of peasants and factory workers and their children. This aspect was much less marked in the two fascist states.

As regards the economies of these dictatorships, party and state control of the economy was most complete under Stalin. This was achieved through his five-year plans and the activities of Gosplan, which, by 1938, had 54 separate departments. In Fascist Italy, though, Mussolini's corporate state adapted rather than destroyed the previous system, while in Nazi Germany, despite *Gleichschaltung*, private enterprise was maintained, although there was also some state direction. In the two fascist states, Mussolini's and Hitler's priorities were to develop autarky and obtain extra territory, so they were content to ally themselves with big business.

While Stalin's industrial policies were successful in turning the Soviet Union into a European superpower, there were important differences between these three regimes as regards agriculture. As has been seen, Stalin's policy of forced collectivisation crippled Soviet agriculture for decades, while Mussolini's 'battle for grain' eventually led to an imbalance in the economy. Hitler tended to avoid any disruption of agriculture.

Creating consent

All three regimes relied to a large extent on coercion and terror. In the Soviet Union there were the secret police, while in Nazi Germany there were the SA, SS, SD and the Gestapo, and in Fascist Italy there was the OVRA. Although Stalin's system was more thorough and extensive, most historians agree that the worst crimes were committed by the Nazi terror machine.

Apart from the different ways in which propaganda and indoctrination were used to manufacture consent in these three dictatorships, the use of terror and purges is another important area of comparison. Purges were especially significant in Stalin's Soviet Union, perhaps partly because, unlike Mussolini and Hitler, Stalin was not the original inspiration behind the new regime and, as a result, was more fearful of potential rivals. Even after the Night of the Long Knives, Hitler did not carry out an extensive purge of the party leadership. However, another important difference between Stalin and Hitler was that the Stalinist purges also had a definite 'correction and rehabilitation' element while the Nazi terror was almost entirely focused on physical extermination.

The significance of war

Apart from the fact that all three dictatorships had their origins – to a greater or lesser extent – in the effects of war, they also performed in different ways under the impact of war. Ultimately, war was the vital test for these regimes: the Second World War led to the collapse of two of them, while Stalin's Soviet Union emerged as Europe's superpower, despite the tremendous human and material losses experienced in that country. This was in part because the Soviet Union was the most successful in adjusting to the demands of total war, by mobilising the entire economy and workforce. As well as extensive state control over the economy, the Soviet Union treated women as an equally important part of the workforce, whereas the Fascist and Nazi states, because of fascist ideology and its emphasis on traditional female roles, were late or half-hearted in getting women involved in war work.

In Fascist Italy, the economy was soon broken by the strains of war and military defeat, while in Nazi Germany the economy was only able to function efficiently during the early successes of *Blitzkrieg*, which brought new supplies of raw materials. As the war continued, and German conquests ended, Hitler's Third Reich soon fell far behind the USSR as regards military production. The Soviet success was largely the result of Stalin's economic policies from 1928 onwards, which had turned the Soviet Union from a mainly agricultural country into a modern industrial state capable of resisting and defeating Nazi Germany.

Select bibliography

General

There are several good texts that deal with the dictatorships in general and their corresponding ideologies. These include S. Lee, *The European dictatorships 1918–1945*, London, 1987, and K. D. Bracher, *The age of ideologies*, London, 1984. For fascism, F. Carsten, *The rise of fascism*, London, 1967, gives a sound overview. More up-to-date surveys are R. Thurlow, *Fascism*, Cambridge, 1999; S. Payne, *A history of fascism 1914–1945*, London, 1995; and R. Eatwell, *Fascism*, London, 1995. For Russia and the Soviet Union, comprehensive coverage is provided by R. Pipes, *The Russian Revolution*, volumes 1 and 2, London, 1990, and by M. McCauley, *The Soviet Union since 1917*, London, 1981. I. Deutscher, *Trotsky*, Oxford, 1970, provides an interesting slant in his three-volume biography. Finally, interesting comparisons are given by I. Kershaw and M. Lewin (eds), *Stalinism and Nazism: dictatorships in comparison*, Cambridge, 1997, and A. Bullock, *Hitler and Stalin: parallel lives*, London, 1991.

Lenin and Stalin

B. Williams, *Lenin*, London, 1997, is a useful up-to-date biography. There are many texts on the Russian Revolution and Lenin's rule: particularly sound are R. Pipes, *Russia under the Bolshevik regime*, London, 1994, and J. D. White, *The Russian Revolution*, London, 1994. J. Daborn, *Russia. Revolution and counter-revolution*, Cambridge, 1991, provides a good overview of the period 1917–24, as well as a useful set of documents.

Excellent treatment of Stalin and his regime, and the main historical arguments is to be found in C. Ward, *Stalin's Russia*, 2nd edn, London, 1999. I. Deutscher, *Stalin. A political biography*, Harmondsworth, 1966, remains an interesting read. W. Laqueur, *Stalin. The glasnost revelations*, London, 1990, provides a useful update. Also worthy of study is R. A. Medvedev, *Let history judge: the origins and consequences of Stalinism*, New York, 1971. Two useful overviews are M. McCauley, *Stalin and Stalinism*, London, 1995, and A. Wood, *Stalin and Stalinism*, London, 1997. Also good on the early Stalin era is S. Fitzpatrick, *The Russian Revolution*, 2nd edn, Oxford, 1994. A. Nove, *An economic history of the USSR*, London, 1969, and R. C. Tucker, *Stalin in power: the revolution from above 1928–41*, New York, 1990, provide a good insight into the various policies adopted by Stalin.

Mussolini and Fascism

A useful, albeit somewhat dated, overview is provided by D. Mack Smith, *Italy*, New York, 1959; more up-to-date is his *Mussolini*, London, 1981. Two sound treatments on Mussolini and Fascist Italy are to be found in D. Thompson, *State control in Fascist Italy, 1925–43*, Manchester, 1991, and J. Whittam, *Fascist Italy*, Manchester, 1995.

Hitler and Nazism

I. Kershaw, *The Nazi dictatorship. Problems and perspectives of interpretation*, 3rd edn, London, 1993, and I. Kershaw, *Hitler, 1898–1936. Hubris*, London, 1998, provide an excellent overview of the main historical debates. Although rather dated, A. Bullock, *Hitler. A study of tyranny*, London, 1964, is a sound introduction. Good on Nazi rule are M. Broszat, *The Hitler state*, London, 1981; K. D. Bracher, *The German dictatorship*, London, 1973; and H. Mommsen, *From Weimar to Auschwitz*, London, 1991.

An excellent up-to-date survey of Nazi economic policy is given by R. J. Overy, *The Nazi economic recovery 1932–38*, 2nd edn, Cambridge, 1996; while T. Mason, *Social policy in the Third Reich*, London, 1993, is very good on the impact of Nazi social policies. There are many texts dealing with Nazi policy towards Jewish people: a very readable account is provided by P. Neville, *The holocaust*, Cambridge, 1999. Also useful are C. Browning, *The path to genocide*, Cambridge, 1992, and P. Burrin, *Hitler and the Jews: the genesis of the holocaust*, London, 1994. A more controversial treatment is provided in D. Goldhagen, *Hitler's willing executioners: ordinary Germans and the holocaust*, London, 1996.

Chronology

Russia/USSR 1917–45

1917   *March:* Tsar abdicates following revolution; Russia becomes a republic; provisional government formed and Petrograd Soviet is revived; start of period of 'dual power'.

      April: Lenin returns from exile and issues his 'April theses'.

      July: July Days uprising forces Lenin into exile; other Bolshevik leaders arrested and Bolshevik Party banned.

      August: government loses support from soldiers and workers, who turn to the Bolsheviks.

      September: Bolsheviks win majorities in Petrograd Soviet and town and city elections.

      October: Lenin persuades Bolshevik Central Committee to overthrow the provisional government; leading Bolsheviks, including Zinoviev and Kamenev, are not in favour.

      November: Bolshevik Revolution organised by Trotsky; power handed over to All-Russian Congress of Soviets; Lenin becomes chairman of new government (Sovnarkom), with Trotsky as commissar for foreign affairs and Stalin commissar for nationalities; decrees quickly issued on peace, land and workers' control.

      December: peace talks begin with Germany; Left SRs form coalition with Bolsheviks; the Cheka created.

1918   *January:* Civil war begins between Reds and Whites; constituent assembly refuses to ratify decrees and is dissolved; Trotsky begins to form Red Army.

      March: Treaty of Brest-Litovsk signed, ending Russia's involvement in the First World War; Left SRs end coalition with Bolsheviks; Bolsheviks renamed the Communist Party.

      April: start of foreign intervention in civil war.

      May: Czech Legion revolt.

      June/July: start of war communism; Tsar and his family executed; Left SRs stage insurrection against Communist government.

      August: foreign intervention increases.

      October: assassination attempts on Lenin and other Communist leaders; start of Red Terror.

      December: Vesenkha set up.

1919   *January:* Orgburo set up.

      March: Communist Third International (Comintern) set up; Politburo set up.

1920   *March:* Poland invades Soviet Russia.

      September: Whites defeated in Crimea; civil war effectively over.

1921   *March:* Treaty of Riga ends Russo-Polish War; Kronstadt Rising; Tenth Congress of Communist Party accepts the NEP, and ban on factions and other parties.

      July: famine breaks out in parts of Soviet Russia.

Chronology

1922   *April:* Stalin becomes general secretary of the CPSU.

      May: Lenin suffers first stroke.

      December: Lenin writes his Testament, after another stroke; the triumvirs begin plans to prevent Trotsky from becoming leader.

1923   *January:* Lenin writes a Postscript, recommending Stalin's dismissal; triumvirs begin campaign against Trotsky.

      March: Stalin's behaviour causes Lenin to make known his criticisms.

      July/August: series of strikes against the NEP.

      October: 'scissors' crisis; the Statement of the 46; Trotsky forms Left Opposition.

1924   *January:* Thirteenth Party Conference condemns views of Trotsky and the 46; Lenin dies.

      May: Central Committee persuaded by Zinoviev and Kamenev not to dismiss Stalin or publish Lenin's Testament and Postscript.

      November: triumvirs begin new campaign against Trotskyism; Stalin announces 'socialism in one country'.

1925   *January:* Trotsky forced to resign as commissar for war.

      October: Zinoviev and Kamenev fall out with Stalin.

1926   *April:* Zinoviev and Kamenev begin talks with Trotsky.

      July: United Opposition declares its existence.

1927   *January:* Trotsky and Kamenev expelled from the Politburo.

      October: Trotsky and Zinoviev expelled from the Central Committee.

      November: Trotsky and Zinoviev expelled from the Communist Party.

      December: 'collectivisation congress' takes place; United Opposition defeated.

1928   *January:* forced grain requisitions.

      April: Stalin begins attacks on *kulaks*; Stalin begins to fall out with Bukharin and the right.

      May: Stalin's 'second revolution' welcomed by Zinoviev and Kamenev.

      June: party membership of Zinoviev and Kamenev restored.

      August: serious break between Stalin and Bukharin.

      October: First Five-Year Plan begins.

1929   *February:* Trotsky expelled from the Soviet Union.

      April: draft five-year plan approved by party congress.

      November: Bukharin and members of the right expelled from important party and state positions; Stalin now clearly in control.

      November/December: Stalin launches collectivisation.

1930   *January:* forced mass collectivisation begins.

      March: Stalin calls a temporary halt to collectivisation.

1932   *September:* Ryutin trial; Politburo refuses Stalin's request that Ryutin be executed.

      November: Franco-Soviet pact signed; first signs of famine in parts of the Soviet Union.

1934   *February:* Kirov's popularity obvious at Seventeenth Party Congress.

      September: Second Five-Year Plan begins.

      December: Kirov assassinated.

1935   *January:* Zinoviev and Kamenev arrested.

      May: Franco-Soviet pact to protect Czechoslovakia.

      August: Stakhanovite Movement begins.

1936 *August:* Trial of the Sixteen.

September: Yezhov becomes head of NKVD; the Purge begins.

December: 'Stalin constitution' adopted.

1937 *January:* Trial of the Seventeen.

May: purge of the Red Army begins.

1938 *March:* Bukharin, Rykov and Yagoda executed after Trial of the Twenty-one; Great Terror under way.

September: Third Five-Year Plan; USSR becomes increasingly concerned about Czechoslovakia.

1939 *March:* Stalin ends the Great Terror and Great Purge.

August: Nazi–Soviet Non-Aggression Pact concluded.

November: Russo-Finnish War begins.

1940 *July:* Baltic states made part of the USSR.

August: Trotsky assassinated.

1941 *June:* Germany invades Soviet Union; the Great Patriotic War starts.

December: Soviet counteroffensive at Moscow.

1942 *August:* the Battle of Stalingrad.

1943 *February:* German Sixth Army surrenders in Stalingrad.

November: Tehran conference begins.

1944 *August:* last German troops expelled from Soviet territory.

1945 *February:* Yalta conference.

May: Red Army enters Berlin; Germany surrenders.

Italy 1918–45

1919 Factory occupations begin the *biennio rosso*.

January: pope allows formation of a Catholic party (PPI); first *Arditi* Association in Rome.

March: Mussolini forms Fascist Combat Group; D'Annunzio seizes Fiume.

1920 *September:* wave of factory occupations in the north, after which *squadristi* violence becomes more widespread.

1921 *May:* Fascists gain 35 seats after electoral alliance with Giolitti.

August: Mussolini signs 'pact of pacification' with Socialists and outmanoeuvres the *ras*.

October: Mussolini creates National Fascist Party (PNF).

1922 Fascist violence increases.

May: Fascists take over Ferrara.

July: Fascists take over other towns; left-wing general strike begins.

August: Fascist violence forces Socialists to call off general strike.

October: March on Rome; the king asks Mussolini to become prime minister.

November: Mussolini given emergency powers for one year.

December: Fascist Grand Council established.

1923 *January:* Fascist squads become a national Fascist militia (MVSN).

March: Nationalist Party merges with Fascists.

June: pope forces PPI leader to resign.

July: Acerbo electoral law passed.

August: the Corfu Incident takes place.

December: Chigi Palace Pact concluded.

1924 *January:* the Ceka set up by Mussolini.

March: Ceka violence becomes widespread.

April: Yugoslavia cedes Fiume to Italy in the Pact of Rome; Fascists win majority in general election.

June: Matteotti murdered; the Aventine Secession.

December: ras force Mussolini to become dictator.

1925 *January:* Mussolini announces dictatorship.

February: new wave of *squadristi* violence against the left.

May: Locarno Treaty signed by Italy; Dopolavoro created.

July: press control increased.

August: central government control over local government established.

December: Mussolini becomes head of government.

1926 *January:* Mussolini has power to issue decrees without parliamentary approval.

July: ministry of corporations set up, signalling start of the corporate state; ONB created.

October: all opposition parties as well as trade unions banned.

1928 *May:* rigged elections take place.

1929 *May:* Lateran Agreements with papacy concluded.

1933 *April:* Institute of Industrial Reconstruction set up.

1934 *July:* Italy opposes Hitler's attempted *Anschluss* with Austria.

1935 *January:* accord with France signed.

March: Stresa Front formed with Britain and France.

October: invasion of Abyssinia begins.

1936 *March:* Italy leaves League of Nations.

May: conquest of Abyssinia completed.

June: Italy decides to join Hitler in helping nationalists in Spanish Civil War.

October: Rome–Berlin Axis formed with Nazi Germany.

1937 *November:* Anti-Comintern Pact signed with Germany and Japan.

1938 *March:* German *Anschluss* with Austria accepted.

July: Charter of Race issued.

September: Munich conference takes place; anti-Semitic laws introduced.

1939 *April:* Mussolini orders annexation of Albania.

May: Pact of Steel with Germany signed.

1940 *June:* Italy enters Second World War.

August: British Somaliland attacked.

September: Egypt attacked.

October: Greece attacked.

November: Italian navy defeated at Taranto.

1941 *March:* Italy defeated in naval battle at Matapan.

April: most of Italy's East African colonies lost.

December: Italy declares war on the USA.

1943 *March:* wave of anti-Fascist strikes takes place.

July: Allies invade Sicily and bomb Rome; Mussolini dismissed by king.

September: Mussolini rescued by Germans; forms Salò Republic in north Italy.

1945 *April:* German troops withdrawn; war in Italy ends; Mussolini executed.

Germany 1918–45

1918 *October:* Kiel mutiny begins wave of revolutionary outbreaks across Germany.

November: kaiser abdicates; Germany signs armistice; republic declared.

1919 *January:* Spartacist rising in Berlin defeated; coalition government for new Weimar Republic elected.

March: second communist uprising defeated.

April: socialist republic in Bavaria collapses.

June: new government signs Treaty of Versailles.

August: new Weimar constitution accepted.

September: Hitler joins DAP.

1920 *February:* DAP changes its name to NSDAP (Nazi Party); 25-point programme drawn up.

March: Kapp's attempted *Putsch* fails.

1921 *July:* Hitler becomes leader of NSDAP; SA set up.

1923 *January:* French occupy the Ruhr.

September: Stresemann becomes chancellor.

November: Munich beer hall *Putsch*; Nazi March on Berlin fails.

1924 *January:* Hitler begins prison sentence in Landsberg castle; starts to write *Mein Kampf.*

December: Hitler released; Nazis win 14 seats in election.

1925 *February:* Nazi Party relaunched; SS formed.

1926 *February:* Hitler re-establishes control over the party at the Bamberg conference.

1928 *May:* number of Nazi seats drops to 12 in elections.

1929 *October:* Stresemann dies; Wall Street Crash begins the Great Depression.

1930 *March:* coalition government collapses.

September: Nazis become second largest party in general election.

1932 *April:* Hitler wins 13 million votes in presidential elections.

July: Nazis become largest party in *Reichstag* with 230 seats.

August: von Hindenburg refuses Hitler's demands to be made prime minister.

November: Nazis drop to 196 seats in election.

December: Hitler makes deal with von Papen.

1933 *January:* von Hindenburg agrees to appoint Hitler as chancellor; Hitler immediately sets date for new election in March.

February: Nazis raise funds from prominent businessmen; *Reichstag* fire; communists blamed and banned; the constitution is suspended.

March: Nazis fail to win overall majority; Day of Potsdam takes place; deals with the Nationalists concluded and threats made against the SPD; the Enabling Act pushed through.

April: Jewish shops boycotted; Jews sacked from state jobs.

May: all trade unions banned; the 'burning of books' takes place.

June: SPD banned; first loans made to encourage women to leave work and marry.

July: all opposition parties dissolved; Germany becomes a one-party state; Reich Church formed; concordat made with Catholic Church.

October: Germany withdraws from disarmament conference and League of Nations; Editors' Law passed.

1934 *January:* Nazis take over local government; non-aggression pact with Poland signed.

April: People's Courts set up.

June: Night of the Long Knives takes place.

August: von Hindenburg dies; Hitler becomes president; army swears oath of loyalty.

September: Schacht announces 'new plan'.

1935 *January:* Saarland returned to Germany.

March: Hitler reintroduces conscription; extension of armed forces announced.

June: Anglo-German Naval Agreement signed.

September: Nuremberg race laws passed.

1936 *March:* the Rhineland reoccupied.

July: Hitler intervenes in Spanish Civil War.

September: Four-Year Plan begins.

October: Rome–Berlin Axis signed with Italy; Anti-Comintern Pact concluded with Japan.

1937 *November:* Hossbach Memorandum; Schacht resigns as economics minister.

1938 *March: Anschluss* with Austria takes place.

September: Sudetenland crisis; Munich Agreement.

November: Kristallnacht attacks on Jews.

1939 *March:* Czechoslovakia invaded.

May: Pact of Steel signed with Italy.

July: talks begin with USSR.

August: Nazi–Soviet Pact concluded.

September: Poland invaded; the Second World War begins.

1940 *April:* Denmark and Norway invaded.

May: the Low Countries and France invaded.

September: Germany fails to win Battle of Britain.

1941 *April:* Greece and Yugoslavia invaded.

June: Operation Barbarossa (invasion of the USSR) begins; 'special action' operations on the eastern front begin.

December: Japanese attack on Pearl Harbor, bringing the USA into the war.

1942 *January:* the Wannsee conference decides on the 'final solution'.

November: Germany defeated at El Alamein in North Africa.

1943 *January:* Germany defeated at Stalingrad.

1944 *June:* D-day landings in Normandy.

July: von Stauffenberg's Bomb Plot fails.

1945 *January:* Soviet troops cross into Germany.

April: Hitler commits suicide.

May: Germany surrenders; war in Europe ends.

Index